The Civil Works Administration

D0153193

The Civil Works Administration, 1933-1934

The Business of Emergency Employment in the New Deal

BONNIE FOX SCHWARTZ

Princeton University Press ★ Princeton, New Jersey

TULSA JUNIOR COLLEGE
Learning Resources Center
Southeast Campus

Copyright © 1984 by Princeton University Press

Published by Princeton University Press, 41 William Street,
Princeton, New Jersey 08540

In the United Kingdom: Princeton University Press,
Guildford, Surrey

All Rights Reserved

Library of Congress Cataloging in Publication Data will be
found on the last printed page of this book

ISBN 0-691-04718-9

Publication of this book has been aided by the Whitney
Darrow Fund of Princeton University Press

This book has been composed in Linotron Goudy Type

Clothbound editions of Princeton University Press books are
printed on acid-free paper, and binding materials are chosen
for strength and durability. Paperbacks, although satisfactory
for personal collections, are not usually suitable for
library rebinding

Printed in the United States of America by Princeton
University Press, Princeton, New Jersey

To my mother and father

THREE weeks before Thanksgiving, 1933, President Franklin D. Roosevelt created the Civil Works Administration and pledged to provide public jobs for 4 million people within thirty days. Although Congress had already appropriated $.5 billion for direct federal relief and $3.3 billion more for public works during the New Deal's First Hundred Days, neither of these programs had proved satisfactory to meet the impending winter emergency. Relief, even work relief, always had connotations of dependency and usually involved a humiliating investigation by a social worker into each client's needs. Public construction projects required careful planning by technical experts to ensure the honest, efficient application of tax dollars. By the fall of 1933, the President and his advisors realized the urgency to offer some new form of aid that might somehow eliminate the time-consuming procedures of case work and elaborate planning. They hoped the CWA would tide the country over one more winter until other agencies could take effect in the spring.

More than a stop-gap, however, the Civil Works Administration stands out in the history of twentieth-century reform as a unique program to cope with unemployment. For the first time, the federal government dared to provide the jobless with real work that was outside the realm of charity. In sharp contrast to the dole, the CWA offered jobs and paid the same minimum hourly wages as the Public Works Administration, based on scales negotiated in collective bargaining agreements. Under the CWA, the federal government also assumed the complete responsibility to undertake projects, hire workers, and place applicants according to their skills. By January, 1934, over 4 million Americans were on the payroll of the most massive work-relief experiment ever undertaken. Architects, engineers, scientists, teachers, surveyors, masons, carpenters, mechanics, unskilled laborers, all found a job in the ranks. Despite record-freezing cold, gangs of construction and repair men fanned out over the landscape, building and widening roads, clearing sites for recreation centers, and grading runways for airports. Hundreds of miles of ditches were opened to install water mains and sewer conduits, while schools, hospitals, libraries, and other public buildings got replastered walls, new coats of paint, and even decorative murals. Hardly a community failed to receive some lasting benefit—a paved street, an athletic stadium, a new playground. The CWA sent visiting nurses to the poor in city slums and bookmobiles to remote regions of the South. It pumped $1 billion of purchasing power into the stagnant economy. But, above all, it left an immeasurable impact on people. No longer on relief, CWA employees took pride in working for the government.

Although a study of the CWA's obvious achievements seemed noteworthy, I found the real story lies in a challenge to some previous assumptions about the role that social work leaders and other urban liberals played in the New Deal relief agencies. I began with a review of the efforts of welfare officials to provide aid and lift morale, but along the way I became more impressed by the significant role of "corporate liberals"—engineers, industrial managers, economic planners, and statisticians—who had called for accurate data on the jobless, national employment exchanges, and planned public works since the progressive era. These businessmen and efficiency experts, many of them independent Republicans and holdovers from the Herbert Hoover "New Era," came to dominate the CWA from Washington down to the state and county offices; and they ran the program more like an emergency employment corporation rather than charitable made work. By January, 1934, the social work initiative had given way to the priorities of industrial management, as CWA orders called for engineering standards, systematic safety campaigns, accurate data collection, and unit-cost accounting. Labor policies permitted union hiring for skilled jobs and representation on local boards to determine wage rates and redress grievances. In the eyes of these efficiency types,

CWA employees had rejoined the active work force and were no longer relief clients.

Social workers had good reasons to feel uneasy with the civil works experiment. The agency had pushed their traditional welfare methods into a corner, such as the Women's Division, which provided aid to women as dependents rather than as unemployed members of the labor force. While social workers continued to dispense direct relief, they found that major CWA responsibilities had gone to other professionals and that their one crucial task seemed to be that of watchdog against political misuse of the work program. This fact is generally overlooked by liberal historians who have regarded fiscal conservatives, like Budget Director Lewis Douglas and Southern Democrats in the Congress, as the villains of the 1934 appropriation battle for more CWA funds. Social workers, too, had their grievances. They saw the CWA as a disruption of proper case-work counseling, and they resented the engineers for usurping their hard-won role as chief dispensers of federal aid to the unemployed. The indignation on the part of some welfare leaders helps to explain their failure to lobby vigorously for additional funds to extend the CWA to 1935. When the CWA folded, social workers would take charge once again of work relief under the Federal Emergency Relief Administration, and the Works Progress Administration incorporated this reaction. The unemployed returned to the status of relief clients, were hired according to need, and paid "security wages." Not for almost forty years, until the Emergency Employment Act of 1971, would a mere tenth of 4 million jobless enjoy the status of public employees.

I suspect that this study will comfort neither the liberal historians, who have championed the New Deal social welfare programs, nor their recent revisionist critics. The liberals have been far too appreciative of their welfare-state heroes, crediting too much to the social workers and the infectious spirit of Harry Hopkins, and they have neglected to see the CWA, and even the FERA, from the perspective of 1933, when federal relief officials (a surprising number of holdovers from the Hoover

Administration) carried out policies in the spirit of the management innovations of the 1920's. They have rarely taken a
hard look at how the CWA actually functioned on the state
and local levels beyond the standard treatment of political battles between Republicans and Democrats. At the same time,
the revisionists have relied largely on the liberals' accounts to
condemn New Deal work relief for its ties to the tradition of
"charities and corrections," its penchant for "security wages,"
and its determination to keep projects from encroaching on the
private sector. The most influential critique, *Regulating the Poor*,
by Frances Fox Piven and Richard A. Cloward, has characterized the CWA and WPA as contrivances to "enmesh people
in the work role, the cornerstone of social control in any society." But Harry Hopkins and his CWA staff would have
been thoroughly mystified by the assertion that emergency
employment on civil works projects was deadening or confin-
ing toil. Influenced by Frederick W. Taylor, the technicians
who managed the CWA, in particular, would have scoffed at
such grim notions and pointed to the menace at hand—the
tyranny of idleness, the five years of depression which had
shattered the lives and morale of millions of working Americans. Regarding a day's work as liberating and inspiring, they
saw their first priority was to get the unemployed back on the
job.

Throughout the many years that I have worked on this project, I have accumulated numerous debts. Many archivists and
librarians have been most helpful. Robert M. Kvasnicka at the
National Archives gave me access to the CWA and FERA Papers and alerted my attention to valuable collections in the
Federal Records Center, Suitland, Maryland. I also wish to
acknowledge the aid of the staff of the Franklin D. Roosevelt
Library, Hyde Park; Andrea Hinding at the Social Welfare
History Archives; Archie Motley at the Chicago Historical Society; and Don Flowers of the North Carolina State Records
. Building, Raleigh. Special appreciation must go to the staff of

the Columbia University Libraries, the Oral History Collection, and particularly Eileen McIlvaine at the Reference Desk.

Mr. Arthur "Tex" Goldschmidt consented to an interview and generously shared his personal papers of the Emergency Exchange Association with me.

The manuscript has benefitted from the insights of many scholars. At Columbia University, Professors Walter P. Metzger, Stuart Bruchey, Charles V. Hamilton, and Andrew Beveridge posed important questions and made useful comments. Professors James T. Patterson and John Braeman read the entire manuscript with great care and offered valuable suggestions. My dissertation sponsor, Professor William E. Leuchtenburg, sparked my interest in programs for the unemployed, first in my home town of Philadelphia and then under the New Deal. For many years, he provided his unique, devoted service as advisor, editor, and critic.

At Princeton University Press, Gail Filion Ullman generously gave advice and assistance, and R. Miriam Brokaw added her excellent copy editing skills. Professor Jane Stevens of the Columbia University School of Library Service offered valuable help with the index.

Friends and associates have aided me in very special ways. Mark Gelfand took time from his book to exchange ideas. Since our first year at Columbia, Marion Fishel Deshmukh has been a constant source of encouragement. And Eleanor Mefford and Mazal Dwarka took excellent care of my daughter and enabled me to go to the library with a clear head.

The years put into such a project would be dreary and lonely without a family. Although my children, Marjorie and David, have not personally participated in this effort, I must note their influence. Their schedules have taught me to budget my time and to make the most of naps and play dates. And their presence has inspired me to finish the work I began long before they arrived. My parents, Eva and Nathan Fox, lived through the Great Depression and shared their memories of those hard times. Mother was a canvasser on the CWA Unemployment Relief Census Project in Philadelphia. My father accompanied me on numerous trips, typed hundreds of note cards, and typed and retyped countless versions of each chapter, including the final draft. Joel, my husband, has sacrificed his own research and writing time to give his talents to every phase of this book. His willingness to live with the CWA for over a decade was far beyond the call of duty.

B.F.S.

New York City
Summer, 1983

CONTENTS

ACRONYMS

AAA	Agricultural Adjustment Administration
AASW	American Association of Social Workers
AFL	American Federation of Labor
AFT	American Federation of Teachers
AIA	American Institute of Architects
AICP	Association for Improving the Condition of the Poor (New York City)
ANA	American Nurses Association
AOPEE	Association of Office and Professional Emergency Employees (New York City)
APWA	American Public Works Association
ASA	American Statistical Association
BAT	Bureau of Apprenticeship and Training
CEA	Council of Economic Advisors
CETA	Comprehensive Employment and Training Act
COS	Charity Organization Society (New York City)
CWA	Civil Works Administration
CWS	Civil Works Service
EEA	Emergency Exchange Association (New York City)
FAECT	Federation of Architects, Engineers, Chemists, and Technicians
FERA	Federal Emergency Relief Administration
FERA-WD	Federal Emergency Relief Administration Work Division
FESB	Federal Employment Stabilization Board
GAO	General Accounting Office
HABS	Historic American Buildings Survey
IERC	Illinois Emergency Relief Commission
JOBS	Job Opportunities in the Business Sector
MDTA	Manpower Development and Training Act
NCSW	National Conference of Social Work
NEC	National Emergency Council
NIRA	National Industrial Recovery Act
NRA	National Recovery Administration
NRS	National Re-employment Service
NSC	National Safety Council
OEO	Office of Economic Opportunity

OMAT	Office of Manpower, Apprenticeship, and Training
PACH	Public Administration Clearing House
PAS	Public Administration Service
PECE	President's Emergency Committee for Employment
PEP	Public Employment Program
POUR	President's Organization for Unemployment Relief
PWA	Public Works Administration
PWAP	Public Works of Art Project
RFC	Reconstruction Finance Corporation
SERA	State Emergency Relief Administration (California)
SERB	State Emergency Relief Board (Pennsylvania)
TERA	Temporary Emergency Relief Administration (New York State)
TVA	Tennessee Valley Authority
TWI	Training Within Industry (WPA)
UMW	United Mine Workers
USECC	United States Employees Compensation Commission
USES	United States Employment Service
UTA	Unemployed Teachers Association (New York City)
UWA	Unemployed Writers Association
VA	Veterans Administration
WPA	Works Progress Administration

ABBREVIATIONS

Manuscripts

AGF	Adjutant General Files
AW	Aubrey Williams Papers
CWA	Civil Works Administration Papers
DJ	Department of Justice Papers
EB	Edward Bruce Papers
ER	Eleanor Roosevelt Papers
EW	Ellen Woodward Papers
FB	Frank Bane Papers
FDR-OF	Franklin D. Roosevelt Papers—Official File
FERA	Federal Emergency Relief Administration Papers
FHL	Fiorello H. La Guardia Papers
FW	Frank Walker Papers
GP	Gifford Pinchot Papers
HH	Henry Horner Papers
HLH	Harry L. Hopkins Papers
HLL	Harry L. Lurie Papers
JMC	John M. Carmody Papers
JL	Julian Levi Papers
JWB	Josiah W. Bailey Papers
NCERA	North Carolina Emergency Relief Administration Papers
NEC	National Emergency Council Papers
NT	Norman Thomas Papers
RFW	Robert F. Wagner Papers
USES	United States Employment Service Papers
VAO	Victor A. Olander Papers
WD	War Department General Staff Papers
WGM	William G. McAdoo Papers

Periodicals

AER	*American Economic Review*
AHR	*American Historical Review*
Annals	*Annals of the American Academy of Political and Social Science*
APSR	*American Political Science Review*

BTS	*Bulletin of the Taylor Society*
ENR	*Engineering News-Record*
JAH	*Journal of American History*
JPE	*Journal of Political Economy*
MLR	*Monthly Labor Review*
NCSW	National Conference of Social Work, *Proceedings*
PSQ	*Political Science Quarterly*
SAMJ	*Society for the Advancement of Management Journal*
SSR	*Social Service Review*
SWT	*Social Work Today*

The Civil Works Administration, 1933-1934

CHAPTER ONE

Origins of Civil Works: Unorthodox Social Work and Progressive Engineering

IN OCTOBER, 1933, as President Franklin D. Roosevelt's New Deal Administration settled in for its first winter, the federal government undertook a nation-wide relief census. For the first time, officials in Washington dared to count the exact number of families receiving aid from public funds, the number of persons in these families, the total cost to government, and gather other information to calculate the national dimensions of unemployment and dependency. When the statistics were finally tabulated, the Relief Census documented the shattering impact of four years of depression. More than 12.5 million Americans—ten percent of the population—were living on public aid. Four states alone, Pennsylvania, New York, Ohio, and Illinois, claimed a third of these persons, and an eighth resided in five cities with a million or more inhabitants. The count included over 5.25 million children under sixteen years of age. One seventh of all youngsters from six to thirteen years old depended on relief, an experience comparable to school in its impact upon a future generation. And almost .25 million infants were starting life out on the dole.[1]

The Relief Census presented an ironic contrast to the first federal census of 1790, which counted 4 million farmers and artisans busy at work. The 1933 Census found three times as many individuals living in idleness and despair. The purposes of the two, however, offer striking analogies in furnishing basic information for government action. The 1790 statistics served

[1]Corrington Gill, "A Study of Three Million Families on Relief in October, 1933," *Annals*, CLXXVI (November, 1934), 25–36.

to allocate representatives to the new Congress, to levy direct taxes to support the federal government, and to estimate military strength. The 1933 figures revealed data for use in the administration, not of a new government, but of new federal agencies attempting to provide emergency relief and work with few precedents to guide them. The Relief Census would assist in allocating funds, pointing to areas of extreme need, estimating the size and nature of individual and family needs, and planning programs to rehabilitate the jobless and their dependents. A century and a half of time had witnessed the growth of an industrial economy and a complex urban society far different from the 1790's. The federal government would have to undertake new responsibilities based on new attitudes toward the unemployed, who looked to Washington as a last resort for help.

I

Americans traditionally regarded a man out of work as lazy and worthless. Whether times were good or bad, if a person had no job, he was to blame. Some basic character flaw accounted for his destitution. As a result, those temporarily unemployed fell in with the improvident and physically disabled, all under the same stigma of dependency. This concept of "charity and corrections" influenced whatever forms of relief existed from colonial times through the twentieth century.

Elizabethan Poor Laws and the Puritan work ethic shaped colonial and early American practices of caring for the needy. Although the poor remained within the community and received "outdoor relief" in their own homes, public "overseers" meted out assistance harshly, feeling that charity only encouraged dependency. The pauper's oath, disfranchisement, or refusal of a marriage license served to humiliate recipients so that only the truly desperate applied. Payments took the form of food orders or donated clothing, just enough to maintain subsistence. This "relief in kind" implied that dependents did not have judgment and represented an unwillingness to trust them with money.[2]

In the optimistic, self-reliant nineteenth century, Jacksonian reformers preferred to isolate social deviants by replacing "outdoor assistance" with "indoor relief" and the establishment of almshouses. Instead of tending to the poor at home, community leaders created institutions to educate them in good habits. More than charity, the needy required supervision to avoid the temptations of liquor, gambling, and other vices. Once behind the walls of the asylum or "house of industry," residents could learn discipline under a precise, rigorous routine.[3] Even during periods of economic crisis, when overloaded almshouses were supplemented by *ad hoc* relief committees, charitable groups still insisted that relief only prolonged idleness. Acknowledging that the Panic of 1819 had created "personal inconveniences," the New York Society for the Prevention of Pauperism pointed out that "no man who is temperate, frugal and willing to work need suffer or become a pauper for want of employment." The New York Association for Improving the Condition of the Poor, founded in 1843 at the end of another severe depression, stressed personal regeneration over material aid. Although its directors noted how Manhattan's wretched slums had contributed to demoralization, they emphasized that individuals could be reformed by learning economy, industry, and temperance.[4]

---

[2]Edith Abbott, "Abolish the Pauper Laws," *SSR*, VIII (March, 1934), 1–16; Josephine C. Brown, *Public Relief, 1929–1939* (New York: Henry Holt and Company, 1940), pp. 3–17.

[3]David J. Rothman, *The Discovery of the Asylum* (Boston: Little, Brown and Company, 1971), pp. 155–205.

[4]Samuel Rezneck, "The Depression of 1819–1822, A Social History," *AHR*, XXXIX (October, 1933), 28–47; Benjamin J. Klebaner, "Poverty and Its Relief in American Thought, 1815–1861," *SSR*, XXXVIII (December, 1964), 286; Samuel Rezneck, "The Social History of an American Depression, 1837–1843," *AHR*, XL (July, 1935), 665–682; and "The Influence of Depression upon American Opinion, 1857–1859," *Journal of Economic History*, II (May, 1942), 18–21.

After the Civil War, unprecedented industrial expansion and intellectual affirmation of "survival of the fittest" sharpened the preference for private charity over public relief. Any clamor for public works during the 1873 depression smacked only of radical demands during the Paris Commune, while widespread revulsion against Boss Tweed's patronage gave the public dole connotations of political corruption. Wasteful expenditures by such dishonest bosses encouraged reformers in eight major cities, including New York and Philadelphia, to abolish municipal outdoor relief in the Gilded Age. In this era of individualism, Social Darwinists looked upon charity as a necessary evil, suited only to those who could not compete—the aged, the sick, the orphaned. Only private philanthropy, established on a permanent basis, could distinguish between such "worthy poor" and the indolent, who would not work if given aid. "Human nature is so constituted," remarked the social work pioneer Josephine Shaw Lowell in 1884, "that no man can receive as a gift what he should earn by his own labor without a moral deterioration."[5]

The first extensive use of "made work" for the unemployed during the Panic of 1893 was undertaken in this punitive spirit. Presuming the jobless were probably "work shy," local authorities applied the "work test" to determine the "genuineness and desert of the applicant." Enthusiastic supporters held that an honest day's labor prevented pauperism and gave the able-bodied indigent a chance to improve their characters by making them self-supporting. "Work-for-relief" programs provided an excuse for those getting aid to "earn" whatever they received. Projects involved only rough physical labor and were generally useless. One local relief official conceded that the typical task "may be necessary or unnec-

[5]Leah Hannah Feder, *Unemployment Relief in Periods of Depression* (New York: Russell Sage Foundation, 1936), pp. 169–171, 325–331; Herbert G. Gutman, "The Failure of the Movement by the Unemployed for Public Works in 1873," *PSQ*, LXX (June, 1965), 254–277; Samuel Rezneck, "Distress, Relief, and Discontent in the United States during the Depression of 1873–1878," *JPE*, LXIII (December, 1950), 499–502.

essary; it may be useful here and now or in anticipation of a future need; invented or *ad hoc.*" Meager payments in kind enabled overseers to stretch limited resources and dissuaded all but the most desperate. Careful to avoid competition with the private market, advocates indeed followed Josephine Shaw Lowell's philosophy that "to be a benefit rather than an injury work relief must be continuous, hard, and underpaid."[6]

The severity of the 1893 depression, however, combined with the reform spirit of the progressive movement to prompt a major shift in outlook by the turn of the century. Although this new perspective did not totally deny that individual frailties caused personal destitution, it did stress the impact of the factory system and low wages, which prevented even the thrifty from saving. Settlement house leaders like Jane Addams and Lillian Wald practiced community service and came to understand slum-living first hand. Statistical researchers such as Robert W. De Forest and Lawrence Veiller provided sophisticated studies of tenement crowding, and Robert Hunter voiced the widespread conviction that "social evils must be remedied and certain social wrongs must be put right." Frances Kellor's *Out of Work* (1915) urged that commissions gather accurate data to understand fully the plight of the jobless.[7]

This spirit of scientific inquiry also brought technological experts to see the root causes of unemployment in the chronic disorganization of the market place. Engineers, economists, and enlightened industrialists, influenced by Frederick Winslow Taylor's scientific management, realized that periodic fluctuations in business had forced many laborers out of work and below the subsistence level. Captivated by the efficiency

[6]Henrietta Liebman, "Work Relief in Certain States, 1930–33," FERA, *Monthly Report* (May, 1936), p. 35; Samuel Rezneck, "Unemployment, Unrest, and Relief in the United States during the Depression of 1893–1897," *JPE*, LXI (August, 1953), 330.

[7]Roy Lubove, *The Professional Altruist* (New York: Atheneum, 1969), pp. 8–10; Robert Bremner, *From the Depths* (New York: New York University Press, 1966), pp. 131–163.

movement, technicians called attention to disorders in the industrial system which created dramatic "labor turnovers" and
threw men out of work involuntarily.[8]

Armed with these new explanations for the phenomenon of
unemployment, two groups in particular—social workers and
social engineers—offered new professional approaches to the
traditional dispensation of poor relief. The recession of 1914–
1915, the mobilization and relief efforts during the First World
War, and the economic downturn of 1921–1922 would provide each group with opportunities to demonstrate and refine
its expertise.

II

Although social workers had often operated in the public sector, for example, in staffing legislative commissions of inquiry
to upgrade housing and factory safety standards, their professional methods remained centered on the individual "client"
and were practiced predominantly under private auspices. By
the turn of the century, case work had begun to emerge as the
"nuclear skill" of the profession. Good-hearted, casual home
visitors, who voluntarily dispensed a little charity, were grad-
ually displaced by full-time, trained professionals, well read in
sociology, with degrees from the University of Chicago or the
New York School of Social Work. These investigators attempted to "diagnose" social ills and prescribe treatment for
particular needs. They determined the amount of relief according to a "means test," which involved a searching inquiry into
personal finances and family resources with scientific budgeting. By establishing a relationship with each client, case
workers could render informed advice on how to secure a job
and other questions. They understandably disapproved of pub-

[8]Frederick Winslow Taylor, *Principles of Scientific Management* (New York: Harper and Brothers, 1911), p. 8; Samuel Haber, *Efficiency and Uplift* (Chicago: University of Chicago Press, 1964), pp. 99–116.

lic relief with its lax, often corrupt administration, its unsightly breadlines, and crowded municipal flophouses.[9]

Case workers confronted the first challenge of mass unemployment during the recession of 1914–1915. Instead of offering free soup or a mattress for the night, settlement houses, federated charities, and private neighborhood groups in many cities coordinated their activities in "programs of community planning." Despite the emergency, professionals remained committed to adequate investigations and personalized case work for individual clients and their families. Within this approach, the United Charities of Chicago devised street cleaning and clearance of vacant lots for 1,729 married men with dependents. New York's Association for Improving the Condition of the Poor arranged with the Bronx Botanical and Zoological Gardens to place clients at $2.00 a day for three days a week. If men refused this opportunity, the Association turned down further relief claims. Minneapolis Associated Charities undertook a local dam project and paid heads of families $1.60 plus carfare for an eight-hour day, three days a week, with wages in kind or in grocery orders. Such modest attempts resembled the nineteenth-century work test with "jobs" as a precondition for family assistance.[10]

The World War I mobilization enhanced the status of the private charities and their commitment to case work. Community war chest drives stimulated private fund-raising, particularly the idea of combining all contributions in one pledge. Although welfare officials gave relief to soldiers' families who

[9]Allen F. Davis, *Spearheads for Reform* (New York: Oxford University Press, 1967), pp. 65–70; Lubove, *Professional Altruist*, pp. 47, 52–54, 119–124; Frank J. Bruno, *Trends in Social Work, 1874–1956* (New York: Columbia University Press, 1948), pp. 183–191; Fred R. Johnson, "Unemployment from the Angle of Case Work," *Survey*, XXX (November 13, 1915), 162–173.

[10]Feder, *Unemployment Relief*, pp. 218–219, 250–251; Joanna C. Colcord, *Community Planning in Unemployment Emergencies* (New York: Russell Sage Foundation, 1930), p. 8; "Scrambling To Care for the Unemployed," *Survey*, XXXIII (January 30, 1915), 453–455; William H. Matthews, "Wages from Relief Funds," *ibid.*, XXXIV (June 12, 1915), 245–247.

had not received their allotment, the amount of aid depended on need.[11]

After the Armistice, during the 1921–1922 recession, private agencies turned their fund-raising and disbursement apparatus to the unemployed. Financial federations, the successors of the war chests, solicited contributions; and councils of social agencies coordinated local relief. Despite added client loads, dedicated case workers staunchly maintained standards, as suggested by the meticulous procedures of the Philadelphia Society for Organized Charity. A first interview focused on the applicant's immediate plight: why unemployed, previous earnings, jobs held in the last three years, how the family coped, children's health, and job prospects. A "curtailed" investigation still required information from the last two employers, one relative on each side of the family, the church, and the medical service. The case worker also checked neighborhood references, including tradesmen, school officials, the physician, and the clergyman. Even when municipal funds supplemented the private effort, social workers insisted on limited public involvement. The Minneapolis Associated Charities referred the unemployed to City Hall, but sent along staff members to advise on procedures. A long-standing agreement between Boston's Family Welfare Society and the city Board of Overseers had public authorities watch over families who required continuous cash allowances while private organizations conducted home visits. When private agencies developed work projects, they did so for special clients rather than as a general policy. The Philadelphia Society for Organized Charity had five programs, which allowed for diversity and a crude placement of applicants according to their capabilities. Laborers wielded picks and shovels, while opportunities for skilled repair work were available at the Pennsylvania Hospital, College Settlement, and the Lighthouse Settlement. Officials preferred to keep projects small

[11]Horatio G. Lloyd, "The War Chest Plan," *Annals,* LXXIX (September, 1918), 286–298; Foster Rhea Dulles, *The American Red Cross* (New York: Harper and Brothers, 1950), pp. 136, 146–147, 166.

enough to remain an adjunct of good case work rather than a substitute for it. [12]

With renewed prosperity in the mid-Twenties, social workers solidified their commitment to case work and private fundraising. The return of most of the able-bodied to industry permitted time to focus on chronic dependents, like the handicapped, orphans, and widows. While Freudian ideas stimulated an exploration of the ways in which individual psychosis hampered a person's ability to find and keep a job, the publication of Mary Richmond's classic *What Is Social Case Work?* in 1922 gave an authoritative definition to this painstaking process "which develops personality through adjustments consciously effected individual by individual, between men and their social environment." At the same time, private charities experienced the influence of bureaucratic management, as businessmen participated in the administration of relief. They helped make rationalized fund drives an accepted strategy during the 1920's, and even expanded the federation movement to a national scale. These achievements in casework orthodoxy and private charity organization would provide the first line of defense against the Great Depression in 1929. [13]

III

While social workers served through private agencies, a new generation of technicians had moved from the factory production lines to the public arena. In the progressive era, Frederick W. Taylor's disciples preached the gospel of rationalized public administration and encouraged engineers to enter government service, particularly to clean up the wasteful corruption of boss

[12]Feder, *Unemployment Relief*, pp. 311–313, 316; Philip Klein, *The Burden of Unemployment* (New York: Russell Sage Foundation, 1923), pp. 78, 80–81, 137.

[13]Lubove, *Professional Altruist*, pp. 119–124, 221; Mary Richmond, *What Is Social Case Work?* (New York: Russell Sage Foundation, 1922), pp. 98–99; Clarke Chambers, *Seedtime of Reform* (Minneapolis: University of Minnesota Press, 1963), pp. 85–106.

politics. Victories of insurgent mayors like New York's John Purroy Mitchel and Rudolph Blankenburg in Philadelphia placed many Taylorites in office to confront a painful example of national inefficiency, the recession of 1914–1915.[14] Administering municipal departments like public works, streets, and sanitation, efficiency experts found opportunities to offer a scientific response to mounting "labor turnovers." At the first National Conference on Unemployment in New York City, held February 27 and 28, 1914, speaker after speaker dwelled on the concept of "regularizing employment." Henry S. Dennison, a business executive and Taylorite, drew up "Standard Recommendations for the Prevention and Relief of Unemployment," which found joblessness "a concomitant of the disorganization rampant in the industrial system." "It is almost impossible to conceive that under good management there is any necessity for such violent changes in the number of employees as we saw in Philadelphia during the winter of 1913–1914," added Morris L. Cooke, the city's director of public works. As the recession deepened, New York's Mayor Mitchel appointed a committee on unemployment and relief chaired by U.S. Steel magnate Elbert H. Gary. Viewing direct relief as debilitating, Gary preferred putting the idle to work to increase overall efficiency and productivity. In Philadelphia, Mayor Blankenburg invited business leaders to confer with his cabinet; and public works director Cooke assigned Joseph H. Willits, a Wharton School professor and fellow Taylorite, to study the city's jobless. Although these committees failed to initiate permanent reforms, they did suggest statistics gathering, soundly

[14]Samuel P. Hays, "The Politics of Reform in Municipal Government in the Progressive Era," *Pacific Northwest Quarterly*, LV (October, 1964), 157–169; Augustus Cerillo, Jr., "The Reform of Municipal Government in New York City: from Seth Low to John Purroy Mitchel," *New-York Historical Society Quarterly*, LVII (January, 1973), 51–71; Bonnie R. Fox, "The Philadelphia Progressives: A Test of the Hofstadter-Hays Theses," *Pennsylvania History*, XXXIV (October, 1967), 391.

managed employment bureaus, and long-range planning of public works for the future.[15]

The engineers' contribution to the war mobilization, coupled with the public's growing fascination with technical expertise (and chief engineer Herbert Hoover), gave Taylorites an influential if minority viewpoint on unemployment in the 1920's. When the 1921 recession brought renewed demands for relief, Hoover, as Secretary of Commerce, initiated the Conference on Unemployment to deal with this "technical problem that could be solved by socially responsible engineers." Inviting business academics, trade association leaders, progressive engineers, and other efficiency experts, he called for "cooperative planning" and set an agenda to determine the exact number out of work, devise emergency measures, and study possible reforms. The Conference acknowledged "unemployment as a national problem requiring national planning," but looked to local communities to implement its recommendations, which included public works, employment offices coordinated by a federal service, and cooperative agencies.[16]

Although renewed prosperity distracted attention from this movement, the Unemployment Conference did stimulate thinking

[15]John B. Andrews, "A Practical Program for the Prevention of Unemployment in America," *American Labor Legislation Review*, V (June, 1915), 176–192; J. Feldman, "The New Emphasis in the Problem of Reducing Unemployment," *BTS*, VII (October, 1922); Morris Llewellyn Cooke, "Casual and Chronic Unemployment," *Annals*, LIX (May, 1915), 197; (New York City) Mayor's Committee on Unemployment, *Report* (New York, 1916); Donald A. Ritchie, "The Gary Committee: Businessmen, Progressives and Unemployment in New York City, 1914–1915," *New-York Historical Society Quarterly*, LVII (October, 1973), 33; Joseph H. Willits, *Steadying Employment* (Philadelphia: American Academy of Political and Social Science, 1916).

[16]Joan Hoff Wilson, *Herbert Hoover: Forgotten Progressive* (Boston: Little, Brown and Company, 1975), pp. 46–47, 90; Edwin T. Layton, Jr., *The Revolt of the Engineers* (Cleveland: Case Western Reserve University Press, 1971), p. 67; Ellis Hawley, "Herbert Hoover, the Commerce Secretariat, and the Vision of an 'Associative State,' 1921–1928," *JAH*, LXI (June, 1974), 116–140; Carolyn Grin, "The Unemployment Conference of 1921: An Experiment in National Cooperative Planning," *Mid-America*, LV (April, 1973), 83–97.

about a systematic response to joblessness. Urging the establishment of statistical analysis to monitor and provide timely warnings of business fluctuations, the Conference sponsored four surveys during the 1920's on business cycles and unemployment, seasonal operations in construction, recent economic changes, and the planning and control of public works. Committees recommended the creation of permanent datagathering services and a federal agency to coordinate scattered public works to supplement the private sector in periods of depression. Repudiating charity and worthless "made work" and convinced that such *ad hoc* creations never absorbed more than a fraction of the able-bodied, experts around Commerce Secretary Hoover conceived of public works as self-liquidating construction projects, already on the drawing boards and funded in capital budgets. Civic improvements would be undertaken by contract with private industry or force account (where the government unit did the planning and hiring) and supervised by engineers and construction executives. A true public works program would attempt to "imitate the general economic order, trying very hard to use methods which big industry uses— speed, high production, competency." Implicit in this formulation was the selection of a work force qualified by skill and training, not by months on the breadline—and the foremen's right to fire incompetents regardless of their dependents and family budget. This orthodoxy, however, like case work, would soon be tested by the need to meet the immediate demands of millions of unemployed.[17]

IV

When the Great Depression struck, the ground broken by social workers and engineers in the large cities had not changed

[17]President's Conference on Unemployment, *Report* (Washington: Government Printing Office, 1921); Richard A. Feiss, "The Engineering Approach to the Problem of Continuous Employment," *BTS*, VI (October, 1921), 187– 194; Conference on Unemployment, *Seasonal Operations in the Construction Industries* (New York: McGraw Hill, 1924); Leo Wolman, *Planning and Control*

the reality that only local relief arrangements existed to cope with the emergency: the almshouse, poor board, neighborhood settlement, and family aid society. In the fall of 1929, social workers concentrated in the private agencies rallied as they had in the past and launched a valiant attempt to carry staggering numbers of clients. New York City's Association for Improving the Condition of the Poor, which had pioneered in work relief in 1914–1915 and 1921–1922, instituted similar projects but managed to place only 1,564 men for a short time. Relief applications piled up, as anticipation of the second winter (of 1930–1931) prompted the AICP to cooperate with the Charity Organization Society and establish an Emergency Work Bureau. Seward Prosser of Bankers Trust Company headed a group of financiers who collected over $8 million to last six months. Despite the careful screening of applicants and efficient organization, the program covered only a fraction of those who applied. Inadequacies of the Prosser Committee, plus the public's revulsion against breadlines, applecarts, and street beggars, made city intervention imperative. Reluctantly driven to action, municipal authorities under Mayor "Jimmy" Walker proved inept and corrupt, as New Yorkers asked for state and federal relief.[18]

Philadelphia provided the most diversified effort under a volunteer Committee for Unemployment Relief chaired by Horatio Gates Lloyd, a partner of Drexel and Company, the city branch of the House of Morgan. Lloyd, along with social work leaders Karl De Schweinitz and Jacob Billikopf, organized a program of relief, work relief, loans, a shelter for homeless

of Public Works (New York: National Bureau of Economic Research, 1930); Arthur D. Gayer, Public Works in Prosperity and Depression (New York: National Bureau of Economic Research, 1935), pp. 5–6, 12–13.

[18]The Reminiscences of Frank Bane, Social Security Project (October, 1965), pp. 3–5 in the Oral History Collection of Columbia University (hereafter cited as Bane COHC). Irving Bernstein, The Lean Years (Baltimore: Penguin Books, 1960), pp. 292–298; "How the Cities Stand," Survey, LXVIII (April 15, 1932), 71; Joanna C. Colcord, William C. Koplovitz, and Russell H. Kurtz, Emergency Work Relief (New York: Russell Sage Foundation, 1936), pp. 36–60.

men, and school breakfasts. Despite sound management and community coordination, the Committee rapidly exhausted its funds. City appropriations eventually supplemented private donations, although Lloyd took charge of all disbursements to guard against political interference. By the second winter, the number of applicants had steadily mounted, municipal resources dried up, and $5 million from a United Campaign barely lasted three months. A small state subsidy enabled the Committee to struggle on until June, 1932, when Lloyd decided to disband, fearing he would cruelly mislead dependent families by continuing. Although long advocates of local relief, Lloyd and his associates came to champion direct, federal assistance.[19]

Detroit, which suffered the most acute industrial crisis of any American city, could offer little more than mass public aid. With a virtual absence of private charities, the city elected Mayor Frank Murphy in 1930 on a platform of public relief to the unemployed. Murphy reorganized the department of welfare, set up an emergency committee to register the jobless, and created a Homeless Men's Bureau. With little time to distinguish individual needs and no money to spare for work relief materials, Detroit muddled through the winter of 1930–1931 on meager food allowances and petty cash. By the second year, Murphy voiced a desperate plea to Washington for help.[20]

The collapse of local relief signaled the inability of cities and counties to expand public works to absorb the able-bodied unemployed. Construction had peaked in 1928, and municipal and county governments could not possibly accelerate building activities enough to compensate. Administrative red tape accounted for some delays, while the collapse of the Wall Street bond market and the reluctance of private underwriters to purchase city notes aborted new civic improvements. With taxes in arrears and mounting relief costs, officials deferred or simply

[19]Bonnie R. Fox, "Unemployment Relief in Philadelphia, 1930–32: A Study of the Depression's Impact on Voluntarism," *Pennsylvania Magazine of History and Biography*, XCIII (January, 1969), 86–108.

[20]Sidney Fine, *Frank Murphy, The Detroit Years* (Ann Arbor: University of Michigan Press, 1975), pp. 257–387.

eliminated plans. Public works departments slashed even their maintenance work, and within two years local treasurers were forced to beg for subsidies from Washington.[21]

Fully aware of the cities' plight, Senator Robert F. Wagner of New York initiated the first federal response, a modest program based on recommendations of the 1921 Unemployment Conference. His bills called for a system to gather statistics on the jobless, a national board to plan public works, and a federal-state employment service financed by grants-in-aid from Washington. Although Commerce Secretary Hoover had supported these concepts, President Hoover feared that such "drastic action" would only create panic. Stressing local initiative and a balanced federal budget, Hoover disregarded many of his technical advisors who supported the "Wagner Bills." He forced the emasculation of the statistics and public works programs and prevented the establishment of a new employment service. The July, 1930, compromise law provided that the Bureau of Labor Statistics collect and publish monthly figures on employment, wages, and hours in manufacturing, construction, agriculture, and other leading areas; but Hoover declined to request an adequate appropriation and simply named an Advisory Committee on Employment Statistics with Leo Wolman, an authority on the planning and control of public works, to chair the subcommittee on measurement. When Wolman recommended gathering additional data on part-time work in manufacturing and railroad transportation, a quinquennial employment census, and a $200,000 appropriation, his requests fell on deaf ears.[22]

The Employment Stabilization Act, reluctantly signed by Hoover in February, 1931, adhered to advanced planning and did nothing to stimulate immediate building activity. The new Federal Employment Stabilization Board would collect an out-

[21]Gayer, *Public Works in Prosperity and Depression*, pp. 36–40; Mark I. Gelfand, *A Nation of Cities* (New York: Oxford University Press, 1975), p. 46.

[22]Bernstein, *Lean Years*, pp. 267–269; J. Joseph Huthmacher, *Senator Robert F. Wagner and the Rise of Urban Liberalism* (New York: Atheneum, 1968), pp. 61–63.

line of projects and expenses for the next six years from heads of federal agencies and also gather data on state and local construction. In case of an economic downturn, the President, upon recommendation of the Board, might ask Congress for a special public works appropriation. Hoover, however, conceived of the FESB as a statistical body, and his director, Donald H. Sawyer, advocated local public works. Sawyer believed that large-scale, carefully designed federal projects would not help the jobless significantly until 1933, when business would undoubtedly revive and government competition would harm the free market. Furthermore, Sawyer's chief of public construction agreed that expanded federal activity would weaken individual and community responsibility.[23]

Senator Wagner's desire to coordinate a system of federal-state employment exchanges never got off the ground. To bring order to the chaotic labor market and reform the ineffective United States Employment Service, he proposed a new USES within the Labor Department. The President would appoint a director to establish a national system of employment offices, publicize information, set up a clearing house for labor, impose uniform standards, and help transport workers to new jobs. States had to create similar agencies in conformity with federal regulations to qualify for grants-in-aid. Many Taylorites supported this bill, including Joseph Willits, who had studied unemployment in Philadelphia, and Bryce M. Steward of the Industrial Relations Counselors, Inc. But Hoover opposed even this federal involvement, convinced that existing laws and agencies were sufficient.[24]

Still, Hoover realized that the White House had to become involved, if only indirectly, in emergency relief to the unemployed. When the nation confronted the second winter of depression, he created the President's Emergency Committee for Employment in October, 1930. Hoover appointed as chair-

[23]*Ibid.*, pp. 273–274; D. H. Sawyer, "Municipal Construction as Unemployment Relief," *Annals*, CLXII (July, 1934), 133–135.
[24]Bernstein, *Lean Years*, p. 275; Huthmacher, *Senator Wagner*, pp. 75, 78.

man Colonel Arthur Woods, former New York City police commissioner and secretary of the 1921 Unemployment Conference. Only a token number of social workers participated in the PECE compared to the array of technical experts, many from the 1921 gathering, who made up the majority. Members came primarily from business, public administration, and industrial research, and included Edward Eyre Hunt, planner of the 1921 meeting, Joseph H. Willits, and Leo Wolman. The Committee conceived of its role as a moral leader "for coordinated action" built upon a "feeling of local responsibility and local initiative." Woods and his associates appealed to enlightened businessmen to "spread the work," hold the line on wages, and establish rational priorities for releasing employees. They circulated pamphlets, which described programs used in past recessions, and sponsored radio addresses by business executives, welfare administrators, and engineers. Following the 1921 recommendations, the Committee gathered data on the unemployed, but relied on private organizations, like the Association of Community Chests and Councils and the Family Welfare Association, to do the leg work. When PECE's own studies revealed that exhausted public funds created a "vicious cycle of municipal bankruptcy and human suffering," however, Colonel Woods urged deliberate federal action. In a draft message to Congress, he called for accelerated public works, especially roads; advanced planning of federal projects, including slum clearance, low-cost housing, and rural electrification; and a national employment service. When Hoover rejected these proposals and addressed the nation with his usual optimism, Woods saw the Committee through until April, 1931, and then resigned.[25]

In August, as the country geared up for the third winter, the President's Organization on Unemployment Relief took over

[25]Edward Eyre Hunt, "From 1921 Forward," *Survey*, LXII (April, 1929), 6; E. P. Hayes, *Activities of the President's Emergency Committee for Employment (October 7, 1930-August 19, 1931)* (Concord, New Hampshire: Rumford Press, 1936); Edward Ainsworth Williams, *Federal Aid for Relief* (New York: Columbia University Press, 1939), pp. 27–29.

as chief morale booster. More conservative and business-oriented than its predecessor, POUR excluded from its membership those independent economists and social workers who had sided with Colonel Woods. Its director, Walter S. Gifford, president of A.T.&T., executive chairman of New York's Charity Organization Society, and wartime director of the Council of National Defense, reaffirmed the importance of local efforts for which POUR would serve only as a clearing house. Owen D. Young of General Electric headed the Mobilization of Relief Resources and spirited a nation-wide drive for funds to be "administered and distributed in the communities where they were raised." "There is to be no campaign of a national fund of any character," he emphasized. James R. Garfield, who chaired the Committee on Public Works, took a more orthodox line than Hoover. Speed, insisted Garfield, would result in inefficient projects; and he found no justification for unsound, make-shift ventures, which would only shake federal credit, increase taxes, and weaken local initiative. As head of the Administration of Relief Committee, Fred Croxton appealed to national private agencies like the Family Welfare Association to outline a cooperative program for state and local organizations to meet the winter emergency.[26]

While the Hoover Administration still exhorted a maximum effort on the local front, community relief administrators, backed by social work professionals, reached near unanimity that the federal government had to intervene directly. The American Public Welfare Association (formerly the American Association of Public Welfare Officials) assisted POUR in mobilizing local private organizations to coordinate and enlarge their facilities, but ended up pointing to the bankruptcy of the Hoover approach. Director Frank Bane, former Virginia Commissioner of Public Welfare, turned to members of the Public Administration Clearing House and International City Managers As-

[26]Brown, *Public Relief*, pp. 74–77; Bernstein, *Lean Years*, pp. 460–461; Harry Hopkins, *Spending to Save* (New York: W. W. Norton and Company, 1936), p. 57.

sociation to draw up a platform which included: state and federal responsibility for relief, public funds handled exclusively by public agencies, uniform eligibility standards, accurate statistics on needs and expenditures to ensure efficient administration, and work relief as the only satisfactory answer to unemployment. No longer ambivalent on the issue of public aid, the social work profession now stood in the forefront of the drive for federal relief. In October, 1931, a group of charity leaders headed by Linton B. Swift, director of the Family Welfare Association, organized the Social Work Conference on Federal Action to set guidelines for Congressional legislation. Senators Robert M. La Follette, Jr., and Edward P. Costigan sought their advice for subcommittee hearings to consider the extent, causes, and consequences of unemployment. A parade of social workers trooped up to Capitol Hill with grim details of thousands of case loads and collapsed local resources, which provided a powerful brief for federal action.[27]

Hoover's final response came in July, 1932, when he signed the Emergency Relief and Construction Act, authorizing the Reconstruction Finance Corporation (which had made loans to banks, railroads, and insurance companies) to furnish $2 billion in loans to the states for public works and $300 million for relief. Although the act called for "reproductive" public projects, it represented a tacit admission that private and public works at the state and local level had failed and that emergency action rather than long-term planning had to begin. Because of its strict definition of "self-liquidating" and stringent financial requirements, however, RFC public works promotion had little effect. States and localities with good credit could borrow elsewhere, and those with weak ratings could not plunge into further debt. Advances for relief also had limitations. No more than fifteen percent of the total could go to any one state, and the loans would bear interest at three percent to be deducted

[27]American Public Welfare Association, APWA, Our Autobiography (1941); Bruno, Trends in Social Work, pp. 297–306; Joanna C. Colcord, "Social Work and the First Federal Relief Programs," NCSW, Proceedings (New York: Columbia University Press, 1943), pp. 382–394.

from regular federal appropriations for highways beginning in 1935, which amounted to a heavy mortgage on future local works programs.[28]

The RFC Emergency Relief Division, under Fred Croxton and six field representatives, absorbed the operations of POUR in Washington, while the American Public Welfare Association helped the governors prepare loan applications and set up local administrations. Most states had no organization to receive loans, much less control their expenditure. Upon request, Bane sent members of his staff to forty-three states to advise on improving existing welfare offices and help establish many *de novo* public welfare departments. To upgrade standards and develop sound management techniques, they promoted new legislation and suggested revisions for laws already on the books. APWA men also tried to recruit qualified personnel for counties that had never acquired such expertise. This infusion of professionalism, however, failed to secure any major RFC relief disbursements. Croxton dribbled out relief loans like a conservative banker; and the policy of small advances for short periods did not allow time for welfare officials to evaluate unmet needs, nor to formulate plans beyond immediate help for the starving. "Relief for the unemployed was a tail reluctantly attached to the corporation relief provided by the RFC," concluded *Survey* writer Gertrude Springer. With no power to set nation-wide standards and procedures, the RFC lacked any local influence except over bookkeeping.[29]

A Conference on the Maintenance of Welfare Standards convened in Chicago in November, 1932, after Franklin D.

[28]Donald S. Watson, "Reconstruction Finance Corporation," *Municipal Year Book, 1937* (Chicago: International City Managers Association, 1937), pp. 375–381; Brown, *Public Relief*, pp. 125–130.

[29]APWA, *Our Autobiography*; Louis Brownlow, *A Passion for Anonymity* (Chicago: University of Chicago Press, 1958), pp. 272–274; Gertrude Springer, "How Federal Relief Gets into Action," *Survey*, LXVIII (October 15, 1932), 506–507; Russell H. Kurtz, "American Relief Caravan," *ibid.*, LXIX (January, 1933), 11–12; Gertrude Springer, "The New Deal and the Old Dole," *Survey Graphic*, XXII (July, 1933), 349.

Roosevelt's election triumph, to consider reforms in the administration of unemployment relief on a national scale. Sponsored jointly by the APWA, the Public Administration Clearing House, and the University of Chicago School of Social Service Administration, the Conference attracted representatives from all levels of government, schools of social work, and private charities. Its chairman, Louis Brownlow of PACH, tossed out the formal agenda to permit a free-wheeling discussion of the current relief crisis. Frank Bane attacked RFC procedures, which had disbursed only $67 million of the $300 million meant for the states. Before adjourning, the delegates adopted a set of principles: government responsibility for relief at all levels, effective state administration units to direct and supervise expenditures, public funds handled only by established public agencies, and allocations to secure properly qualified personnel to uphold standards. This platform set the tone for Congressional hearings during the winter of 1932–1933 to draft legislation for federal aid for relief.[30]

The New Deal's First Hundred Days saw breakthrough legislation for the unemployed in both public works and federal aid for relief. Title II of the National Industrial Recovery Act appropriated $3.3 billion for the Public Works Administration. With wide authority to initiate its own projects, the PWA could also make allotments to other federal agencies and offer loans and grants to states and public departments to stimulate nonfederal construction. But under Interior Secretary Harold L. ("Honest Harold") Ickes' penchant for meticulous planning and zeal against the pork barrel, PWA projects took months to get off the drawing boards, with little immediate impact on the unemployed. Moreover, the PWA practice of subcontracting to private firms, like Stone and Webster, and Bechtel, who were not restricted to hiring from relief rolls, meant that the needy

[30]Brownlow, *Passion for Anonymity*, pp. 273–274; testimony of Frank Bane, U.S. Congress, Senate, Subcommittee of the Committee on Manufacturers, *Hearings, Federal Aid for Unemployment Relief* on S. 5125, 72nd Cong., 2nd Sess., January 3 to 17, 1933 (Washington: U.S. Government Printing Office, 1933), pp. 27–36.

would have to look elsewhere. That help finally came with the Federal Emergency Relief Act of May, 1933, which marked the first time that Washington assumed direct responsibility for aiding the unemployed. It authorized $.5 billion in outright grants to the states. Half the money was available on a matching basis, with one federal dollar for each three spent in the state during the preceding three months. The remainder went into a discretionary fund for areas with needs so desperate and resources so depleted that the FERA administrator could suspend the matching provisions. This "supplementary aid" represented a new concept in federal relief. Where the RFC had reviewed loan applications like a bank, the FERA took a compassionate look at the local social welfare crisis.[31]

V

Under the unorthodox leadership of Harry L. Hopkins, the FERA would not only meet the urgent demands of the unemployed, but also break down established procedures for aiding those out of work. A frail-looking yet dynamic little man, Hopkins had always been an outsider to the charity world. He came up through the volunteer tradition and never shared the professional social workers' commitment to a thorough investigation of each relief client. After graduation from Grinnell College, he left his native Iowa for New York City, where he "apprenticed" for a brief time under Dr. John A. Kingsbury, general director of the Association for Improving the Condition of the Poor. During the 1914–1915 recession as work relief agent for the AICP's Bureau of Family Rehabilitation and Relief, he saw the importance of providing jobs, not just case files, for the unemployed. At the outset of the 1929 depression, Hopkins joined Manhattan's Gibson Committee of

[31]William E. Leuchtenburg, *Franklin D. Roosevelt and the New Deal, 1932–1940* (New York: Harper and Row, 1963), pp. 70–71, 120; Arthur M. Schlesinger, Jr., *The Coming of the New Deal* (Boston: Houghton Mifflin Company, 1965), pp. 283–284; Harry L. Lurie, "A Program for National Assistance," December 9, 1933, HLL 2; Robert E. Sherwood, *Roosevelt and Hopkins* (New York: Harper and Brothers, 1948), p. 52.

the Red Cross and plunged ahead to provide work relief. With no planning board, no questionnaires, and no case work, the committee arbitrarily gave a job to any man who asked. Harshly criticized for these irregularities by several social work agencies, which claimed it unprofessional to hand out work tickets without checking the background of each applicant, Hopkins snapped, "Go to hell!"[32]

Hopkins brought this brash, innovative spirit to his handling of unemployment relief in New York State, when Governor Roosevelt appointed him to direct the Temporary Emergency Relief Administration in 1931. As head of the largest state relief fund ($25 million), Hopkins organized the "most daring" public program ever undertaken. When field reports told of outmoded county practices, he used state rules and regulations to set rigorous uniform standards. He defined broad criteria for eligibility; forbade discrimination on the basis of politics, religion, or race; and stipulated cash rather than payments "in kind." Hopkins always kept the focus on work relief, including programs for the white collar and professional unemployed. Aware of the expense, he countered that jobs on public projects preserved the individual's self-esteem and brought benefits to the community. Hopkins also insisted that local offices hire full-time, qualified executives; and he required a periodic accounting of funds, needs, case loads, and expenditures to ensure honest, efficient disbursal. Despite the enormous sums handled (over $83 million by January, 1933), TERA remained untouched by corruption or political scandal and drew praise from social workers throughout the nation as an agency which made "relief a social work function."[33]

[32]By the early 1920's, when case workers had established themselves as the official spokesmen for the social work profession, the school-trained and apprentice-trained had little in common except a general commitment to serve the needy. See Lubove, *Professional Altruist*, pp. 118–119; Sherwood, *Roosevelt and Hopkins*, pp. 24–62.

[33]Searle F. Charles, *Minister of Relief* (Syracuse: Syracuse University Press, 1963), pp. 20–22; Emma O. Lundberg, "The New York State Temporary Emergency Relief Administration," *SSR*, VI (December, 1932), 545–566; Gertrude Springer, "The Lever of State Relief," *Survey*, LXVIII (January 15, 1932), 407–410.

When President Roosevelt gave the oath of office to Hopkins as Federal Emergency Relief Administrator, on May 22, 1933, social workers and public welfare advocates hailed the appointment. Having led the fight for federal aid, they looked upon FERA as their own and anticipated the expansion of case work procedures on a nation-wide scale as well as the establishment of uniform state and local public relief departments. Hopkins understood these goals, and he turned to Frank Bane and C. M. Bookman, former president of the American Association of Social Workers, for advice during the early hectic weeks. But Hopkins' first concern was the immediate needs of over 4,720,000 on relief rolls. Impatient with bureaucratic red tape, he disbursed $51 million in matching grants to forty-five states within a month, and the first discretionary allotment to Texas on June 27. Hopkins tapped existing state and local administrations; and, following established grant-in-aid procedures, he quickly ordered the remaining states to designate a public administration to cooperate with Washington. Anxious for funds, most governors quickly complied and requested legislatures to appropriate at least token sums for operations. FERA orders further required each state to draw up a comprehensive plan to determine the amount of aid, provide for a full-time, qualified director and county supervisors, and set up an auditing and statistical division.[34]

Called upon to handle the most serious relief crisis, the majority of states brought little practical experience to the task. In 1933, large-scale relief was as much an innovation on the state level as in Washington. Most departments had been in existence for less than ten months! To qualify for the old RFC loans, governors had hurriedly created emergency relief administrations by executive order or by *ad hoc* extensions of bureaus

[34]Colcord, "Social Work and the First Federal Relief Programs," 384–394; Bane COHC, pp. 10–11; Williams, *Federal Aid*, pp. 78–80, 83; James T. Patterson, *The New Deal and the States* (Princeton: Princeton University Press, 1969), p. 50; "Harry Hopkins," *Fortune*, XII (July, 1935), 59; Russell H. Kurtz, "On the Governor's Doorsteps," *Survey*, LXIX (October, 1933), 344–345.

of child welfare. They diverted personnel who had been dispensing widows' and orphans' assistance, hastily borrowed overseers from archaic poor boards, and even took volunteers from private charities. These local officials brought diverse philosophies representing all traditions of service, from the most punitive pauper relief customs to the most sophisticated professional techniques. To manage these thousands of administrators and ensure control over millions of dollars in disbursements, Hopkins created a regional staff. With a distaste for large organization charts, he chose a small group of field representatives, who shared his commitment to government responsibility for the unemployed, his passion for hard work, and his zest for experimentation.[35]

Aubrey Williams, who ultimately became one of Hopkins' top aides, shared his chief's experience in state-wide public service and detachment from professional case work. A native of Birmingham, Alabama, Williams had done volunteer settlement work among textile hands and black convict laborers. When World War I broke out, he went off to France with the YMCA, joined the Foreign Legion and later the AEF, and stayed on after the Armistice to study philosophy. During the 1920's he headed the Wisconsin State Conference of Social Work and worked closely with Governor Robert M. La Follette, Jr.'s, progressive administration to sponsor many social reforms, including an experiment in work relief. In 1931, he left to assist Frank Bane and the American Public Welfare Association establish state commissions to handle RFC relief loans. As an APWA field man in the South, Williams spent three months in Mississippi carving out county public welfare departments from scratch and securing competent local administrators. Against continued abuse from the press, he encouraged county officials to give each head of a family three dollars' worth of work per week. Williams then helped to create the Texas Relief

[35]Brown, *Public Relief*, pp. 177–181; Williams, *Federal Aid*, pp. 78–80; Springer, "The New Deal and the Old Dole," 348; Sherwood, *Roosevelt and Hopkins*, p. 49.

and Rehabilitation Commission under Governor James "Pa" Ferguson, by cajoling an unenthusiastic legislature for adequate funding. Again, he made sure that county boards handled all public money, and he drew guidelines for a social welfare department, employment bureau, and work relief program. These achievements brought applause from social workers throughout the country and the attention of Harry Hopkins, who appointed him FERA field inspector for the Southwest and then assistant administrator of the Division of Relations with the States, which coordinated all field repesentatives.[36]

The corps that Hopkins assembled to work under Williams epitomized the new "business of relief" that had emerged in the 1920's. Instead of "ladies bountiful" or graduates of social work school, they were lawyers and public administration experts, who had moved beyond neighborhood agencies and case work to rationalized fund-raising and systematic disbursement. Most were Republicans or independents, supported Hoover in 1928, and had served the PECE, POUR, and RFC Relief Division. Robert Kelso, a Harvard Law School graduate, directed community fund organizations, administered relief in Boston and St. Louis, and published several books, including *The Science of Public Welfare* in 1929. Rowland Haynes headed the War Camp Community Service from 1918 to 1920, directed the Cleveland Recreation Council and Welfare Federation, and worked for PECE and POUR. An alumnus of the New York Bureau of Municipal Research, Arch Mandel served in a succession of institutions which spearheaded the campaign for efficiency in city government: the Dayton Bureau of Municipal Research (1913–1916), the Detroit Bureau of Governmental Research (1916–1923), and the Dayton Research

---

[36]"Harry Hopkins," *Fortune*, XII (July, 1935), 59, 64; John A. Salmond, "Aubrey Williams; Atypical New Dealer?" in John Braeman, Robert H. Bremner, and David Brody, eds., *The New Deal: The National Level*, Vol. I (Columbus: Ohio State University Press, 1975), p. 221; Aubrey Williams, "Social Work in the Southwest," *SSR*, VII (September, 1933), 375–382; Joanna C. Colcord and Russell H. Kurtz, "Unemployment and Community Action," *Survey*, LXIX (March, 1933), 122–125; and *ibid.* (April, 1933), 168–170.

Association (1923–1926). Pierce Williams, a commercial attaché in London and Paris during the war, was associate director of the Association of Community Chests and Councils from 1923 to 1929. He wrote two books on corporate contributions to organized charities and from 1929 to 1932 was executive director of Commerce Secretary Hoover's favorite "think tank," the National Bureau of Economc Research. Williams, too, became a regional advisor for the RFC and stayed on under Hopkins. Others came to the FERA from the federations. Travers Edmonds was graduated from Yale, helped the Red Cross during World War I, directed civilian relief to Siberia, and wound up as executive secretary of the Iowa Tuberculosis Association from 1920 to 1933. Howard Hunter, an organizer for the Boy Scouts of America, led Community Chest campaigns in Connecticut and Michigan; and Alan Johnstone, a graduate of Harvard Law School, ran the Baltimore Community Fund and returned to his native South Carolina to head the state relief administration.[37]

Although initially appointed to inspect and report, these men soon exercised wide authority over state and local relief, imposing vast changes in America's system of public welfare. At first, each had a desk in Washington to answer questions through correspondence, while making sporadic forays to trouble spots. When this routine could no longer keep up with the urgent demands of overwhelmed, inexperienced officials, each representative took on a fixed number of states in a particular region. Constantly traveling about their assigned area, they contacted social workers and familiarized themselves with welfare politics in the legislatures. They came to know the petty quarrels that blocked appropriations and regional prejudices toward public aid. When state officers appeared hopelessly in-

[37]Key Personnel of the CWA," HLH 49; "Robert Wilson Kelso—Middle Westerner from Boston," Michigan AASW, *Compass Needle*, September, 1935, pp. 23, 40; Rowland Haynes, "Research and Social Work," NCSW, *Proceedings* (Chicago: University of Chicago Press, 1931), pp. 506–514; Arch Mandel, "Budgetary Procedure under the Manager Form of City Government," *Annals*, LXII (November, 1915), 163–168.

competent, field men requested governors to make new appointments. Trusting their judgment of local performances, Hopkins supported their recommendations and threatened to withhold funds when governors were unresponsive. In six states, he "stepped in" to create an entirely new department. By the end of the summer, FERA had laid out a nation-wide pattern for local relief, based upon new public agencies entirely separate from the old poor boards, on one hand, and charity units caring for mothers' aid and other statutory benefits, on the other. They swept away nineteenth-century traditions and set forth a "democratic interpretation of relief" that every citizen, not just orphans, widows, and the disabled, had a right to public assistance. Recognizing that personal distress resulted from a world-wide depression, they emphasized that federal aid must carry no stigma, no implication of favor, and no expectation of gratitude. Furthermore, they stipulated cash payments. "I cannot accept the projecting of nation-wide relief arrangements on a grocery order as anything but bad and undesirable," declared Williams before the National Conference of Social Work. "I have more confidence in what Mrs. John Smith can do with a five dollar bill."[38]

To determine eligibility and the amount of aid required by each family, Hopkins and Williams looked to social workers to dispense FERA money at the county level. Although disdainful of case-work techniques, they still preferred the integrity of dedicated professionals to ensure that relief went to those in need and to protect the FERA against political interference. Investigators applied the "means test" and drew up minimum standard budgets, listing essentials, local prices, and family size and income. They made certain that assistance equalled the "budget deficit" or whatever portion could be offered from available funds. Under the FERA, average general benefits per

[38]Frank Bane, Memo on Field Work, FB 20; Williams, *Federal Aid*, pp. 71, 161–162; Springer, "The New Deal and the Old Dole," 348–349; Bane COHC, pp. 15–16; Aubrey Williams, "The New Deal: A Dead Battery," p. 35, AW 44; Aubrey Williams, "A Year of Relief," NCSW, *Proceedings* (Chicago: University of Chicago Press, 1934), p. 158.

family rose 93 percent between May, 1933, and May, 1935, with the largest gains in Southern and Mountain states, where public aid had been virtually unknown before the depression. Social workers understandably hailed FERA as the most advanced relief program, yet Hopkins and Williams felt uncomfortable with direct cash payments as the accepted means to alleviate the unemployed. All along, they considered the dole a temporary expedient, to keep the jobless from starving until some form of work and wages could be provided.[39]

Hopkins was always looking for a more creative response, which he found among experts outside of social work, who shared his interest in public service and concern for wasted manpower. One was Corrington Gill, a young, handsome statistician, who took charge of FERA's new Division of Research, Statistics, and Finance. A graduate of the University of Wisconsin, where he majored in economics and statistics, Gill went East as a reporter and manager for the Washington Press Service and then organized the statistical department for the Federal Employment Stabilization Board under President Hoover in 1931. Gill directed the first comprehensive study of national business conditions as an index to long-range planning of federal public works. When Gill presented his findings to an FERA staff meeting, Hopkins invited him to join the team.[40]

In the summer of 1933, Hopkins also appointed Jacob Baker,

[39]Russell H. Kurtz, "Two Months of the New Deal in Federal Relief," *Survey*, LXIX (August, 1933), 284–290; Gordon Hamilton, "Case Work Responsibility in the Unemployment Relief Agency," *The Family*, XV (July, 1934), 135–141; Enid Baird and Hugh P. Brinton, *Average General Relief Benefits, 1933–1938* (Washington: United States Government Printing Office, 1940); Walter Wilbur, "Special Problems for the South," *Annals*, CLXXVI (November, 1934), 53.

[40]Schlesinger, *The Coming of the New Deal*, p. 268; Williams, "The New Deal: A Dead Battery," p. 72; Aubrey Williams, "Standards of Living and Governmental Responsibility," *Annals*, CLXXVI (November, 1934), 37–39; *New York Times*, July 14, 1946, p. 37; "Gossip," *Survey*, LXIX (August, 1933), 303; Corrington Gill, "The Effectiveness of Public Works in Stabilizing the Construction Industry," *American Statistical Association Proceedings*, XXVIII (March, 1933), 196–200.

a bald, thick-set, amiable engineer, to head the Division of Work Relief and Special Projects. With the most varied background of any man in Hopkins' circle, Baker had taught science in rural schools, then knocked around as a rancher and a day laborer. Before World War I, he had been a personnel expert with Bethlehem Shipbuilding Corporation and San Joaquin Light and Power Corporation of California; a consulting industrial engineer in Los Angeles and Chicago; and a partner of House, Baker, Associates of Chicago, where he assisted many of Samuel Insull's mid-boom mergers. In 1926, Baker helped organize and direct under the American Fund for Public Service an educational publishing house (today the Vanguard Press) in New York City.[41]

In Manhattan, soon after the Crash, "Jake" got involved with some friends in a self-help cooperative experiment and advocated public employment for the jobless. During the fall of 1932, he joined discussions at the New York City Taylor Society, where economists, engineers, lawyers, and businessmen explored the possibility of "bringing idle machines, raw materials, dwellings, and farms into a working relation with idle men and women eager and able to work."[42] With Baker in the forefront, they came up with a plan for the Emergency Exchange Association to get the unemployed through the winter by enlisting scientific management experts to direct "the cooperative manufacture of goods and rendering of services for

[41]William F. McDonald, *Federal Relief Administration and the Arts* (Columbus: Ohio State University Press, 1969), pp. 37–38; *New York Times*, September 20, 1967, p. 47.

[42]Jean Christie, "Morris Llewellyn Cooke: Progressive Engineer" (unpublished Ph.D. dissertation, Columbia University, 1963), p. 127; "Plan for the Industrial Organization of the Unemployed in New York City," JMC 75.

Volunteer directors of the Emergency Exchange Association included: Stuart Chase, economist; John Kirkland Clark, president of the New York State Board of Bar Examiners; John M. Carmody, president of Society of Industrial Management; Frank D. Graham, Princeton professor of economics; Henry S. Person, managing director of the Taylor Society; and Leland Olds, assistant to the chairman of the New York State Power Authority. Emergency Exchange Association, "Plan," no date, Columbia University Business Library.

themselves." Organized on a neighborhood basis, members would barter their labor, goods, or services as directed by technicians, many of whom were also jobless. Since the destitute had no purchasing power and their products and labor would be mutually consumed, reasoned the planners, the Exchange would not compete with commercial business and could supplement charitable agencies. Of greater importance, this rational work relief effort would sustain the morale and productive efficiency of the unemployed until they could re-enter the job market. Launched in February, 1933, the EEA functioned as a coordinator of community groups in New York, where its director, Jacob Baker, came to the attention of Hopkins, then head of New York State's TERA.[43]

Hopkins called Baker to Washington to hammer out a clearcut policy of genuine work relief within the FERA. When the federal government first assumed the burden of mass relief, an estimated 1,900,000 people had crude make-shift jobs on scattered state and local projects. Since the FERA made funds available to pay weekly stipends, Baker used this wedge to incorporate public works priorities into a work relief program. He encouraged more sophisticated projects and attempted to raise job standards commensurate with the skills of the unemployed. With limited success, Baker ordered all localities to submit proposals to state emergency relief administrators for approval. To improve the quality of work and diversify jobs, Baker also initiated federal projects, although communities hesitated to accept them.[44]

Attempts to upgrade work relief under the FERA fell far short of Baker's goals. Since few projects originated in Washington, the Work Division could only suggest that localities improve those already in progress. Many areas had little expe-

[43]Emergency Exchange Association, "The Crisis in Relief and the Mutual Exchange System," no date, Columbia University Business Library; *New York Times*, December 23, 1932, Sec. VIII, p. 2; December 24, 1932, pp. 1, 6; and December 28, 1932, p. 19.

[44]Williams, *Federal Aid*, pp. 99–108; McDonald, *Federal Relief Administration*, pp. 37, 47–48.

rience, virtually no plans, and only a half-hearted commitment. Field representatives found some jobs little better than the traditional "made work" for the malingering poor, and local officials still applied the "means test" to applicants for both direct and work relief. One qualified for either as long as personal resources could not provide for the necessities of life, and the "budget deficit" figured heavily in determining the amount of aid. The relation of total weekly earnings to need usually resulted in "staggering" workers and made continuity of employment virtually impossible. Furthermore, limited funds often provided the excuse to skimp on materials, while jealous public works departments and private contractors fought to confine projects to low-priority civic improvements. Pointing to projects of little value, the over-reliance on unskilled labor, inadequate supervision and materials, and general inefficiency, Corrington Gill found that FERA work relief "left much to be desired."[45]

Gill also based his conclusions on statistics he had gathered under FERA auspices by initiating the first nation-wide census of unemployment relief families. When individuals first appealed for aid in large numbers, they were jumbled together on emergency relief rolls. The FERA studied 12.5 million out of work, and for the first time, the amorphous mass of jobless took on a social texture of specific skills and diverse economic backgrounds, of ages, sexes, colors, family compositions, and previous occupations. Breaking down the data, Gill showed the broad spectrum of distress: the special needs of drought-stricken farmers compared with the desperation of jobless city workers, including a staggering 1 million idle factory hands, an enormous pool of trained workers wasting away on the dole. "We are now dealing with all classes," acknowledged Harry Hopkins before the National Conference of Social Work. "It is no longer a matter of unemployables and chronic dependents, but

[45]Arthur Edward Burns and Peyton Kerr, "Survey of Work Relief Wage Policies," *AER*, XXVII (December, 1937), 711–713; Corrington Gill, "The Civil Works Administration," *Municipal Year Book, 1937* (Chicago: International City Managers Association, 1937), p. 420.

your friends and mine. . . . The whole picture comes closer to home than ever before." Case workers now fussed over proper procedures for an applicant who owned a car, and Gertrude Springer discussed alternative techniques for clients with bank accounts. Their comments focused on "the new poor," unfamiliar with welfare and often embarrassed by their plight.[46]

Ominous reports of growing anger and resentment came to Hopkins' attention. "Relief was going out in great amounts but men were growing restless," observed a neighborhood case worker. FERA field reporters sensed the psychological impact of four years of depression, noting a "dangerous feeling of hopelessness and dependence—a spreading of listlessness." The unemployed did not want handouts; they wanted jobs. In her first letter, dated August 6, 1933, Lorena Hickok, Hopkins' roving reporter, conveyed unnerving news. She was struck by "unions of the unemployed," which had formed in the anthracite coal fields of Northampton County, Pennsylvania, called the Unemployed Council (under Communist influence) and the moderate Unemployed League. One of the League's chief complaints was that food orders "made us feel like charity cases." Miss Hickok added that such organizations of jobless could cause "plenty of trouble" if not handled properly. What they really wanted was "made work—for cash relief." "There are lots of things we could do around here," said the County League secretary. "We could fix up the river fronts, we could plant trees. We could repair buildings. . . . We'd all be better off and feel more like human beings." The Republican County chairman concurred, "If they're not in a fighting mood, they're getting

---

[46]Joanna C. Colcord and Russell H. Kurtz, "Unemployment and Community Action," *Survey*, LXIX (November, 1933), 390; Corrington Gill, *Wasted Manpower* (New York: W. W. Norton and Company, 1939), p. 155; and "A Study of Three Million Families on Relief," 25–26; Harry L. Hopkins, "The Developing National Program of Relief," NCSW, *Proceedings* (Chicago: University of Chicago Press, 1933), pp. 65–71; Gertrude Springer, "When Your Client Has a Car," *Survey*, LXIX (March, 1933), 103–104; "What? Clients with Bank Accounts?" *ibid.* (October, 1933), 347–348; "White Collar Temperament," *ibid.* (December, 1934), 374–375.

hopeless." Hopkins and his aides agreed that despite the enormous outpouring of funds and devoted, sympathetic administration, drastic changes would have to be brought to the relief system itself.[47]

VI

"Relief as such should be abolished," wrote Aubrey Williams to Harry Hopkins in late October, 1933. After dispensing over $1.5 billion in direct aid, Hopkins and his associates were still dissatisfied with FERA programs to help the unemployed. "What most of them needed was not case work but a job," Hopkins explained later. In the belief that men "have a deep yearning to express themselves through achievements," Williams sketched out his notion for an alternative employment program far bolder than the FERA Work Division and designed to incorporate those jobless who were too proud to ask for relief yet unable to benefit from public works. He would combine the present FERA activities and a part of the PWA program in one undertaking and eliminate the "harsh extremes" of both. His plan would "lift the status of relief to the employment level," scrap the "means test" and "budget deficit," and pay a daily wage for useful work reasonably suited to the applicants' skills and training. At the same time, Williams would avoid the prohibitive costs, elaborate plans, and red tape of orthodox public works by making the federal government the contractor under an "Emergency Employment Corporation."[48]

The fall of 1933 offered a propitious moment to lay this scheme on the President's desk. The sharp business revival of the summer had spent itself, as production and employment figures turned down once again. Although an estimated 3 million had returned to work during the Blue Eagle hoopla, the National Recovery Administration had not brought about an

[47]Hickok to Hopkins, August 6, 1933, HLH 61; Harry Hopkins, "The War on Distress," *Today*, I (December 16, 1933), 8, 9, 23.

[48]Memo, "On the Re-employment of the Unemployed," A. Williams to Hopkins, October 30, 1933, CWA 64; Hopkins, *Spending to Save*, pp. 133–134; Williams, "The New Deal: A Dead Battery," 73.

upturn as quickly as its proponents had anticipated. Industry failed to hire rapidly enough to offset new high school and college graduates entering the labor market. The class of 1933 "will go out into the world unemployed before they have ever had a job," commented a journalist. Relief rolls, which dropped sharply from their March peak, began to lengthen again in October. Buried in blueprints and contract specifications, the Public Works Administration had not yet absorbed many jobless nor stimulated industry by extensive material purchases. Unforeseen delays had emerged with the passage of state and local enabling legislation, debt limits, bond elections, and advertising for bids and contracts. The PWA seemed bogged down in technicalities, leaving most idle men with no immediate prospect for jobs until 1935; and FDR's first winter in office promised to be as dismal as any of his predecessor's. With Thanksgiving and Christmas not far off, Hopkins and his aides thought the time right to offer Williams' plan.[49]

Before Hopkins conferred with the President, however, he sounded out relief and administrative experts in the Midwest. On October 28, he arrived in Chicago to have lunch with Robert M. Hutchins, President of the University of Chicago, and to attend a football game. He was greeted at the LaSalle Street Station by Frank Bane and Louis Brownlow. Brownlow recalled how they urged Hopkins to use every means to induce the President to set up some emergency scheme to get more of the unemployed immediately on the payroll and "indeed, so far as relief was concerned, to abandon the means test for the time being." Hopkins reflected on their discussions en route to Kansas City, where he talked to Missouri's unemployment director, Harry Truman, who had made quite a stir with an honest and extensive road-building campaign.[50]

Hopkins found out what was really going on in the country

[49]Hopkins to Baker, October 18, 1933, CWA 92; "A Hard Winter Ahead," *Nation*, CXXXVII (October 18, 1933), 424; Beulah Amidon, "After College—What?" *Survey Graphic*, XX (June, 1933), 400–402; A. Williams to Hopkins, December 11, 1933, CWA 53.

[50]Brownlow, *Passion for Anonymity*, pp. 286–287; Sherwood, *Roosevelt and Hopkins*, pp. 50–51.

and brought the facts home to Roosevelt. At a luncheon meeting, he outlined Williams' scheme, which he explained would
not conflict with the Public Works Administration because it
would undertake smaller projects that could be started quickly
and terminated on short notice. This new agency would restore
the idle to wage-earning consumers, since the recipients would
spend the money immediately. Hopkins estimated he could offer
4 million jobs. "Let's see," said the President. "Four million
people—that means roughly $400 million." Roosevelt, too, re-
alized how slowly Ickes had started the PWA and decided to
take the money out of his appropriations. The whole effort
could tide the unemployed over one more winter until large-
scale public works would finally take up the slack.[51]

President Roosevelt formally created the new CWA by Executive Order on November 9, 1933. He diverted $400 million
from the PWA budget to finance short-term, light construction and named FERA head Harry Hopkins in charge of the
operations through his state and county relief organization. While
FERA would continue to supply direct relief, particularly to
special groups like transients, drought victims, and self-help
cooperatives, the CWA would employ 4 million on public projects. Conceived as an emergency stop-gap to create jobs, the
Civil Works Administration was an uneasy hybrid of social-
work compassion and engineering know-how. Initiated by welfare reformers, it stood out as the most advanced federal work
relief experiment ever undertaken. As an employment agency,
however, the CWA would have to rely on engineers, management experts, and labor mediators. Having already surrounded
himself with welfare executives detached from case work, Hopkins would now look for technicians who had moved far from
their professional orthodoxy and were willing to get thousands
of public projects underway within thirty days.[52]

[51]Schlesinger, *Coming of the New Deal*, p. 269; Sherwood, *Roosevelt and Hopkins*, pp. 48, 51.

[52]United States President, Executive Order, "The Creation of the Civil
Works Administration," November 9, 1933, CWA 53.

CHAPTER TWO

The Civil Works Organization: From Social Welfare to Social Engineering and Management

WHEN Harry Hopkins left the White House on Friday afternoon, November 2, 1933, after a luncheon meeting with President Roosevelt, he "fairly walked on air." Instead of taking two or three weeks of persuasion, FDR had acceded at once to his proposal for a new federal work relief program and even ordered Hopkins to get it going by the following week! Coming down to earth, the FERA Administrator quickly summoned his top aides, field men, and intimate advisors. He telephoned Aubrey Williams in New Orleans, interrupting his speech before the Community Chest, to give him the news that "his program" was going to start with $400 million. Hopkins then asked Louis Brownlow and Frank Bane to drop everything in Chicago and come to Washington, and he ordered FERA field men Pierce Williams and Howard Hunter back from the hustings. They all convened Saturday night at the old Powhattan Hotel; then on Sunday morning Jacob Baker, Corrington Gill, and other FERA staffers joined them for round-the-clock sessions in the unheated headquarters of the Federal Emergency Relief Administration in the Walker-Johnson Building, Eighteenth Street and New York Avenue. In cold, sparsely furnished rooms, amid unpainted partitions, Hopkins and his associates sketched out rules and regulations to put 4 million at work within thirty days.[1]

[1]Robert E. Sherwood, *Roosevelt and Hopkins* (New York: Harper and Brothers, 1948), pp. 51–52; Louis Brownlow, *A Passion for Anonymity* (Chicago: University of Chicago Press, 1958), pp. 287–288; Searle F. Charles, *Minister of Relief* (Syracuse: Syracuse University Press, 1963), p. 48.

Confronted with the largest administrative challenge in the peacetime history of the United States, Hopkins proceeded as he had only a few months before with federal relief, by "improvisation or emergency conversion." Back in the spring of 1933, when Washington had no cadre of trained public administrators to carry out the New Deal's social welfare policies, Hopkins had built the FERA by drafting left-over Hoover men from the Reconstruction Finance Corporation and Federal Employment Stabilization Board and coopting state and county relief officials to expedite local programs. But to manage the CWA's army of 4 million unemployed, who would join the federal payroll almost overnight, Hopkins would have to create an instant policy staff, an instant corps of project engineers, instant payroll and auditing departments, and other modern management apparatus which the federal government had long neglected. From FERA would come the only source of trained welfare administrators. The American Society of Civil Engineers, American Engineering Council, Taylor Society, and private construction firms would lend project managers, inspectors, and safety engineers to run a work force equal to that of General Motors, U.S. Steel, and twenty other mammoth corporations. Only the Veterans Administration, Treasury Department, and Public Administration Service could supply enough disbursers and accountants to balance the books on a mass of temporary "civil servants," five times the size of the federal work force in 1930.[2]

This massive draft of "outsiders" would eventually change the fundamental character of Hopkins' work relief experiment. He would move forward with no preconceived plans, organization charts, or formal directives, but the new recruits would insist on precise controls to maintain professional standards. Although Hopkins and his social work colleagues played a major role in promoting and getting civil works off the ground, they

[2]Lieutenant Colonel John C. Lee, "The Federal Civil Works Administration," 5, 12 (prepared for the information of the War Department, 1934), HLH 49; Louis Brownlow Diary, November 22, 1933, p. 23, University of Chicago.

quickly discovered that its implementation—the very business that raised the CWA above charity and made work—would largely be taken over by technicians drafted for the emergency.[3]

I

Even before President Roosevelt's Executive Order formally designated Hopkins the Civil Works Administrator on November 9, 1933, the "minister of relief" launched the CWA with a small group of trusted associates from the Federal Emergency Relief Administration. Hopkins, his FERA division chiefs, and the field men, all assumed dual offices for both organizations. Jacob Baker, head of the Work Division, took over all CWA engineering services, and Corrington Gill had charge of the Division of Finance, Research, and Statistics for the two agencies. Though they continued to make FERA grants-in-aid to the states for direct relief, their immediate attention shifted to the work program.[4] Agreeing they had little time to prod each state into line, they made the CWA a federal operation from top to bottom. Hopkins rather than the governors appointed all state civil works administrators, who in turn picked county heads. In effect, he deputized the state emergency relief officials to serve in a federal capacity, accountable only to him, his assistants, and the field representatives. At the same time, Hopkins "federalized" those already "employed" on state and local projects under the FERA Work Division. The first *Rules and Regulations*, issued on November 15, 1933, immediately

[3]Paul A. Kurzman, *Harry Hopkins and the New Deal* (Fair Lawn, New Jersey: R. E. Burdick, Inc., 1974), pp. 180–182; Arthur W. MacMahon, John D. Millet, and Gladys Ogden, *The Administration of Federal Work Relief* (Chicago: Public Administration Service, 1941), pp. 189–190; Jacob Baker, "The Range of Work Relief," *Public Works Engineers Year Book, 1935* (Chicago: Joint Secretariat American Society of Municipal Engineers and International Association of Public Works Officials, 1935), pp. 62–65.

[4]United States President, Executive Order, "The Creation of the Civil Works Administration," November 9, 1933, CWA 53; telegram, Hopkins to all governors, November 11, 1933, CWA 73; Betters to Gill, November 20, 1933, CWA 92; Hopkins to all department heads, November 27, 1933, CWA 53.

transferred 2 million "relief workers" to the CWA. At one stroke, "clients" became wage earners who would receive cash for their labor to spend as they saw fit.[5]

The CWA's second 2 million were recruited with the assistance of W. Frank Persons and his staff of the new United States Employment Service. Long the goal of social workers and progressive technicians, a national system of public employment exchanges had finally gotten underway when President Roosevelt signed the Wagner-Peyser Act in June, 1933, providing for federal aid to and coordination of already existing state and local agencies. Reconstituted during the summer as a bureau within the Department of Labor, the USES had scarcely begun referring workers for PWA projects when Hopkins dumped the CWA burden on its shoulders.[6] To meet the winter deadline, Persons created a special division, the National Re-employment Service. Almost overnight, NRS state directors set up local offices in armories, public schools, and other temporary offices, manned by volunteers, emergency relief personnel, and even CWA employees.[7]

[5]Corrington Gill, *Wasted Manpower* (New York: W. W. Norton and Company, 1939), pp. 163–166; Edward Ainsworth Williams, *Federal Aid for Relief* (New York: Columbia University Press, 1939), p. 110; telegram, Hopkins to all governors, November 11, 1933, CWA 73; Donald Stone to Charles Ascher, February 19, 1975, copy in possession of author; Civil Works Administration, *Rules and Regulations, Number 1* (November 15, 1933); Russell H. Kurtz, "Relief from Relief," *Survey*, LXIX (December, 1933), 404.

[6]Raymond C. Atkinson, Louise C. Odencrantz, and Ben Deming, *Public Employment Service in the United States* (Chicago: Public Administration Service, 1938), pp. 21–22; John Charnow, *Work Relief Experience in the United States* (Washington: Committee on Social Security, Social Science Research Council, 1943), p. 32.

[7]When the civil works program started, only a skeleton crew existed in most states, with 1,986 USES centers and a paid personnel of 1,959. By December, 1933, 3,428 local USES and NRS affiliates had 18,538 workers putting in long hours overtime just to keep abreast of requisitions. United States Employment Service, *Twelve and One-Half Million Registered for Work, 1934* (Washington: United States Government Printing Office, 1935), p. 6; telegram, Gill to all state civil works administrators, December 4, 1933, CWA 73; telegram, A. W. Motley to Mary LaDame, November 24, 1933, USES 609.

Across the country, 9 million eventually applied for the 2 million slots. Advertisements in newspapers during the last week of November directed people to report to federal buildings, courthouses, civic auditoriums, and other make-shift quarters. After midnight, November 28, when offices opened in New York City, about 500 people formed a thin line outside the Manhattan USES, 124 East 28th Street, but by dawn long files extended to Fourth Avenue below 27th Street. Approximately 5,000 crowded the sidewalk and spread onto the street by the Brooklyn station, while mounted police had to keep 2,000 behind barriers near the Long Island City center. In all, 15,000 jammed offices throughout the five boroughs that first day. In Chicago, a reported 70,000 assembled before sunrise on November 23, when the city opened forty-one park field houses and the Eighth Regiment Armory to register CWA applicants. By evening over 32,000 had filled out forms. An estimated 150,000 flocked to sign up the first week in North Carolina, although the state CWA estimated only a third would get on the payroll.[8]

"These fellows have to be hired and fired like everybody else on any contract job," declared Hopkins, as he assured applicants that the USES would follow procedures for public employment rather than those for dispensing relief. Earlier work programs accepted only heads of families with dependents, automatically turned away single youths, and examined the family budget and "relative needs." USES officials, in contrast, classified workers solely on the basis of skill, training, and experience. Several persons from one family could be signed on, while others with many dependents might be passed by. Like all federal agencies, the CWA prohibited discrimination be-

---

[8]Testimony of Harry Hopkins, U.S. Congress, House of Representatives, Committee on Appropriations, *Hearings, Federal Emergency Relief and Civil Works Program* on H.R. 7527, 73rd Cong., 2nd Sess., 1934, p. 20; Aubrey Williams, "Putting Four Millions to Work," NCSW, *Proceedings* (Chicago: University of Chicago Press, 1934), p. 410; *New York Times*, November 28, 1933, p. 26, November 29, 1933, p. 6; *Chicago Tribune*, November 23, 1933, p. 7, and November 24, 1933, p. 9; *Raleigh News and Observer*, December 8, 1933.

cause of race, religion, and color; but preference for war veterans figured in the eligibility because of stipulations in the Recovery Act. "We took the exact regulations of the Public Works Administration," Hopkins later explained, "because we were using Public Works funds." CWA rules favored ex-service men with dependents, then non-service men with the same qualifications, followed by able-bodied ex-veterans with no dependents, and, last, married men who had not seen military duty. The Veterans Placement Service, a division of the USES, saw that proper attention went to ex-service men, and its staff cooperated closely with local veterans' groups, like the American Legion, Veterans of Foreign Wars, and Disabled American Veterans. Finally, to provide for continuous work after an initial assignment, preferential classification also went, not particularly to the neediest, but to employees on projects previously started or completed.[9]

To speed up the hiring, CWA authorities in Washington set quotas for the states to fill by December 15, 1933, when the unused portion would go to other states. Hopkins and his staff meted out jobs rather than funds to keep the number on the payroll from being skewed by local variations in project costs due to regional differences in hourly wages, materials, and the money and equipment contributed by local sponsors. They decided on the ratio of three-fourths in accordance with each state's population and one-fourth on the basis of its total relief case load. State administrators used the same scheme to determine county quotas. As a compromise between relief needs and population densities, this formula favored urban-industrial areas, where unemployment figures ran highest, and gave eleven states 57 percent of all jobs. Thirty-nine percent of the total went for

[9]Hopkins, Address, November 27, 1933, HLH 3; CWA, *Rules and Regulations, Number 1*; Civil Works Administration, *Rules and Regulations, Number 2* (November 15, 1933); testimony of Harry Hopkins, House of Representatives, *Hearings, Federal Emergency Relief and Civil Works Program*, pp. 25--26; H. Robert Braden to Persons, December 11, 1933, USES 233; P. A. Burket to George K. Brobeck, December 2, 1933, USES 609; Miles Coleman to Congressman Kent Keller, December 30, 1933, CWA 13.

the heaviest concentration of jobless in ninety-three large cities, generally confined to New York, Illinois, Ohio, Pennsylvania, Michigan, California, Indiana, Massachusetts, New Jersey, Texas, and Wisconsin.[10]

Early hiring policies proved easy compared to the procedures needed to generate suitable projects (ultimately 300,000) to occupy 4 million workers. Unlike the Public Works Administration, which sub-contracted to private firms in the construction industry and got bogged down in engineering specifications, open bids, and legal negotiations, the CWA operated by "force account," where the federal government itself did the planning, purchasing, hiring, and firing. Although vulnerable to political corruption and patronage spoils, this method did provide Hopkins the necessary speed. "If you contract this stuff out, you will never get these fellows to work," he declared. Hopkins envisioned CWA undertakings as "stop-gap public works," somewhere between conventional projects and charitable made jobs, that had to commence immediately in November and terminate on short notice. At the same time, he had to avoid competition with private enterprise and conflict with the PWA. "No City Halls, schools, state institutions, or sewage disposal plants will be built," ruled Hopkins, drawing a definite distinction from Harold Ickes' program. But Hopkins determined to make the jobs socially useful. "We are not going to permit CWA funds to be used for garbage collection or for cleaning of streets or for snow removal," he warned.[11]

Despite Hopkins' desire for central control over project standards, the winter emergency forced him, from the start, to

[10]Betters to Hopkins, November 23, 1933, CWA 92; CWA Minutes, December 4, 1933, HLH 49; Hopkins to all state civil works administrators, November 12, 1933, CWA 73.

[11]Carl H. Chatters and Irving Tenner, *Municipal and Governmental Accounting* (New York: Prentice Hall, 1947), p. 396; Daniel W. Mead, *Contracts, Specifications and Engineering Relations* (New York: McGraw Hill, 1916), pp. 157–158; Fellows to D. C. Culler, February 14, 1934, CWA 10; Hopkins, Address in Baltimore, November 27, 1933, HLH 3; Hopkins to all governors and state emergency relief administrators, November 3, 1933, CWA 64.

delegate to state and local administrators authority to initiate projects. He charged local CWA executives to use their imagination and suggested park and playground construction, feeder roads, water mains and sewer extensions, excavations, and special projects for white collar and professional workers. But the responsibility remained with local officials to generate ideas. County offices received proposals from municipal public works departments, parks departments, social service agencies, boards of education, and similar public bureaus. They examined plans to see if they met basic requirements: that the work be confined to public property, be constructive, and have a cost ratio of seventy to thirty percent for labor and materials. Proposals that met these standards went to the state CWA administrator, who checked budget estimates for accuracy and gave the go-ahead to the locality to start hiring and to purchase tools, equipment, and materials.[12]

The CWA ordered local sponsors to furnish supplies to maximize the amount of federal money to go for wages. Although states, counties, and municipalities leased trucks, tractors, stone crushers, and concrete mixers, by the middle of November they faced an immediate crisis in procuring enough small tools. Chicago officials feared rioting might break out because they had signed men on without adequate supplies. "We could not buy any more tools," reported Hopkins. "They [manufacturers] have been down here lately trying to get us to use the [NRA] code authorities to get them to allow them to work overtime." Refusing to be delayed, Hopkins drew on all available stocks, such as those held by railroads, by Sears, Roebuck, and Montgomery Ward, and especially by the military. In late November, 1933, Hopkins asked the Secretary of War to make available picks, shovels, wheelbarrows, and other small equipment stored in Army depots. The War Department rushed supplies to Chicago and ordered local officers in San Francisco, New Orleans,

[12]CWA, *Rules and Regulations, Number 1*; Civil Works Administration, *Rules and Regulations, Number 3* (November 15, 1933); Henry R. Bitterman, *State and Federal Grants-in-Aid* (New York: Mentzer, Bush and Company, 1938), p. 311.

St. Louis, New York, Columbus, and San Antonio to issue tools to the respective state CWA. "We opened up warehouses from World War I," recalled Arthur "Tex" Goldschmidt, Baker's assistant. After meeting this emergency in selected cities, the War Department furnished the CWA with a list of supply areas upon which the state civil works administrators could call for available stocks.[13]

With workers equipped for real jobs, Hopkins determined to pay them real wages—the first respectable earnings many relief recipients had seen in years. Before the CWA, over 2 million people on FERA Work Division projects had collected an average of $20 a month based on social workers' figures of the budget deficit. "At the very time they are engaged on genuine public works," complained Hopkins, "they are receiving an income so totally inadequate that it is demoralizing and pauperizing." When Jacob Baker took over the Work Division in July, 1933, he attempted to institute a "fair wage policy" but still left the responsibility to state and local officers to determine standards and stipulate a daily wage or hourly equivalent. In August, the FERA established a $.30 per hour minimum. Although this order placed work relief benefits on an hourly basis with a maximum of eight per day and thirty-five per week, it still allowed local authorities to hold down total "earnings" by restricting the number of hours a worker could perform. For the CWA, Hopkins proposed to increase these FERA "relief wages" by raising the rates and hours, adding enough total

[13]Federal Emergency Relief Administrator to Chairman Senate Committee on Appropriations in Response to Senate Resolution, Number 115, *A Report on Expenditures of Certain Funds, May 1, 1935* (Washington: United States Government Printing Office, 1935), p. 112; Lt. Col. J. K. Crain to Assistant Secretary, War Department, November 24, 1933; R. E. Callan to War Department General Staff, November 28, 1933; C. J. Peoples to Assistant Secretary of War, November 29, 1933; all in AGF 2408; testimony of Harry Hopkins, House of Representatives, *Hearings, Federal Emergency Relief and Civil Works Program*, p. 28; CWA Minutes, November 23 and December 11, 1933, HLH 49; Hopkins to Secretary of War, November 23, 1933, CWA 73; Hopkins to Branion, November 23, 1933, CWA 4; interview with Arthur "Tex" Goldschmidt, Assistant Civil Works Administrator, September 14, 1976.

income to make the recipients self-respecting wage earners.[14]

Since the CWA's initial funds came from the Public Works Administration, Hopkins applied the PWA wage formula, which divided states into three zones with hourly minimums of $1.00, $1.10, and $1.20 for skilled labor in the southern, central, and northern regions respectively and the unskilled receiving $.40, $.45, and $.50 per hour. These rates followed suggested "floors" established by the blanket code of the National Industrial Recovery Act. Each person could put in up to thirty hours a week with an eight-hour-day maximum. Since PWA rates applied only to skilled and manual labor, CWA rules set special rates for semi-skilled, clerical, and other white collar employees (approximately $18.00, $15.00, and $12.00 per week for the northern, central, and southern states). Hours of labor were carefully limited to provide enough for most workers to live on but not to destroy the incentive to seek private employment. Each CWA jobholder could accumulate up to thirty hours per week, and clerical and professional employees could work as many as thirty-nine hours.[15]

Meeting the first CWA payroll for the 1 million employees who would line up on Friday afternoon, November 23, meant, said Harry Hopkins, that "the United States is going to draw more checks every month than it ever did in its life before," and they would have to be disbursed with great speed. "The greatest possible flow of dollars shall proceed into local channels of trade and business that recovery may be forwarded and relief be eliminated," Hopkins wired the governors. To expedite his payrolls, Hopkins and his aides decided to use the largest federal disbursing system, the Veterans Administration, with

[14]CWA, *Rules and Regulations, Number 1*; Corrington Gill, "The Civil Works Administration," *Municipal Year Book, 1937* (Chicago: International City Managers Association, 1937), p. 420; Hopkins to Ickes, November 6, 1933, CWA 53; Arthur Edward Burns and Peyton Kerr, "Survey of Work Relief Wage Policies," *AER*, XXVII (December, 1937), 711, 713–714; Julius Stone, "Draft Report on Work Relief," January 5, 1934, CWA 69.

[15]CWA, *Rules and Regulations, Number 1*; Viola Wyckoff, *The Public Works Wage Rate* (New York: Columbia University Press, 1946), pp. 91–92.

its decentralized regional offices and check-writing machinery. VA Administrator General Frank T. Hines designated a special officer in each state as the disbursement nucleus, who also handled purchases for CWA equipment and materials. In addition, Hines made 4,000 bonded agents available to every county, and they were authorized to give out U.S. Treasury checks to meet local payrolls.[16]

On November 8, 1933, when Hopkins had announced his intention to distribute the first paychecks within two weeks, officials from the Treasury and General Accounting Office warned that it was physically impossible to engrave, print, and distribute the necessary forms. But a special order from President Roosevelt commanded all federal agencies to stop work so that "every operation in every department concerned be expedited to the fullest extent possible that the U.S. Government may meet its obligation to these Civil Works employees." The Bureau of Printing and Engraving scheduled three shifts a day, and the Government Printing Office took on its largest single order up to that time to get out enough check paper. Airplanes and special delivery services rushed blank checks to CWA disbursing offices, and on the desired date, over 1 million CWA employees collected their first earnings. The President urged banks to cooperate by promptly cashing checks at par upon proper identification with cards issued to CWA workers. By mid-December, the Banking Code Committee passed a resolution to prohibit banks from charging to honor CWA checks. Gill also requested that payrolls be staggered to spread out the cashing of checks throughout the nation. Compared with 1933, when the federal government wrote 33 million paychecks each

[16]FDR to CWA, November 16, 1933, CWA 53; interview with Goldschmidt, September 14, 1976; Harvey C. Mansfield, *The Comptroller General* (New Haven: Yale University Press, 1939), p. 150; Hopkins to all governors, November 3, 1933, CWA 64; Civil Works Administration, *Rules and Regulations, Number 2* (November 15, 1933); CWA Minutes, November 27, 1933, HLH 49; U.S. Congress, House of Representatives, Committee on Expenditures in the Executive Departments, *Hearings, Relief of Disbursing Officers* on H.R. 151, 74th Cong., 1st Sess., April 10, 1935, p. 1.

year, the CWA that winter made 60 million individual payments totalling approximately $720 million.[17]

Along with a new wage policy, the CWA would depart from past work relief programs concerning liability compensation to those injured on the job. Traditional hostility toward relief had generally precluded the protection of persons on made work projects under existing accident compensation laws. After the Crash, several state legislatures had excluded "relief labor" from coverage. New York, the leader in much social welfare innovation, amended its laws to place injured Temporary Emergency Relief Administration employees back on direct aid based on budgetary needs rather than have them receive compensation. New Jersey statutes defined work relief as "casual employment" not compensable in a regular sense, and Pennsylvania removed the liability of public charitable institutions by collecting a contribution of $.25 per week per employee for the state treasury solely for this purpose. Several years of depression and more experience in work relief administration had modestly changed this assumption of liability. In May, 1933, a New Jersey law empowered the state emergency relief director to provide for medical treatment and hospital care and to give awards comparable to, but not exceeding, the maximum for a similar injury or death under the state workmen's compensation act. But these weekly allowances were based on need. The Pennsylvania General Assembly also extended medical treatment and hospitalization but no cash payments unless total disability continued for a minimum of six months. These two state laws illustrated a continued reluctance to regard injury on relief work as tantamount to an injury "on the job."[18]

[17]FDR to CWA, November 16, 1933, and Hopkins to Joint Committee on Printing, November 29, 1933, CWA 53; *New York Times*, November 24, 1933, p. 36; Gill to Hopkins, December 14, 1933, CWA 92.

[18]William M. Aicher, "Workmen's Compensation on Work Relief Projects," FERA, *Monthly Report* (July, 1935), pp. 2, 5–6; E. Glenn Callan, "Some Workmen's Compensation Problems of Persons on Work Relief," *SSR*, VIII (June, 1934), 211–225; Marietta Stevenson and Susan Posanski, *Federal and State Welfare, Relief, and Recovery Legislation, 1933–1934* (Chicago: Public Administration Service, 1935), p. 6; Roger F. Evans, "The Place of Work in

The CWA broke completely from this tradition. "If the federal government is required by an emergency to furnish employment to citizens," reasoned Hopkins, "it has the obligation to afford conditions of employment which would prevail among the great proportion of the working population." He applied to civil works job holders the medical and compensation features of the Federal Employees Compensation Act of 1916. CWA disability and death benefits could total up to two-thirds the rate earned at the time of injury, with a maximum of $116.16 per month. For administration, the CWA initially relied on the United States Employees Compensation Commission, which operated through its own offices in each state. But the organization of a claims section to investigate and adjust the 167,000 cases ultimately brought forward forced the USECC to delegate special authority back to the CWA, which created its own compensation department within the Finance Division and recruited top executives from private industry, like Ray Koehler, Vice President of A.T.&T., and insurance companies.[19]

Hopkins and his staff could take considerable pride in their remarkable transformation of work relief policies implemented in record time. By Christmas week, almost 4 million Americans were at work on the CWA. They had been lifted out of idleness and dependency, given a chance to wield a hammer,

Unemployment Relief," State Emergency Relief Board, *Unemployment Relief in Pennsylvania, September, 1932-October, 1933* (Harrisburg: State Emergency Relief Board, 1933), pp. 90–91.

[19]Testimony of Harry Hopkins, U.S. Congress, Senate, Committee on Appropriations, *Hearings, Federal Emergency Relief and Civil Works Program* (A Bill Making an Additional Appropriation to Carry Out the Purpose of the Federal Emergency Relief Act of 1933, for Continuation of the Civil Works Program and for Other Purposes) on H.R. 7527, 73rd Cong., 2nd Sess., 1934, p. 121; Civil Works Administration, *Rules and Regulations, Number 5* (December 12, 1933); Edward Ainsworth Williams, "Intergovernmental Relations under the Emergency Relief Program," FERA, *Monthly Report* (May, 1936), p. 16; Hopkins to I. G. Miller, January 5, 1934, CWA 53; CWA Minutes, December 4, 1933, HLH 49; McClure to all department heads, November 11, 1933, CWA 92.

ply a trowel, or sight a transit on projects which thousands of communities needed; to backslap on payroll lines instead of linger outside relief stations; to receive decent wages to take back to their families; and even to enjoy protection by accident compensation. To achieve these results, Hopkins and his men had built an organization of some 4,000 civic units, starting with the FERA and drafting personnel from any federal agency within reach—the United States Employment Service, the United States Employees Compensation Commission, the Government Printing Office, the Veterans Administration, and the War Department. "The logistics of the thing!" exclaimed "Tex" Goldschmidt. Many skeptics had doubted the federal government's ability to accomplish this mission, but Hopkins and his staff had proved them wrong. [20]

II

No sooner had the CWA gotten off the ground than the staff at the Walker-Johnson Building began to sense that the huge, decentralized operation needed tighter controls to maintain project standards. The approaching winter and mad rush to fill the quotas had forced state civil works authorities to revert back to old work-relief criteria for projects and had hampered the initiation of suitable new ones. The first CWA rules, issued on November 15, 1933, had permitted the wholesale transfer of all projects already in operation under the FERA Work Division, which meant that all the substandard made-work jobs which Hopkins and his associates had sought to improve now had the CWA imprint. New applications received consideration primarily if they could be implemented in the shortest time and by their potential to absorb the greatest number of idle hands. Uncertainty about the program's duration and little time for advanced planning further limited the quality

[20]Roy Lubove, *The Struggle for Social Security, 1900–1935* (Cambridge: Harvard University Press, 1960), pp. 45–65; interview with Goldschmidt, September 14, 1976; Gill, *Wasted Manpower*, p. 169.

of projects, while the unusually severe winter delayed work schedules.[21]

Haste during the first weeks caused technical requirements to go unchecked, with specifications and approvals often passed over the telephone. Choked with applications, the New York State office conceded that the process of approval had become superficial. Seven or eight officers "okayed" as many as a thousand applications in a week. California's civil works administrator later admitted "a failure to recognize the basic and essential features of project eligibility and of the inadequacy or irreconcilability of the estimates submitted." Sticking to federal orders that projects begin immediately and require only a small portion of material outlay, state officals tended to load up with highway construction and repairs. Hopkins feared a proliferation of questionable undertakings. "There are some pretty important people I have seen lately who tell me this is just covering up on work relief," he confided to his aides, "that this is not work projects." The Illinois Municipal League complained that "federal money is being wasted on state projects such as digging ditches . . . ," while a Democratic congressman from Los Angeles accused President Roosevelt of "having men do unnecessary work moving boulders and dirt from one side of the road to another." Hopkins' field man, Robert Kelso, reported that his New England states needed city engineers instead of welfare officials to assume "some advisory control," and Howard Hunter admitted seeing some "lousy" projects in the Midwest. The staff grew particularly uneasy about all the road work, reminiscent of convict labor and shabby "made jobs." Shrewdly aware that everyone could see outdoor projects, Hopkins realized how the CWA was particularly vulnerable to criticism.[22]

[21]Williams, "Intergovernmental Relations," 14–15; and *Federal Aid*, pp. 123–124; Gill, *Wasted Manpower*, p. 168.

[22]CWA Minutes, December 6 and 7, 1933, HLH 49; Alexander Leopold Radomski, *Work Relief in New York State, 1931–1935* (New York: Kings Crown Press, 1947), p. 221; California CWA, *Final Report* (March, 1934), p. 30; telegram, Illinois Municipal League to Hopkins, November 23, 1933, CWA 13; Congressman J. H. Hoeppell to FDR, November 27, 1933, CWA 4; Kelso

In a few short weeks, civil works had obviously gone beyond welfare administration to issues of engineering and management. Highway construction, the development of safe airports, building schools, and laying out of sewer lines all required technical skills; and interested professionals as well as the public began to question the "engineering integrity" of the program. Hopkins did not expect civil works to be compared with contract jobs, but his balance sheets, when examined during the November, 1934, election, would have to show reasonable services rendered for the $900 million spent. He therefore turned to a former engineer, Jacob Baker, head of the FERA Work Division, to take charge of all CWA engineering services; and Baker immediately drafted an old associate from the New York Emergency Exchange, John Michael Carmody, who was then a mediator for the National Labor Board, to come over to the Walker-Johnson Building as chief engineer.[23]

Carmody, like Baker, had a long interest in unemployment from the perspective of scientific management. Active in the Taylor Society for nearly twenty years, a member of the executive committee of the Management Division of the American Society of Mechanical Engineers, and past president of the Society of Industrial Engineers, he had taken part in special studies looking to technical solutions for unemployment. As editor of *Factory and Industrial Management,* Carmody differed with many of his conservative associates and supported early bills for public works and federal relief. In 1930, he wrote

---

to Hopkins, November 16, 1933, CWA 92; Hunter to Hopkins, December 8, 1933, CWA 81; Carmody to Baker, February 4, 1934, CWA 56; testimony of Harry Hopkins, Senate, *Hearings, Federal Emergency Relief and Civil Works Program,* p. 39.

[23]Perry Fellows, "Engineers in Government," *SAMJ,* II (May, 1937), 43; and "Municipal Engineers and the Relief Administration," *Public Works Engineers Year Book, 1935* (Chicago: Joint Secretariat American Society of Municipal Engineers and International Association of Public Works Officials, 1935), pp. 177–179; Conrad Van Hyning, "Work Programs from the State Point of View," *ibid.,* pp. 66–67; Hopkins to all department heads, November 19, 1933, CWA 53; Emergency Exchange Association to Carmody, December 11, 1933, and Carmody to Frank W. Sutton, February 28, 1934, JMC 73.

several articles advocating a role for engineers and businessmen in getting the idle back to work. "This is not a job for social workers only, nor for politicians, however highly placed," declared Carmody. "It is a job calling for the organizing brains of competent manufacturers."[24] Carmody joined informal discussion groups with economists, college professors, and local public officials at New York's City Club, although he recalled, "The management society had gone too completely Hoover to suit me." In late 1932, Jacob Baker invited him to join the Emergency Exchange, which Carmody later regarded as one of the Taylorite "action groups [that] would be called on during the next six months [of 1933] for little more than local activity but at the right moment could be amalgamated into a national agency." Carmody saw this opportunity when Baker asked him to join the CWA engineering division.[25]

On the job just before Thanksgiving, Carmody assembled his own technical staff to parallel Hopkins' field representatives from the FERA. According to Carmody, "No engineers and no production or construction men were in the picture the day the first 2 million were shifted over." "The relief part of the show . . . got a head start," he remembered. "They had stirred up a good many projects and had undertaken them locally without much clearance." Carmody quickly brought in expe-

[24]Carmody to Baker, January 4, 1934, CWA 56; Carmody to McClure, May 15, 1934, JMC 73; John M. Carmody "Unemployment Solutions," *Factory and Industrial Management,* LXXIX (June, 1930), 371; "Intelligent Unemployment Relief," *ibid.* (July, 1930), 67; and "Curing Unemployment— Whose Job Is It?" *ibid.* (October, 1930), 752.

[25]Carmody later scribbled on the "Plan for the Industrial Organization of the Unemployed in New York City" the following: "This is the Emergency Relief Association of New York, which really became the basis for the Civil Works Administration in Washington in 1933. Almost everybody who was connected with the New York program wound up in Washington and some of them *actually* outlined the CWA," JMC 75.

"CWA Reminiscences," April 24, 1958, JMC 73; Jean Christie, "Morris Llewellyn Cooke: Progressive Engineer" (unpublished Ph.D. dissertation, Columbia University, 1963), p. 126; The Reminiscences of John Michael Carmody, Vol. II, pp. 293–295, in the Oral History Collection of Columbia University (hereafter cited as Carmody COHC).

rienced engineers, industrial managers, and construction men who shared his recognition that technicians had to guide government intervention in the stricken economy:

> The industrial engineers that I had brought in had had some business but there wasn't any of them who wasn't glad to come. There wasn't one who wasn't glad to stay. They worked in the field. I could call them at seven or eight o'clock at night or even mid-night and get a response from them. They were glad to work. They enjoyed it. They were enthusiastic. All of us were. I recall nothing that approached it.[26]

For his chief assistant, Carmody chose Perry Fellows, another enthusiast for applying scientific management techniques to the unemployment crisis. As a municipal engineer in Detroit for nine years, Fellows had come to regard early made-work programs as "slavery," and he chaired a research committee for the Society of Industrial Engineers which promoted local public works for the jobless. Calling for a new "human branch of engineering," Fellows agreed with Hopkins' goal to give the unemployed productive jobs commensurate with their skills and training, which would "communicate to all the workers a sense of social dignity and value to their task."[27]

In this spirit, Carmody and Fellows added to the regional staff and state and county offices men who shared their desire for more engineers in public service. To the Southwest, they sent Russell Hackett, who had an engineering degree from Stanford, served as a military engineer in World War I, and worked for the Pacific Coast Power Company and the Washington State Highway Department. Thomas Hibben, an army

[26]McClure to all department heads, November 27, 1933, CWA 92; Carmody to Frank Sweetser, February 6, 1934, and to Erwin Schell, February 28, 1934, JMC 73; Carmody COHC, Vol. II, pp. 299, 301–302, quote from p. 307.

[27]S. J. Hudd to Carmody, December 28, 1933, JMC 73; Perry Fellows, "Economic Atmosphere Charged with Tremendous Potentials," *Society of Industrial Engineering Bulletin,* XIV (July, 1932), 15–16; "Engineers in Government," 42–43; "Worthwhile Work," *SAMJ,* I (May, 1936), 65; and "Standards of Efficiency in Governmental Activities," *ibid.,* IV (January, 1939), 18–19.

major during the war, inspector for the Interior Department, and private architect in New York City from 1924 to 1933, covered the Midwest. Joseph Hyde Pratt, who earned a Ph.D. from Yale, held the rank of colonel in World War I, and directed the North Carolina Highway Commission, took charge of the South. James C. Lindsey, a graduate of Reed College, member of the Taylor Society, and an industrial engineer for the Puget Sound Power and Light Company, served in the Pacific Northwest. The regional staff made formal recommendations for state CWA engineers and confirmed their choices for county positions. Carmody enlisted technical organizations, like the Taylor Society, American Engineering Council, and other construction and management groups, to participate in the planning and administration of local projects.[28]

At his desk in Washington, the chief outlined standards and procedures for tighter project control, which the field staff implemented in the states. Carmody insisted on "good plans" which left "nothing to the imagination," the cornerstone of efficient municipal engineering since the progressive era. While Hopkins preferred to settle things with a quick phone call, Carmody demanded blueprints, detailed specifications, and supervision schedules. CWA applications, which had started in November with a blank sheet of paper and a few lines for description of the project, now required a complete analysis with drawings, itemized costs, and estimates. The state engineers, who reported directly to Carmody's field men, still had final approval on all state and locally sponsored projects, and field engineers advised Hopkins' representatives as well as conducted their own investigations. But Carmody's men functioned as an independent inspectorate. They visited state headquarters to check on personnel, organization, and construction activities; and they held local conferences to discuss procedures relating to the types of projects in operation, elimination

[28]Carmody COHC, Vol. II, pp. 298–299; Key Personnel of the CWA, HLH 49; "CWA Reminiscences," April 24, 1958, JMC 75; Carmody to Fellows, December 4, 1933, CWA 72; Memo on Field Representatives, CWA 73; American Engineering Council to Hopkins, January 27, 1934, CWA 65.

of useless projects, and methods to improve CWA work. They also set guidelines for inspection reports, requiring data on cost justification, whether the project was over- or under-manned, if supervision and equipment were sufficient, and bills for materials. In their zeal, the engineers strongly urged more investment in building supplies and materials to enhance the quality of projects, but Carmody had to disagree "on the grounds that the organic policy of the CWA is to employ needy people rather than to complete public projects no matter how worthy." Still the chief could not quite relinquish all public works priorities and confided to his men: "If the program goes forward, it is entirely likely that with proper engineering supervision we may be able to work out such a plan."[29]

In a further attempt to bring projects under more reliable control, and at the same time put people to work quickly, Hopkins decided to take over 1 million "federal" CWA jobs and placed them under the engineers' direct supervision. To coordinate these programs, Jacob Baker set up a special office under Julius F. Stone, Jr., a chemist and experienced relief administrator in New York State, who had first come to Washington at Hopkins' request to assist Baker with the FERA Work Division. As the new head of CWA Federal Projects, Stone called on federal agencies to sponsor worthwhile opportunities for the nonmanual and professional unemployed. The Treasury Department, for example, sponsored the CWA's Public Works of Art Project, which hired 3,000 artists, painters, sculptors, etchers, and mural designers. Technicians worked on experiment stations for the Department of Agriculture, Tennessee Valley Authority, and Soil Erosion Service. Surveys conducted

[29]Telegram, Carmody to Joseph P. Shaw, February 16, 1934, CWA 31; Hopkins to all states, December 7, 1933, CWA 67; Hunter to Carmody, January 10, 1934, CWA 81; Reynolds to Hunter, December 4, 1933, CWA 13; Shaw to Carmody, January 10, 1934, CWA 92; Hackett to Carmody, December 9, 1933, CWA 4; Hunter to Hopkins, December 10, 1933, CWA 81; William Ford to Fellows, April 9, 1934, JMC 73; Carmody to Baker, January 27, 1934; and Carmody to R. J. Sheehan, January 27, 1934, CWA 56.

by the Department of Commerce pooled idle white collar workers into the CWA, and the U.S. Department of Health waged campaigns against gypsy moths, grasshoppers, ticks, and other pests. Although the federal sponsor took charge of project execution in the states, Stone had final approval on all proposals and served as liaison between federal project directors and local CWA offices.[30]

A significant number of CWA federal projects came under the dual administration of Stone's assistants and the engineering expertise of War Department officers at bases and depots across the country. The Quartermaster General acted as War Department representative for civil works affairs, and he prepared "Supplemental War Department Civil Works Programs," which included jobs on Army posts, stations, national cemeteries, and National Guard and Seacoast Defense Projects. Stone approved projects totalling $11,510,104 in Regular Army Sections and the National Guard which employed a total of 55,000 CWA workers. At Wright Field, Ohio, CWA workers extended runways, improved drainage ditches, did landscaping, and repainted building interiors. A complete drainage system was installed at Patterson Field, Ohio, a facility previously muddy and unsafe after any severe rain. Fort Knox had its landing field resurfaced, roads repaired, a storm drain installed, and a new nine-hole golf course designed for officers. And projects at Arlington National Cemetery, Fort Myer, the Army War College, and Bolling Field put the Washington, D.C. area unemployed to work.[31]

[30]Civil Works Administration, *Rules and Regulations, Number 4* (November 25, 1933); Betters to Baker, November 20, 1933, CWA 92; CWA Organization Chart, JMC 73; Stone to Illinois CWA, January 20, 1934, CWA 13; Stone to Hunter, February 20, 1934, CWA 81; Carmody to Stone, January 4, 1934, CWA 62; Stone to all federal departments conducting CWA projects, January 18, 1934, CWA 62; TVA-CWA Coordinator to Stone, January 29, 1934, CWA 96.

[31]Hopkins to Dern, November 27, 1933; Major General R. E. Callan to Chief of Staff, February 12, 1934; and Major General L. H. Bash to Deputy Chief of Staff, March 31, 1934, all in War Department General Staff Papers, Box 262; and Dern to Donald Richberg, August 14, 1934, War Department

The most revealing aspect of engineering control over civil works, however, occurred when Carmody and his staff imported industrial safety management into the CWA. Before World War I, safety engineering had emerged in large, integrated firms like U.S. Steel and their "captive" coal mines, where plant managers and their insurance underwriters were appalled by unpredictable compensation suits, the disruption of continuous operations, and the sheer waste of accidents. Safety experts came to regard the accident-prone as particular social types: the worker distracted by "morale problems" at home; the careless or irascible "loner" who did not cooperate with the production team; the illiterate, undisciplined immigrant ignorant of sensible procedures.[32] With his background in the Cleveland steel mills and Davis Coal and Coke Company and his service on the U.S. Coal Commission, Carmody saw the CWA as "the biggest industrial safety job ever attempted," particularly when psychologists and professional safety inspectors warned that the depression had added to the ranks of the

General Staff Papers, Box 309, Record Group 165, National Archives; Major General R. E. Callan to War Department Chief of Staff, December 5, 1933, AGF 2408; Stone to Baker, January 9, 1934, CWA 92.

[32] Arundel Cotter, *United States Steel: A Corporation with a Soul* (Garden City: Doubleday and Company, 1921), pp. 187–197; William Graebner, "The Coal-Mine Operator and Safety: A Study of Business Reform in the Progressive Era," *Labor History*, XIV (Fall, 1973), 483–505; "Iron and Steel Session," *Proceedings of the First Cooperative Safety Congress, 1912* (Princeton: Princeton University Press, 1912), pp. 280–283; M. F. Gartland, "The Personal Element in a Safety Program for the Foundry," *Proceedings of the National Safety Council* (October, 1919), pp. 726–730; Lucian W. Chaney, "The Statistical Factor in the Accident Experience of the Iron and Steel Industry," United States Department of Labor, Bureau of Labor Statistics, *Bulletin, Number 428* (Washington: United States Government Printing Office, 1926), pp. 35–87.

Corporate managers and engineers also participated in the movement for workmen's compensation. See James Weinstein, *The Corporate Ideal in the Liberal State, 1900–1918* (Boston: Beacon Press, 1968), pp. 40–61; Robert F. Wesser, "Conflict and Compromise: the Workmen's Compensation Movement in New York, 1890s–1913," *Labor History*, XI (Summer, 1971), 345–372. Although Carmody discussed his early support of accident compensation laws in Ohio, there is not enough evidence to show the engineers' role in developing CWA compensation provisions. Carmody COHC, Vol. II, pp. 312–313.

accident-prone. The one-time steady worker, unemployed for months or even years, had lost his factory discipline, developed flabby muscles, and became distracted with worries about paying the rent and putting bread on the table. Thousands who had completely forgotten the "techniques of group labor" took on civil works assignments requiring skills they had never learned. "We had a terrific safety problem," noted Carmody, recalling his first days on the CWA:

> I was aware of the kind of thing we were up against. Hopkins might have thought of it later—but he had no knowledge of that sort of thing; nor did many of the others with whom I associated. Almost none of them had the same kind of industrial background that I had had.[33]

After a few days at his desk, Carmody contacted his friend, William H. Cameron, managing director of the National Safety Council, and recruited a top staff man and safety engineer, Sidney J. Williams. A graduate in civil engineering from the University of Wisconsin, Williams had served with the Industrial Commission of Wisconsin from 1913 to 1918 and directed the Public Safety Division of the NSC. With no time for elaborate plans or detailed instructions, Williams, in effect, coopted the National Safety Council into CWA service. The Council not only had the technical expertise but could do the job with minimal preliminaries, as its members welcomed the opportunity to put across safety instruction to 4 million. Circulating lists of qualified candidates for state directors, Williams personally appealed to associates to volunteer. The response was splendid among men "loaned for the work because their companies recognized a real emergency and a real opportunty." Within three weeks, nearly every state had a director, who in turn appointed county officials ultimately totalling 1,800—approximately one

---

[33]Carmody COHC, Vol. II, pp. 312–313; Carmody to Frank Sweetser, February 2, 1934, JMC 73; Hart Ellis Fisher, "When the Employee Returns to Work," *National Safety News*, XXIX (May, 1934), 17–18, 59; William H. Cameron, "What Happened to the Safety World in 1933," *ibid.* (February, 1934), 13–14.

safety man for 2,200 to 3,000 employees, practically the same proportion in modern industrial plants. Williams coordinated the campaign through regional meetings which urged full-time inspectors on projects employing ten or more men, correction of physical hazards in compliance with existing codes, placement of men on jobs suited to their physical and mental powers, instruction of new recruits by foremen, and immediate reporting of accidents to the state safety director. Relying on recognized safety codes, Williams also drafted new recommendations to meet the unique CWA working conditions from construction sites to sewing rooms.[34]

Besides bulletins and letters (and some 80,000 posters), Williams relied on the state directors, who recruited from a half dozen to thirty or forty engineers per state to go into the field. Most moved from project to project, explaining, advising, and in some cases stopping the job until ditches were shored up or banks graded properly. Although professionally trained men were needed at every project site, a shortage was inevitable. Williams sought cooperation from the American Red Cross and the United States Bureau of Mines, who helped instruct some 70,000 persons (more than peak times of World War I) on treatment of minor injuries, pressure points to control severe bleeding, and artificial respiration. The CWA held infections down to the average minimum found in private industry, at a cost from two to four cents per man per week (nearly half that of safety programs run by large corporations). CWA officials had estimated in December, 1933, that without a safety program, the 1 billion man-hours worked might produce at least 800 deaths and thousands of injuries. By reducing the actual number of fatalities to half of those predicted, the CWA saved

[34]Carmody COHC, Vol. II, pp. 309–310; Carmen T. Fish, "The Biggest Industrial Safety Job Ever Attempted," *National Safety News*, XXIX (February, 1934), 19–20; Sidney J. Williams, "Four Million Green Men," *Safety Engineering*, LXVIII (October, 1934), 144; Anne W. Buffum, "Saving Lives on CWA Jobs," *ibid.* (June, 1934), 9; S. Williams to E. G. Padgett, January 2, 1934, CWA 34; W. O. Wheary, "Safety Procedures on Federal Work Relief Programs," FERA, *Monthly Report* (March, 1936), p. 20.

$1.5 million in death benefits and from $6 million to $8.5 million in compensation and medical costs.[35]

III

Engineering project control represented only one half the administrative effort to upgrade the CWA from relief to public employment. The technical dimension would have been incomplete without sophisticated audits on project expenditures—a partnership of engineering and accounting that had grown out of municipal reform in the progressive era. At the turn of the century, engineers and businessmen had come to prominence in city administrations in sharp reaction to the "honest graft" and dubious standards that were hallmarks of the "Tammany" engineer. From the supervision of street paving to garbage collection, the new breed of city managers focused on "executive budgets" to provide a monitor of municipal activity, cost accounting which stressed line-by-line itemization to eliminate lump-sum requests, and organization charts, similar to those in business, which pinpointed responsibility. By the 1920's, this municipal accounting centered on standardized "unit costs" as a scientific yardstick to measure anything from laying asphalt by the square yard to inspecting pot holes per day.[36]

To promote these methods, administrative reformers and fi-

[35]S. Williams to all state directors of safety, January 10, 1934, CWA 92; Carmody COHC, Vol. II, pp. 312–313; Foster Rhea Dulles, *The American Red Cross* (New York: Harper and Brothers, 1950), p. 319; F. G. Padgett to S. Williams, December 28, 1933, CWA 34; S. Williams to Carmody, March 30, 1934, CWA 92; Report, FERA to NEC, December 17, 1934, NEC 152; Curtis Billings, "CWA Offers a Lesson in Accident Prevention," *ENR,* CXIII (October 4, 1934), 426–428.

[36]Barry Dean Karl, *Executive Reorganization and Reform in the New Deal* (Cambridge: Harvard University Press, 1963), pp. 18–21; Morris Llewellyn Cooke, *Our Cities Awake* (Garden City: Doubleday, Page, and Company, 1918), pp. 13–42; Frederick A. Cleveland, *Chapters on Municipal Accounting* (New York: Longmans, Green and Company, 1909), pp. 104–106, 115–117, 122; Louis Brownlow, "The New Role of the Public Administrator," *National Municipal Review,* XXXII (May, 1934), 248–251.

nance experts sponsored national organizations in the 1920's, like the City Managers Association, Municipal Finance Officers Association, and National Committee on Municipal Accounting. The increased welfare expenditures and mounting urban debts after 1929 prompted further reforms to help cities meet their fiscal crises. Professional managers attempted to advance these techniques through the publication of manuals, like the Municipal Finance Officers Association's *Accounting Manual for Small Cities* (1933) and *A Manual of Public Works Records and Administration, Flint, Michigan,* put out by the Public Administration Service. In 1933, the PAS staff installed public works cost-accounting methods in Flint and Ann Arbor, Michigan; Newport, Kentucky; and Niagara Falls, New York, to demonstrate the control of men, materials, and equipment via the unit-cost system. "Citizen interest is at its height and the demands of the time are ripe for bringing about the improvements which have been sought for a long period of years," wrote Carl Chatters, executive director of the Municipal Finance Officers Association.[37]

Inevitably, these experts saw the CWA as an enormous administrative challenge and opportunity to promote progressive financial management through the federal government. The sheer magnitude of its half-billion-dollar payroll necessitated overhauling federal record-keeping, while CWA audits were complicated by the disbursements inherent in the force account. Furthermore, the likely charges of waste and corruption from Republican editorial writers and even members of the President's own party made it imperative to throw every possible accounting safeguard around the agency. With the future integrity of relief and public works at stake, Hopkins drew on personnel from the FERA and adapted traditional methods where expedient. But, in the end, he relied on professionals from outside agencies, like the Public Administration Clearing House

[37]Leonard D. White, *The City Manager* (Chicago: University of Chicago Press, 1927), pp. 266–274; Carl Chatters, "Municipal Accounting," *Municipal Year Book, 1934* (Chicago: International City Managers Association, 1934), pp. 51–53.

and Public Administration Service, and refused to allow obsolete statutes and time-consuming procedures to block his path. Just as the CWA had discarded social case work and long-range planning, it took a fresh approach to federal bookkeeping and budgeting, much to the satisfaction of the management experts whom Hopkins had called in.[38]

During those first hectic days in November, 1933, Hopkins turned to Louis Brownlow, director of the Public Administration Clearing House and one of the most influential of the new public servants. As city manager of Petersburg, Virginia, in 1920, the "first necessary reform" he instituted was a budget system with modernized accounting and a centralized purchasing office. Before he went to manage Knoxville, Tennessee, in 1924, Brownlow hired accountants to provide "prompt and accurate reports that could be keyed in with the control necessary to maintain a sound, efficient, and economical purchasing system." As president of the City Managers Association, in 1922, an organization composed predominantly of engineers, Brownlow personified the growing independent professionalization of municipal administration. His commitment to improve the techniques of government led him to help establish PACH in 1931 as a center for city management information. At Hopkins' invitation, Brownlow brought into the CWA several experts in municipal finance, chiefly from the Public Administration Service, a joint agency made up of ten national associations of public officials organized to improve standards of government.[39]

The most important of Brownlow's recruits was Donald C. Stone, an associate from the University of Chicago, director of research for the PAS and International City Managers Asso-

[38]Lee, "The Federal Civil Works Administration," p. 2; Mansfield, *Comptroller General*, pp. 218–219; Bitterman, *State and Federal Grants in Aid*, p. 312; Louis Brownlow Diary, November 24, 1933, p. 31; Hopkins to Comptroller General, January 5, 1934, CWA 53.

[39]Brownlow, *Passion for Anonymity*, pp. 117, 119, 145, 172; Karl, *Executive Reorganization*, pp. 101, 104–105; Richard Polenberg, *Reorganizing Roosevelt's Government* (Cambridge: Harvard University Press, 1966), pp. 11–12.

ciation from 1930 to 1933, and advisor on the reorganization and administrative improvement of approximately 100 city, county, and state governments from 1930 to 1939. Called in to straighten out CWA accounting, Stone applied professional city-manager techniques to tighten the agency's financial controls. Double-entry bookkeeping, the balance sheet, time cards for payrolls, centralized purchasing, and code numbers (so the bookkeeper would know which item to charge or credit) became the order of the day in civil works. Stone insisted on securing well-qualified personnel and employing sound methods in the "new management," which he and his associates proceeded to spell out.[40]

On December 26, 1933, the Civil Works Administration issued a *Manual of Financial Procedure, Accounting, and Reporting* to provide a complete and uniform system down to the county level. Stone, along with Gustave Moe, chief accountant of PAS, and others from the Public Administration Service and American Municipal Association, drew up the guide in two weeks' time. "The Government Printing Office turned handstands and printed it in something like forty-eight hours," recalled Stone, as over 30,000 copies were circulated among every state and county CWA office. More than simple instructions for setting up proper balance sheets, the *Manual*, in typical PAS tradition, explained how to establish and manage a local CWA office. It contained forty illustrations of various forms and outlined policies for project approval, recruiting workers, payrolls, purchasing, and voucher procedures, together with a plan of accounting for budgetary control. Instructions described all reports which the local unit had to prepare for the state and that the state was to send to Washington. The *Manual* replaced

[40]Louis Brownlow Diary, November 24, 1933, p. 31; Donald Stone, "The Need for Standard Units and Costs in Municipal Management," *Municipal Year Book, 1931* (Chicago: International City Managers Association, 1931), pp. 232–239; "Public Works Management with the Aid of Records and Standards," *ibid., 1932*, pp. 150–153; "The Use of Administrative Reports in the Control of City Activities," *ibid., 1933*, pp. 161–174; and "Reorganizing for Relief," *Public Management*, XVI (September, 1934), 259–262.

fourteen old FERA and CWA forms, established twenty new ones, and left only three unchanged.[41]

A comparison of project applications illustrates the increased emphasis on itemization, the mainstay of scientific cost accounting. The old FERA Work Division and CWA at first had asked only for estimated costs, divided according to relief labor, nonrelief labor, materials, equipment and supplies, and contingent costs; sources of funds; and methods of financing. The revised CWA Form L3A, in contrast, was a "rather comprehensive document," consisting of four pages of itemized fine print. It demanded the names of the public agency sponsoring the plan, the person who prepared the attached drawings and specifications, and the officer who would supervise operations. A half page was provided for a description and location of the project and an equal amount for remarks. Two pages called for data on estimated costs, with one for wages and salaries. Each occupation had a classification: skilled, semi-skilled, supervisory, and other; and for each category the application had to show the average number of employees (by sex), number of man-hours, hourly (or weekly) rates of pay, and total estimated cost. The second page required estimated expenses of teams, trucks, and other major equipment, of materials and supplies, and of other direct expenses. Each nonlabor cost had to be itemized with estimates of quality, cost per unit, and total cost shown for each item and type. Although detailed, the system's standardized entries could enable every civil works unit to obtain "with the least amount of effort complete control over all CWA projects." To make doubly sure, the new procedures were transmitted through regional conferences attended by state and local accounting personnel and presided over by field examiners who had assisted in preparing the *Manual*. Local accounting records were supervised by state CWAs and, in turn, the states were

[41]Stone to Ascher, February 19, 1975; Gustave A. Moe, "Manual of Accounting Procedure Prepared for CWA and PWA," *Public Management*, XVI (February, 1934), 55–56; Civil Works Administration, *Manual of Financial Procedure, Accounting and Reporting for State and Local Civil Works Administrations* (Washington: United States Government Printing Office, 1934), pp. 1–2.

checked periodically by the field staff. These accounting records formed the basis of weekly statistical information required
by the CWA Finance Division in Washington to ensure the
strict compliance essential for the federal program.[42]

Although designed to help the CWA to control expenditures
and monitor projects, the *Manual* was also conceived by its
authors as a means to introduce modern, simplified, and standardized accounting methods throughout the country. Stone called
it a "monumental step in the development of efficient public
works accounting by local government." Although the procedures outlined in the *Manual* were automatically implemented
under CWA rules, they could apply just as handily to public
services in cities and counties yet untouched by the municipal
efficiency movement. Louis Brownlow confided to his diary:

> In hundreds of municipalities the CWA manual has intro-
> duced modern cost accounting, purchasing, and reporting
> procedure for the first time. . . . How to persuade munic-
> ipalities to adopt these procedures for their existing haphaz-
> ard accounting systems, or in many instances for their utter
> lack of accounting systems, is a problem for the American
> Municipal Association, the State Leagues of Municipalities,
> and for the Municipal Finance Officers Association. The
> power of the Federal Government under the circumstances
> to impose the procedure as a mandatory requirement so far
> as the CWA and PWA is concerned may give a better op-
> portunity for the propagation of improved uniform account-
> ing practices than we have ever had.

The success of the *Manual* inspired two more organizations,
the American Society of Municipal Engineers and the International Association of Public Works Officials, to join the PAS
in July, 1934; and the CWA experience became the chief topic

[42]Illinois CWA, *Final Report* (March, 1934), pp. 83–94; FERA, *Report on
Expenditures*, pp. 111–112; CWA, *Manual*, Sec. II, pp. 1–6; Paul Webbink,
"The Vast Relief Machinery: the Method and the Checks," *New York Times*,
November 18, 1934, Sec. VIII, p. 3; CWA Organization Chart, JMC 73.

on the agenda of a nation-wide conference held in September as the first joint project of the two groups.[43]

The ultimate in advanced management thinking in the CWA came with the expansion of its Division of Research and Statistics, whose lineage dated back to those institutional gadflies of progressive reform—the bureaus of municipal research. In August, 1933, Corrington Gill had recruited Emerson Ross, formerly with the RFC, to take charge of economic analysis, and Paul Webbink, a research economist with Senator Robert M. La Follette, Jr., as head of statistics for FERA. During the summer and fall, they concentrated on studying the volume and trends in unemployment. With the civil works program, they vastly increased their research activities as CWA federal projects. Employing over 35,000 white collar workers, the CWA Statistics and Research Division became the service bureau for the professional managers attempting to upgrade public administration. While the National Relief Census and the Employment and Payroll Analysis gathered material on the unemployment crisis and provided the potential brief for continuation of the CWA, other inquiries, like the Real Property Inventory, Urban Tax Delinquency, Building Maintenance Survey, and City and Regional Planning Projects, helped document the extent of municipal bankruptcy and its possible resolution through emergency tax and budgetary reforms.[44]

[43]"Accounting Controls for CWA and PWA Expenditures," *American City*, XLVIII (February, 1934), 5; Lloyd Morey, "Uniform Accounting for Local Governments," *National Municipal Review*, XXIII (July, 1934), 377–379; Louis Brownlow Diary, January 14, 1934, p. 184, quote from January 16, 1934, p. 191.

PAS also prepared a manual for the PWA, and its staff surveyed and recommended financial procedures for the Tennessee Valley Authority. "Public Administration Service Expands," *National Municipal Review*, XXIII (July, 1934), 391–392; Donald Stone, "PAS—Consulting and Research Division," *ibid.* (December, 1934), 706; Federal Emergency Administration of Public Works, *Manual of Financial and Accounting Procedure for Public Bodies* (Washington: United States Government Printing Office, 1934).

[44]"Gossip," *Survey*, LXIX (August, 1933), 303; Emerson Ross, "Research and Statistical Programs of the Federal Emergency Relief Administration," *Journal of the American Statistical Association*, XXIX (September, 1934), 288–

•   •   •

The civil works organization was launched in November, 1933, by Harry Hopkins and a small group of trusted associates, primarily welfare administrators and veterans of earlier campaigns against poverty, who had grown impatient with traditional case work. They recognized that the Great Depression had created a new class of unemployed, among skilled mechanics, white collar workers, and even professionals, who were resentful of the current federal relief program. Through the CWA, Hopkins and his colleagues sought to lift the jobless from demeaning investigations, weekly handouts of powdered milk, surplus flour, and subsistence checks, and meaningless made work designed just to keep the idle moving. Instead, the jobless would sign up at local employment offices, have their applications processed like those in any private industry according to skill and training, work on economically and socially desirable projects, and get paid decent weekly wages. "The difference is very real," remarked Hopkins, comparing traditional work relief to his new venture in public employment:

> Although the individual on work relief gets the disciplinary rewards of keeping fit and making a return for what he gets, his need is still determined by a social worker, and he feels himself to be something of a public ward. . . . When he gets a job on a work program, it is very different. He is paid wages and the social worker drops out of the picture.[45]

294; telegram, Baker to all state administrators, December 15, 1933, CWA 73; Ralph G. Hurlin, "State and Federal Cooperation in the Collection of Social Welfare Statistics," *Proceedings of the American Statistical Association*, XXIX (March, 1934), 94–98; Lurie to Paul Webbink, January 26, 1934, and Webbink to Lurie, February 1, 1934, HLL 2; Louis Brownlow Diary, November 29, 1933, p. 42, and December 3, 1933, p. 50.

[45]Harry L. Lurie, "A Program of National Assistance," December 1, 1933, and Address, December 9, 1933, HLL 2; interview with Goldschmidt, September 14, 1976; Harry Hopkins, *Spending to Save* (New York: W. W. Norton and Company, 1936), p. 114.

By mid-winter, 1934, the one-time charity assistant in New York City had become the largest employer in America, and Aubrey Williams' sketchy "emergency employment corporation" had become a huge public construction and management service run by industrialists and corporate accountants, whose professional methods strongly resembled those at Hoover's Commerce Department or the RFC. Ironically, Hopkins' loose, fluid style attracted experts who brought their own strict controls to his social experiment. Engineers demanded detailed plans, specifications, inspections, and safety precautions. Public administrators required periodic audits, based on unit costs, and insisted on organization charts. Their contribution to the development of the CWA foreshadowed the subsequent evolution of the New Deal, as the Roosevelt Administration confronted the continuing depression crisis. Conceived as the compassionate, activist state, committed to social justice and social welfare, it developed into a more dispassionate service state with professional managers and accountants brought in to draw up organization charts and watch the budgets. John Carmody, Louis Brownlow, and Donald Stone, would all participate in this reorganization in 1939.[46]

The contrast of professional approaches to setting up and running the CWA would appear even sharper in states and counties across the nation, where social workers still clung to case work and politicians looked upon government jobs as patronage for the party faithful. Hopkins' FERA representatives, Carmody's regional engineers, and the field auditors would all confront interest groups at the state and local levels as they struggled to get the CWA and the New Deal through that first hectic winter.

[46]Polenberg, *Reorganizing Roosevelt's Government*, pp. 187–188.

CHAPTER THREE

The CWA in the States: Social Workers and Corporate Liberals vs. the Bosses

LESS than a week after President Roosevelt had designated him the Civil Works Administrator, Harry Hopkins took his plans for federal work relief before the state and local officials in whose hands the success of the program would largely rest. He invited governors, mayors, city managers, and state and county emergency relief administrators to the Mayflower Hotel in Washington on November 13 for a briefing on CWA *Rules and Regulations*. Over 500 in the audience saw FDR discard the text of the speech that Hopkins had prepared and challenge them to aid the recovery. Most were members of existing state emergency relief administrations (SERAs) whom Hopkins had drafted wholesale into the CWA. Originally organized to receive RFC loans and grants-in-aid from the Federal Emergency Relief Administration, most SERAs were composed of social workers and volunteer corporate executives who had dominated welfare activities since the progressive era. But these social workers proved more committed to the case-work approach than Hopkins or Aubrey Williams, and they often resisted mass hiring procedures for the new work program. At the same time, businessmen seemed preoccupied with efficient management and safeguarding the public purse, and they hesitated to commit large sums of money for makeshift projects of questionable value. During the next hectic weeks, both groups would have to compromise old orthodoxies and preside over the painful transition of the CWA from a social-welfare to an engineering-management operation. And, as political independents or progressive Republicans in the Bull Moose tradition, many civil works administrators found themselves contending with regular Democratic and GOP bosses who saw public works as essential to their party's future. A focus on state and county administrations in Illinois, Pennsylvania, and California suggests some of the difficulties which confronted the CWA in the states.[1]

I

On November 10, 1933, Hopkins appointed the Illinois Emergency Relief Commission as the state CWA. Organized in February, 1932, the IERC typified the progressive charities that had matured in the 1920's. Led by independent Republican businessmen and prominent social workers, it embodied the professionalism of private social agencies and federated fundraising. Graham Taylor, head of the Chicago Commons, praised its "high standards of business efficiency and non-partisan public service." When the Commission became the Illinois Civil Works Administration, its chairman, Robert J. Dunham, was designated the head. A Chicagoan of "pioneer stock" and former vice president of Armour and Company, Dunham had retired to devote himself to public service. From the outset, he regarded his CWA job as "purely administrative," objected seriously to the mass hiring, and questioned "so-called morale work," which he considered more appropriate for private charity, where people had an "easy money complex." Committed to an efficient relief program, Dunham clashed with other IERC members, like executive secretary Wilfred Reynolds, on leave from the Chicago Council of Social Agencies. Reynolds favored spending large sums for the unemployed, but he also insisted on the case-work approach. Urging that "Reynolds must be allowed the active and consultative assistance of fellow social workers," Graham Taylor supported his philosophy: "No claim to business efficiency can compensate for the loss of experi-

---

[1] U.S. Federal Civil Works Administration, *Proceedings of the General Meeting and Executive Meeting,* November 15, 1933, CWA Papers; *New York Times,* November 16, 1933, p. 1; U.S. Congress, House of Representatives, Committee on Appropriations, *Hearings, Federal Emergency Relief and Civil Works Program,* H. R. 7527, 73rd Cong., 2nd Sess., 1934, p. 21.

enced service individually rendered by personal representatives of the agencies hitherto consulting with each family." This antagonism quickly paralyzed IERC activities and seriously delayed getting projects underway. Hopkins' field representative, Howard O. Hunter, was so alarmed that he threatened to reduce the Illinois quota by thousands and transfer it to other states in the Midwest.[2]

The Pennsylvania Emergency Relief Board also fit the progressive model, with its presiding officer, Eric H. Biddle, a businessman from suburban Philadelphia and a (Gifford Pinchot) Republican, known for his "immunity from political influence." On November 15, Hopkins named Biddle state civil works administrator, and he assumed the dual leadership of direct and work relief. Despite his lack of welfare experience, the Mainline executive enjoyed the respect of social workers on the SERB. But, like his counterpart in Illinois, Biddle took his responsibilities to the taxpayers quite seriously. On December 15, when he was to have 325,000 Pennsylvanians on the job, Biddle frankly told Hopkins, "If I wanted the quota filled by today it would have been through the approval of projects that would not come up to CWA standards. . . . I had rather not."[3] Two of Hopkins' top aides elaborated on this caution:

[2]Frank Z. Glick, The Illinois Emergency Relief Commission (Chicago: University of Chicago Press, 1940), pp. 23–32, and "The Illinois Emergency Relief Commission," SSR, VIII (May, 1933), 23–48; Wilfred Reynolds, "Organizing Governmental Agencies for Unemployment Relief," NCSW, Proceedings (Chicago: University of Chicago Press, 1933), pp. 506–515; telegram, Hopkins to Dunham, November 10, 1933, CWA 13; Graham Taylor, "Civil Works and Other Relief," Chicago Daily News, November 18, 1933, p. 10; Hunter to Hopkins, December 8, 1933, FERA 81; Graham Taylor, "Big Job Needs United Action," Chicago Daily News, December 9, 1933, p. 8.

[3]Ruth A. Lerrigo, "Pennsylvania's Welfare Set-up," Survey, LXIX (May, 1933), 188–189; Biddle to Hopkins, November 23, 1933, and telegram, Hopkins to Pinchot, November 10, 1933, CWA 39; Arthur Dunham, "Pennsylvania and Unemployment Relief," SSR, VIII (June, 1934), 283; Biddle to Hopkins, December 15, 1933, CWA 39.

A close advisor to Biddle, Roger Evans, from the Philadelphia Chamber of Commerce, also insisted that projects be "recruited and conducted throughout on the basis of qualifications and efficiency." Roger Evans, "The Place of

"Mr. Biddle feels very strongly that it would be a grave mistake to have what he calls 'lousy' projects going all over Pennsylvania just to satisfy a whim for having a certain number of men at work on a certain date."[4]

In California, relief efforts took on the progressive mode, but only after a tortured struggle befitting the state's perverse nonpartisanship. Reconstruction Finance loans were initially handled by the State Department of Social Welfare, directed by Rheba Crawford Spivalo, an assistant of the radio messiah Aimee Semple MacPherson and one of the state's most powerful Republicans. Sheer mismanagement of the department and its politicized local outlet, the Los Angeles Employment Stabilization Bureau, forced Republican Governor James Rolph and the RFC field advisor to create a new bi-partisan State Relief Commission headed by Ray C. Branion, an independent Republican. Branion received his training at the New York School of Social Work, served the New York Charity Organization Society, held high executive positions with the Red Cross, and was national director of the Institute for Crippled and Disabled Men (primarily World War I veterans). Coming to California for his health, he had directed a private relief program in Santa Barbara during the Hoover years, a role which won him the governor's attention.[5]

The choice of Branion to head California's SERA (and eventually the federal relief administration and civil works) not only infuriated Mrs. Spivalo and other GOP regulars, but naturally angered state Democrats, who had seen Roosevelt's victory in 1932 as a means to overcome their habitual "also-ran" status.

Work in Unemployment Relief," State Emergency Relief Board of Pennsylvania, *Unemployment Relief in Pennsylvania, September 1, 1932–October 31, 1933* (Harrisburg: State Emergency Relief Board, 1933), pp. 84–85.

[4]Stone and Goldschmidt to Hopkins, "Pennsylvania Situation," no date, CWA 92.

[5]Hickok to Hopkins, June 27, 1934, HLH 51; *Sacramento Union*, January 24, 1934; Lillian Symes, "Politics vs. Relief," *Survey Graphic*, XXIV (January, 1935), 8; Wayne McMillen to FDR, October 24, 1934, HLH 45; telegram, Harold S. Chase to Hopkins, December 13, 1933, CWA 6; statement of Ray C. Branion, March 12, 1934, in Report of James C. Findlay, DJ.

Frankly regarding the "administration of New Deal relief as a function of the Democratic Party," newly elected U.S. Senator William G. McAdoo wrote Hopkins a lengthy critique on Branion's activities. "He is successfully building a fine Republican machine," read the report, which described how Branion controlled his own "lay committees" for each county. A flood of letters poured onto Hopkins' desk from McAdoo's allies, making similar charges. The senator then summoned Pierce Williams, Hopkins' FERA Western field representative, and warned him that although the use of relief for party needs might seem sordid, this matter had to receive consideration in the practical world.[6]

Some of McAdoo's concern was justified. As head of the new CWA, Branion ran an operation dominated by Republicans. Many GOP men controlled county offices because they were chosen by Republican county boards of supervisors. In other cases, Branion consciously retained personnel from the Hoover RFC days, while trying to make professional appointments wherever possible. One major political target, Joseph Scott, head of the advisory board which approved all CWA projects, was president of the Los Angeles Community Chest, but he also was an "old line Republican" who had nominated Hoover at the 1932 GOP convention. Inevitably some of the staff proved unsuitable and had to be removed. At other times, Branion's efforts at picking nonpartisans placed social workers in jobs requiring technical administrators.[7]

[6]Michael Paul Rogin and John L. Shover, *Political Change in California* (Westport: Greenwood Publishing Corporation, 1970); Robert E. Chinn, "Democratic Party Politics in California, 1920–1956" (unpublished Ph.D. dissertation, University of California, Berkeley, 1958); Memo, December 11, 1933, "On Branion's Activities since his Appointment as State Emergency Relief Administrator," WGM 389; Searle F. Charles, *Minister of Relief* (Syracuse: Syracuse University Press, 1963), p. 56.

[7]Macauley to Hopkins, December 26, 1933, CWA 4; Frances Cahn and Valeska Bary, *Welfare Activities of Federal, State, and Local Governments in California, 1850–1934* (Berkeley: University of California Press, 1936), p. 228; *Sacramento Union*, November 22 and December 18, 1933; telegram, Branion to all county committees, November 13, 1933, CWA 4; Allerton West, "Dirty

Criticism or praise of Branion's handling the California CWA depended on whether it came from a social welfare executive or a McAdoo Democrat. The Los Angeles Democratic Chairman wired Jim Farley: "Unless rectified this [Branion's administration] will cost us Congressional seats and dangerously handicap gubernatorial campaign." In contrast, the manager of the Pacific Branch of the American Red Cross praised the "leadership of high order," and a sympathetic reporter commented that the "unique problem" of putting California's 300,000 quota to work "would test the mettle of any social work administrator."[8]

II

Frequent clashes between social workers, businessmen, and politicians delayed the filling of quotas and vexed Hopkins' advisors at the very time that engineers were trumpeting their special fitness to wage war on the depression. "The engineer is no longer a mere technician useful in executing the plans of others," wrote *American Engineer* in May, 1933. "He is an engineer in the true sense of the term. He is not only an executor or operator but a planner and director." Justifying the role of these professionals on the CWA, *Engineering News-Record* warned "that so unprecedented a program may fail of its primary purpose to distribute a wage so quickly, and . . . great sums of money will be wasted unless useful projects in adequate number are planned promptly and ably." While stressing public service, engineering spokesmen were also prompted by the opportunity to find positions for half of their colleagues out of

---

Work in Sunny California—the Background of the Branion-Williams Case," *SWT*, II (January, 1935), 15; John B. Elliott to McAdoo, January 11, 1934, WGM 390; Hickok to Hopkins, June 27, 1934, HLH 51; P. Williams to Hopkins, February 10, 1934, CWA 118.

[8]H. H. Cotton to James A. Farley, November 22, 1933, and NRA Women's Division to Walker, December 9, 1933, WGM 389; Al Schafer to Hopkins, December 18, 1933, CWA 6; Frederick A. Chase to Joseph Keenan, November 10, 1934, DJ.

work. They appeared ambivalent toward the CWA when social workers or businessmen took charge of projects and praised the agency only insofar as their fellow experts joined Hopkins' staff and state and county offices.[9]

Illinois' Emergency Relief Commission, which handled the CWA through its county committees and downstate relief districts, appeared among the most receptive to the engineers' overtures. The inability of IERC people to fill the state quota plus the rift between Dunham and Reynolds prompted Governor Henry Horner to suggest a draft of outside help. Horner and Dunham approached Professor W. C. Huntington of the University of Illinois, College of Engineering, who formed a volunteer advisory committee of officers from professional societies and top executives of various firms to review specifications.[10] As the volunteers assumed more responsibilities (and upgraded their title to Engineering Advisory Board), they stressed the need for a greater role for Frank D. Chase as chief engineer for the state CWA. By early December, Howard Hunter cautioned Hopkins: "It is just a little too big a job for Dunham and Reynolds and they are likely to get in trouble all of the time." Hunter convinced them to juggle positions, although he disappointedly referred to it as "an administrative reorganization and not an organic separation." Dunham remained titular

[9]"The Engineer and the New Deal," *American Engineer*, III (May, 1933), 5; "A New Call on the Engineer," *ENR*, CXI (November 16, 1933), 602; W. A. Shoudy, "The Engineer and the Depression," *Nation*, CXXXVII (September 13, 1933), 296; "What Is the CWA Doing?" *ENR*, CXII (January 11, 1934), 55.

[10]Hunter to Hopkins, November 23, 1933, HLH 52.

The members included: Daniel J. Brumley, chief engineer of Illinois Central Chicago Railway Terminal; C. B. Burdick, consulting municipal and sanitary engineer; Magnus Gunderson, chief structural engineer in his own firm; Alonzo J. Hammond, president, American Society of Civil Engineers and general chairman, Construction League of the United States; Chester MacChesney, vice-president of Acme Steel; Albert Reichman, assistant chief engineer of American Bridge Company and past director American Society of Civil Engineers; and C. C. Whittier, president of the Chicago Engineers Club. Three were past presidents of the Western Society of Engineers. "Engineering Board in Illinois to Approve CWA Projects," *ENR*, CXI (November 30, 1933), 688.

head of CWA and took charge of FERA direct relief grants; Reynolds became executive director of relief to oversee social services and case work; and Chase became the real head of civil works. An MIT graduate, past president of the Western Society of Engineers, and head of his own corporation, Chase enjoyed the confidence of social workers, business executives, and technicians. His duties expanded rapidly to include receiving, examining, and improving projects; requisitioning workers for Cook County; general supervision of all projects; purchasing all materials; public relations and safety; and auditing, accounting, and statistics.[11]

The Advisory Board also attempted to inject more engineering influence down the line, by creating its own grass roots organization. An engineer was named state purchasing agent, and he had two assistants for Cook County and for downstate. Chicago had its own elaborate engineering division in charge of inspection, public relations, labor adjustments, compensation, safety, and project surveys. For the rest of the state, eight district engineers were chosen (to coincide with relief committees), and each had a staff with a purchasing agent. In choosing subordinates, Professor Huntington conferred with the Illinois Society of Engineers, the Illinois Waterworks Association, and similar organizations. Project designers represented district engineers on each site, while "engineer scouts" visited assigned areas to ascertain the need for additional inspection. A personnel division interviewed all potential employees, who had preregistered with the Western Society of Engineers Employment Service.[12]

[11]Illinois CWA, *Final Report* (March, 1934), p. 26; telegram, Hunter to Baker, November 28, 1933, CWA 13; Hunter to Hopkins, December 4, 1933, and December 22, 1933, FERA 81; telegram, Hunter to Hopkins, February 2, 1934, CWA 12; IERC, *Official Bulletin, Number 144*, December 29, 1933, CWA 118.

[12]Illinois CWA, *Final Report*, pp. 21–24; "Engineering Control Features Illinois CWA Organization," *ENR*, CXII (January 25, 1934), 116; Colonel Daniel I. Sultan, Report on Cook County, no date, p. 6, Illinois State Library, Springfield.

Through tight management, the Board developed varied projects to fill the Illinois quota and counter charges of inefficiency. Just as Hunter announced the December 15 ultimatum, the Cook County engineer came up with a project that absorbed 20,000 workers to level spoil banks of Chicago's sewage treatment system. When the sanitary district could not supply adequate supervision, Chase assumed direct control, as he did when reports from a Harvey sewer construction site told of several abuses. With Washington's deadlines met, the technicians embarked on more diversified projects, like a smoke abatement campaign in Chicago. Since Illinois had responded to CWA assistant chief engineer Perry Fellows' appeal "to reach beyond street labor," the state was rewarded with an increased quota. Understandably, engineers across the country hailed the state as a model. *Engineering News-Record* ran several features applauding the effort and credited the large number of varied projects to the "engineering approach." Alonzo J. Hammond, member of the Board, returned from a national convention in New York and proudly reported:

> I found no state where a complete state-wide organization had been set up comparable to ours in Illinois and upon my explanation of what we were doing there was immediate demand for our organizational chart and a definite movement to [sic] more effectually put into practice similar procedure.[13]

Pennsylvania's experience in creating the CWA offers striking parallels and contrasts. When Eric Biddle became head of civil works, he decided to create an independent staff rather than attempt to impose it upon an already overburdened relief board. Social work leader Arthur Dunham claimed that "demoralization of the relief administration was avoided, and relief

[13]"Illinois Work Expedited by Engineers," ENR, CXII (January 11, 1934), 40; *Chicago Tribune*, December 9, 1933, p. 6; *Chicago Daily News*, December 12, 1933, p. 4; "Engineering Board in Illinois to Approve CWA Projects," ENR, 668; "Illinois Work Expedited by Engineers," *ibid.*, CXII (January 11, 1934), 40–41; "Engineering Control Features Illinois CWA Organization," *ibid.* (January 25, 1934), 11; Alonzo J. Hammond to Dunham, January 25, 1934, HH 92.

workers were protected from the terrific pressure of organizing
the CWA almost overnight." With this arrangement, Biddle
had saved Pennsylvania from the confusion experienced in Illinois. Welfare people could continue their FERA chores un-
disturbed, while engineers and business executives took on the
huge responsibility for the CWA.[14]

Of the twenty-three men Biddle placed in charge of county
and regional (in less populated areas) offices, he boasted: "It
would be hard to find a better crowd. They are all serving
without compensation and, with a few exceptions, are either
engineers with a good background of administrative experience
or executives." Identifications of sixty-five percent revealed
that almost half were engineers, nearly all graduates from prestigious universities. One quarter were corporate directors, many
of their own firms. For Philadelphia, Biddle designated William H. Connell, a Taylorite and old associate of Morris L.
Cooke, whose service to the city had dated back to the reform
Blankenburg Administration of 1912. After heading a private
construction firm, Connell returned to public work as chief
engineer of the Pennsylvania Highway Department under
Governor Pinchot. Tudor Williams, a structural engineer,
worked for the Scranton Railway Company and was a partner
in his own contracting company before handling the CWA in
Lackawanna County. After he earned a mechanical engineering
degree at Cornell, Julius Long Stern came home to Wilkes Barre
and managed the family department store, when Biddle tapped
him for Luzerne County. Considered an "exceptionally able
and reliable contractor," Thomas B. Evans left a profitable
business to run the Montour County CWA office.[15]

[14]Kelso to Hopkins, November 20, 1933, FERA 250; Pinchot to Superintendents of State Employment Offices, November 27, 1933, GP 863; Pennsylvania CWA, *Final Report*, p. 55; Dunham, "Pennsylvania and Unemployment
Relief," 271; Biddle to Hopkins, November 25, 1933, CWA 39.

[15]Biddle to Pinchot, November 20, 1933, GP 2558; *Philadelphia Public Ledger*,
November 19, 1933, p. 8; Biddle to Hopkins, November 25, 1933, CWA 39.

Conclusions are based on a study of fifteen men out of twenty-three listed
in the *Philadelphia Record*, November 19, 1933, Sec. 2, p. 1. Information about
each individual comes from various biographical volumes and county histories.

Most came from the Pennsylvania "establishment," including five "Sons of the American Revolution." All but one were Protestant (predominantly Presbyterian). A third had graduated from the Ivy League universities, and over fifty percent had some college background. Besides memberships in local organizations, like the Masons, Chamber of Commerce, University Club, and other civic groups, many had previously served their communities during the First World War. Tudor Williams was fuel administrator for Lackawanna County, while William James Lowe spoke as a "four minute man" for Liberty Loans and after the Armistice chaired a Committee of National Defense to erect memorials to the boys from Fulton County. Philanthropic efforts included: Merrill Winslow Linn's management of the Lewisburg Welfare Federation, Weston Kelsey's supervision of the Neighborhood House in Carbon County, and Herbert P. Stone's leadership of the Warren County Community Chest. As upper-class businessmen, industrialists, and technicians, they had participated in commission and city manager movements to rationalize local government in the progressive era and the 1920's. Their commitment to a nonpartisan, business-like administration, particularly for public works and relief, made them precisely the candidates Biddle would seek out for county CWAs.[16]

Winfield Scott Downs, ed., *Who's Who in Engineering, 1937* (New York: Lewis Historical Publishing Company, Inc., 1937); Frederick A. Godcharles, *Chronicles of Central Pennsylvania*, Vol. IV (New York: Lewis Historical Publishing Company, Inc., 1944); *Encyclopedia of Pennsylvania Biography* (New York: Lewis Historical Publishing Company, Inc., 1945); William H. Connell, "Public Works and Engineering Services on a Public Service Basis," *Annals*, LXIV (March, 1916), 103–114; Thomas Murphy, *Lackawanna County*, Vol. I (Indianapolis: Historical Publishing Company, 1928), 622–623; Oscar Jewell Harvey and Ernest Gray Smith, *A History of Wilkes Barre*, Vol. V (n.p.; 1930), 217–218; Frederick A. Godcharles, *Pennsylvania*, Vol. V (New York: American Historical Society, 1938), 201.

[16]Godcharles, *Chronicles of Central Pennsylvania*, p. 565; *Encyclopedia of Pennsylvania Biography*, Vol. XXIV (1941), p. 19; Godcharles, *Pennsylvania*, p. 171; Murphy, *Lackawanna County*, p. 622; *History of the Juniata Valley*, Vol. III (Harrisburg: National Historical Association, 1936), pp. 573–574; unsigned report, Weston M. Kelsey, Carbon County CWA, no date, GP 2588; Joseph

Progressive engineering and city-management efficiency extended to the lowest levels of the Pennsylvania CWA. An engineering division under Colonel C. E. Myers checked all construction plans in regard to technical feasibility, unit costs, and other guidelines set by chief engineer John Carmody's staff in Washington. This division, in turn, supervised a field corps, ultimately numbering eighteen district leaders, who assisted county heads in designing projects. Pittsburgh went a step further with a municipal advisory council, seven of whose ten members were engineers or construction executives. Biddle also divided the state into six field areas, each with a "resident area assistant" who served as his contact with the counties. With elaborate accounting to ensure "proper control" over projects, Biddle took pride in his accurate records, which gave the exact status of funds and permitted periodic audits by six field accountants. These sound business methods won wide approval for the agency, particularly among local industrialists, private suppliers, and civic groups. A representative from *Construction Methods*, a frequent critic of CWA inefficiency, visited three sites in the Keystone State and praised "the capable labor management by experienced superintendents and skilled engineering supervision . . . which accomplished results of value." Biddle was especially pleased when the regional engineer commended his staff: "Pennsylvania's CWA was better organized from the standpoint of its engineering organization, both locally and in the central office, than any other state with which he had contact."[17]

In California, engineers came in as a last-ditch effort to sal-

Riesenman, Jr., *History of Northwest Pennsylvania*, Vol. III (New York: Lewis Historical Publishing Company, 1943), pp. 327–328; James Weinstein, *The Corporate Ideal in the Liberal State, 1900–1918* (Boston: Beacon Press, 1968), pp. 92–116.

[17]Federal CWA of Pennsylvania, *General Rules and Regulations, Number 1*, November 20, 1933, CWA 38; *Pittsburgh Post Gazette*, December 16, 1933; Pennsylvania CWA, *Final Report*, pp. 56–57; Biddle to Hopkins, January 10, 1934, CWA 39; "Three Communities Re-employ Labor on PWA and CWA Projects," *Construction Methods*, X (March, 1934), 29–31; quoted in statement of Biddle, January 19, 1934, CWA 38.

vage the CWA amid political opposition to Branion and the growing realization that the combined FERA and civil works had proved unwieldly. Hopkins, Pierce Williams, and Branion agreed that U.S. Navy Captain Edward Macauley, state CWA engineer, should take over the work program, while Branion would retain the separate handling of direct relief.[18] Hailed as a "splendid engineer" by Hopkins, Macauley could also claim a close friendship with President Roosevelt that dated back to 1919, when FDR was Assistant Secretary of the Navy and Macauley commanded the ship that took Woodrow Wilson to France. Since that time, Macauley had become a deft bureaucratic manager, had headed the San Mateo County work relief program, and had earned George Creel's admiration as the "very highest type of executive, . . . a man of unquestioned integrity and courage." More than anyone in California, Macauley could pull rank and put work relief above local party squabbles. In the first hectic weeks, he reorganized California's CWA, creating a new administration overnight to handle the massive work program already underway. He turned to a fellow officer and appointed Captain Frank W. Hibbs as chief engineer. Dividing the state into six geographical sections, Hibbs delegated assistant engineers to take charge and supervise each one. Washington ordered all county CWA directors completely separated from county relief committees, making each director wholly responsible to Macauley. This new arrangement enabled him to review all local administrations and ultimately

[18]California's relief rolls were so large (Los Angeles County alone had 60,000 names per month) that Pierce Williams contemplated having two administrations, one for the north and the other for the south. This arrangement ultimately went into effect after the CWA folded. P. Williams to Branion, November 8, 1933, CWA 4; California CWA, *Final Report*, p. 5; *Los Angeles Times*, March 18, 1934.

Telegram, P. Williams to Hopkins, December 7, 1933, FERA 6; Hopkins to Branion, January 3, 1934, CWA 4; *Sacramento Union*, December 17, 1933. Newspapers reported the administrative change as Branion's idea. *Los Angeles Times*, December 17 and 19, 1933.

shift personnel in forty-one of the state's fifty-eight counties.[19]

The engineers' ability to expand their involvement in Pennsylvania, Illinois, California, and other state civil works administrations left social workers with mixed feelings. Some appeared quite defensive at their apparent inability to handle construction projects and frustrated by the growing realization that the CWA had eclipsed their role as chief dispensers of federal relief. Fearing the proliferation of technical advisors and engineers in the Illinois CWA, Howard Hunter questioned the intention of this group to protect its claims. "They are inclined to set up so much control and restrictions," he warned Hopkins, "that they are likely to lose sight of the very important matter of developing . . . good projects throughout the state." Counting no fewer than 1,029 engineers on the Illinois staff, Hunter charged, "These boys wanted to hire all of the unemployed engineers in the state and have a nice little party of their own." A Chicago air pollution project, with 450 mechanical engineers on the payroll, also provided good evidence. At the same time, Pierce Williams echoed some of Hunter's complaints from the Pacific coast:

> In all of the Western states, . . . the engineering department has been overstaffed. What was needed was not a corps of engineers to inspect projects underway, but practical construction men. Neither the state relief commission nor myself had anything to say about the setting up of this staff.

Privately, other welfare spokesmen admitted that civil works had brought too much confusion to an overburdened FERA.

[19]Telegram, Hopkins to McAdoo, December 15, 1933, WGM 389; CWA Minutes, December 12, 1933, HLH 35; Baker to Branion, November 22, 1933, CWA 4; *San Francisco Chronicle*, December 16, 1933; Creel to Walker, March 27, 1934, NEC 395; telegram, Macauley to Hopkins, December 16, 1933; Baker to Macauley, December 27, 1933; and Hackett to Carmody, December 22, 1933, CWA 4; *Los Angeles Times*, December 20, 1933; California CWA, *Final Report*, pp. 5, 19; P. Williams to A. Williams, December 29, 1933, FERA 26; telephone conversation, A. Williams to Macauley, January 17, 1934, CWA 4.

One relief official later revealed his "own particular criticism of the CWA was its tie up in an administrative way with relief organizations. This I think was a mistake." The desire for effective management and the necessity to appease conflicting interests prompted field representatives to encourage the divorce of direct relief from civil works. In Pennsylvania, where Eric Biddle had no particular loyalty to the social work ethic, the CWA functioned separately from the start. Illinois, California, and other large states would learn by the Keystone example and from their own bad experience with interest group quarrels.[20]

III

The CWA's absorption of state relief boards and the subsequent enlistment of engineering and management expertise meant that political independents and Republicans (albeit Bull Moosers) ran the CWA, particularly in major industrial states. For all their claims of nonpartisanship, they gave the CWA an indelible political dimension. At the same time that social workers and corporate liberals struggled to administer direct relief and jobs, plan projects, fill quotas, and meet payrolls, they found themselves also trying to fend off state and local bosses of both parties. From his field trips in the West, Pierce Williams commented with keen insight:

> Politicians did not especially mind turning relief over to a group of citizens for they felt there was nothing but grief in that job. However, it drove the politicians wild to find themselves without anything to say about who was going to get a job on public work.

[20]Marie Dresden Lane and Francis Steegmuller, *America on Relief* (New York: Harcourt, Brace, and Company, 1938), p. 20; Hunter to Hopkins, December 4, 1933, FERA 81; P. Williams to Hopkins, February 6, 1934, CWA 118; Harry Greenstein, "Work Programs and Relief Measures," *Proceedings of the Delegate Conference, AASW, 1936* (New York: American Association of Social Workers, 1936), p. 71.

Republican and Democratic regulars charged favoritism, patronage building, and graft against the local civil works administrator, regardless of his formal registration.[21]

An independent Republican, Eric Biddle started off the Pennsylvania CWA on a nonpartisan note. "This thing will never work out if politicians butt in on us," he told a Philadelphia reporter. From his brief experience with the SERB, Biddle was prepared for trouble: "What a hell of a job it is to keep politics out of any public administration. I certainly know that it has been the toughest part of the whole relief job and common sense tells me that it is going to get even tougher when we are dealing with jobs." Keystone Democrats lost no time in challenging what they saw as GOP domination. Fifty-three years in the patronage wilderness, they resented the Republican stranglehold on state offices and feared they would exploit CWA placements. Joseph Guffey demanded a Democratic Board of Control to replace Biddle, and Congressman Henry Ellenbogen of Pittsburgh supported this attempt "to eliminate political influence." Guffey also rallied John B. Kelly and other Philadelphia Democrats to attack the local civil works administrator, Republican William H. Connell, as a "Vare Machine lieutenant" despite Connell's long association with civic reform. By December, several other county leaders had dumped charges of favoritism on Hopkins' desk.[22]

To a certain extent, Pennsylvania Democrats had justification for their complaints. From the sample of sixty-five percent

[21]P. Williams to Hopkins, February 6, 1934, CWA 118; Bonnie Fox Schwartz, "Social Workers and New Deal Politicians in Conflict: California's Branion-Williams Case, 1933–1934," *Pacific Historical Review*, XLII (February, 1973), 51–73.

[22]*Philadelphia Public Ledger*, November 20, 1933; Biddle to Hopkins, December 27, 1933, CWA 40.

No Democrat won the Pennsylvania gubernatorial election since 1890. Richard Keller, "Pennsylvania's Little New Deal" (unpublished Ph.D. dissertation, Columbia University, 1960), p. 6.

Philadelphia Record, November 16, 1933, p. 1; Congressman Henry Ellenbogen to Hopkins, November 14, 1933, CWA 39; telegram, Joseph Guffey to Hopkins, November 18, 1933, CWA 40.

of Biddle's appointments, all but one had registered Republican. The lone exception, Hugh Dolan, was an Irish Catholic, but a self-styled "independent." Although most disdained partisanship, many in fact had actively campaigned and later reaped public standing from their CWA connection. Floyd Chalfant, a local newspaper publisher, had served on the State Election Commission in the 1920's and went on to become secretary of commerce under Republican Governor Edward Martin in 1943. Herbert P. Stone sat as Republican borough councilman from 1907 to 1910, while Dr. Charles A. Ernst had run unsuccessfully for Congress as a GOP nominee in 1928. The CWA chief of Chester County, Frank B. Foster, was considered a likely candidate for state senate in the 1934 elections; and former manager of the Bethlehem Bureau of Water and city planner, Robert Lee Fox, later rose to chief engineer and executive director for the city.[23]

Illinois Democrats had similar cause for dismay. While listed as a Republican, Frank Chase appeared to be an independent, since he never held office, shunned campaigns, and joined nonpartisan civic clubs. But his control of the state CWA, accompanied by some local appointments of active politicos, touched a nerve among regular Democrats. A state assemblyman grumbled that his county administrator had run on the GOP line every four years for surveyor, while a Republican engineer in Alton rewarded the faithful in his district. When these charges came to Jim Farley's attention, he relayed them to Hopkins.[24]

Howard Hunter also informed Washington of trouble spots,

[23]Adolph W. Schalck and D. C. Henning, History of Schuylkill County, Vol. II (n.p.: State Historical Association, 1907), pp. 118–119; Godcharles, Chronicles of Central Pennsylvania, p. 19; Riesenman, History of Northwest Pennsylvania, pp. 327–328; Encyclopedia of Pennsylvania Biography, Vol. XXIV (1941), p. 19; Philadelphia Public Ledger, February 11, 1934, p. 6; Who's Who in Engineering, p. 467.

[24]Bane to Hopkins, February 8, 1934, FB 9; Edwin M. Schaefer to Congressman J. C. O'Mahoney, December 19, 1933; W. G. Frank to Edwin M. Schaefer, December 19, 1933; Farley to Hopkins, December 24, 1933, all in CWA 14.

this time in the Democratic Kelly-Nash machine of Cook County. From the CWA's inception, Hunter had worried about Chicago because of its huge relief load and absence of a local IERC office. Urging Hopkins to put in his own man to guard against "political stealing," Hunter wired in disgust:

> We have had to sit up nights watching potential chiseling. . . . It has been the old Cook County custom of figuring in a little profit for some of the boys. These lads can not get it through their heads that this Civil Works business is spending federal money. It is generally taken for granted when they are spending local money there will be a reasonable amount of petty graft and they cannot change their local rules.

Allegations of Democratic inroads followed, with the *Chicago American* and the *Tribune* enthusiastically printing headlines of favoritism, payroll frauds, and graft.[25]

True or false, attacks about the political character of the CWA echoed across the country, even, to President Roosevelt's embarrassment, in his own Dutchess County. Just as Hopkins rejoiced that 4 million were on the payroll, by January, 1934, alleged scandals threatened the entire future of federal work relief. His immediate response was to order all payrolls and purchase accounts opened to the public and to send investigators from the Department of Interior to check some 150 charges of graft. Though Hopkins realized the need to shake up certain state and local CWAs, he agonized over the appropriate action in each case. For small, rural areas, he could send in a trusted social worker and rest easy. In Georgia, for example, Hopkins dissolved the Talmadge-controlled relief board, and assigned Gay Shepperson, "an experienced welfare worker possessed of rare executive ability." But large industrial states and urban counties with huge CWA payrolls and tangled pol-

[25]The IERC ran Cook County from its office in Springfield. Hunter to Hopkins, November 18, 1933, HLH 52; Hunter to Hopkins, December 8, 1933, and January 7, 1934, FERA 81; telegram, Hunter to Hopkins, January 23, 1934, CWA 12.

itics seemed to demand tough, experienced administrators. Hopkins found some among business-minded Bull Moose Republicans, who appeared to run efficient programs, avoid scandal, and keep peace among rival professionals.[26]

Hopkins declined to interfere in Pennsylvania, for instance, because he had confidence in Biddle and because President Roosevelt still entertained the possibility of building a Democrat-progressive Republican coalition in the state. In addition, Biddle had acted the honest broker between social workers and engineers by separating their official duties. He seemed shrewdly sensitive to Democratic charges, inviting Joseph Guffey and disgruntled county chairmen to bring complaints to Harrisburg. At the same time, Biddle managed to keep the GOP Old Guard at arm's length and even ordered an investigation into the Bucks County CWA, which he described as a "feudal fief and [Boss Joseph] Grundy as the Lord of the manor."[27]

In a number of areas, however, where administrative backbiting jeopardized CWA operations and appeared to damage the New Deal's prospects in the upcoming fall elections, Hopkins readily turned to other leadership. On January 27, 1934, he ordered Major Daniel Sultan to Chicago and Major Donald Connelly to Los Angeles, and hinted of future military appointments to other cities. The Army Corps of Engineers seemed a natural choice for Hopkins, given the War Department's recent success in mobilizing the Civilian Conservation Corps and handling "emergency missions of great magnitude involving local cooperation and relief" during the Mississippi flood crisis. Nevertheless, he appeared defensive to the press and argued: "It is federal money and there is no reason for not doing it, nothing to apologize for. I know you people are going to put

[26]Hopkins to FDR, CWA 92; Baker to all field representatives, regional engineers, and state administrators, January 3, 1934, CWA 92; Hopkins to Ronald Ranson, January 4, 1934, CWA 10; *Atlanta Constitution*, January 7, 1934, p. 6.

Hopkins took similar steps in Colorado, Oklahoma, Kentucky, and Texas.

[27]James MacGregor Burns, *Roosevelt: The Lion and the Fox* (New York: Harcourt, Brace and World, 1956), pp. 199–200; Biddle to Hopkins, December 12 and December 13, 1933, CWA 39.

varied interpretations on this, but it is just that these men are good administrators and they know how to deal with the problem." Newspaper editors, on the whole, applauded the move and drew favorable comparisons with the CCC. "They will go into each community 'cold' with no political or other ties," predicted the *Washington Post*. "They will be in a position to stop chiseling and political favoritism."[28]

Engineers and businessmen took umbrage at what they considered a professional insult. "Calling in a number of army engineers to take charge as CWA directors . . . ," wrote *Engineering News-Record*, "casts unjustified reflection on men who have given devoted effort to the work while the army engineers have enough to do in their own offices." In Washington, CWA chief engineer John Carmody worried that some state officials were "jittery," and he defended his "men in the field who are close to the various administrators [and] are themselves in a better position."[29] But in Illinois the reaction was bitter and beyond soothing. Colonel Sultan's assignment to Chicago triggered a dramatic resignation by Robert Dunham and the IERC from their civil works duties. The Commission protested "with a sense of justice to over 700 members . . . who in our judgment have served the best interests of the citizens." The Engineering Advisory Committee seemed equally provoked and more emotional. Howard Hunter reported that Professor Huntington "actually broke down and cried" because of his profound feeling that "we were repudiating the work that his board had been doing."[30]

Hunter, as Midwest field representative, took hold of the

[28]Press Conference, January 26, 1934, HLH 21; Lt. Colonel John C. Lee, Report, no date, HLH 45; Samuel Grafton, "The New Deal Woos the Army," *American Mercury*, XXXIII (December, 1934), 436–443; John A. Salmond, *The Civilian Conservation Corps* (Durham: Duke University Press, 1967); *Washington Post*, January 27, 1934, p. 1.

[29]"The CWA Crisis," *ENR*, CXII (February 1, 1934), 151; Carmody to Hopkins, February 15, 1934, CWA 62.

[30]Telegram, Dunham to Hopkins, January 27, 1934, CWA 13; *Chicago Tribune*, January 17, 1934; Hunter to Hopkins, January 29, 1934; and Hunter to Hopkins, "A Weekly Review of Current Events, January 22 to 27," January 27, 1934, FERA 81.

Illinois CWA on a temporary basis and used the occasion to overhaul its operations from Cairo to the Loop. Though Hunter publicly regretted Dunham's resignation, citing his "devoted service," both Hunter and Hopkins privately welcomed this chance to divorce completely the IERC from civil works. "Let them run the relief show," exclaimed Hunter, "and we will run CWA." Acting the broker, Hunter consulted various interests, including Frank Bane from the American Public Welfare Association; Edward L. Ryerson, a retired businessman and former IERC director; and Charles Merriam from the University of Chicago. After he mollified the engineers, praising their "excellent and honest job," Hunter asked Frank Chase and his entourage to take charge. Hunter conveyed the scene to Washington:

> I had a prayer meeting and held hands and kicked them around. . . . I have the boys pretty well in line, putting it up to them on a loyalty basis, and those boys are pretty high. They are not connected with the political groups and can see the thing on a point of view of national service.[31]

At last the sole executive of Illinois' CWA, Chase organized the state just as Biddle had in Pennsylvania. He appointed new county heads to succeed IERC committees, and in each case local authority would rest with a single individual rather than with a group. District engineers and relief officials recommended candidates, and Hunter thoroughly checked their qualifications, taking pains to favor persons "sympathetic" to the program. Many of those finally named had worked as county project engineers and were already familiar with CWA procedures.[32]

[31]Telegram, Hopkins to Dunham, January 29, 1934, CWA 13; Hunter to Hopkins, January 29, 1934, FERA 81; telegram, Hopkins to Hunter, January 31, 1934, CWA 12; telephone conversation, Hunter and A. Williams, January 27, 1934, FERA 81.

[32]Illinois CWA, *Final Report*, p. 172; Hunter to Hopkins, February 6, 1934, FERA 81; Notes on Conference Called by Howard Hunter, February 23, 1934, HH 92; John E. Cassidy to Walker, March 15, 1934, NEC 403.

In Chicago, Colonel Sultan assumed his duties with marked military efficiency. Cooperating with Frank Chase and his civilian aides, he carved out a distinct Cook County CWA, which operated separately from the main state staff. Sultan established a new procurement office with a nucleus of forty-five persons who conducted all purchases. Its responsibilities included comptroller, requisitions, bid invitations, contracts, and vouchers. To combat payroll irregularities, Sultan designated ten field officers, and by March 1 a centralized reporting system of timekeepers used daily sheets. At the same time, a new legal department sounded out citizens' complaints.[33]

Although Hunter admired these reforms, his reports also conveyed a touch of resentment. "The colonel mustered up quite a corps of Army officials from various centers, which I do not think is such a hot idea," he confided to Hopkins. "The point was to get some people who knew federal regulations . . . but there is a little underground feeling I think that these Army fellows are perhaps too officious." Hunter's feelings persisted, even when he could relax and characterize the Illinois CWA as a "different show." "The Army," he gibed, "had put so much red tape around it that they are practically doing no new business."[34]

Although the Corps of Engineers provided an expedient solution for the CWA, Hunter's repeated "digs" did not rest solely on professional jealousy, but on apprehensions that the Army, too, was advancing its own interests. Although the presence of military officers deflected some political charges, it also constituted "a challenge to civil works leadership in all parts of the country, indicating that if local and civil effort fails,

---

[33]New York City offers an interesting parallel. Emergency agencies had offices dealing with the state situated in Albany and also in Manhattan, making the city in effect a "forty-ninth state." Chronological Review of National Emergency Council Activities, 1933–1937, FW.

Colonel Daniel Sultan, Report on Cook County, pp. 14–19; Illinois CWA, *Final Report*, p. 172.

[34]Hunter to Hopkins, February 6, 1934, and March 20, 1934, FERA 81.

sterner measures and more direct action will be taken."[35] Like
all professional groups which participated in the emergency,
the Corps brought its own style and its own motivations.[36] In
Chicago, Colonel Sultan introduced an elaborate bureaucracy
of junior officers, which dwarfed the Illinois Advisory Board's
staff. Army installations benefitted directly from the CWA to
the tune of $25 million spent on military posts, veterans cem-
eteries, and national guard camps. The War Department later
blew its own horn to New Deal leaders, when Secretary George
Dern praised his outfit's "highly coordinated organization"
which enabled it to "assist the CWA very materially in the
initiation and prosecution of its relief programs."[37]

Although the Corps helped Hopkins and the CWA to get
through the winter, he would have preferred to stay with state
and local civilians. Lt. Colonel John C. Lee appreciated Hopkins' position when he later studied the CWA. The officer
concluded that the War Department was the only possible alternative organization to have undertaken the work relief experiment. Either nine Corps Area Commanders under the Chief
of Staff or the eight Engineer Department Divisions with their
fifty Engineer Districts "could have handled the program with
a reliable effective organization for administration and disbursement." In such an arrangement, however, Colonel Lee

[35]Clipping, Salt Lake City Tribune, January 28, 1934, CWA 62.

[36]Army officers had a reputation for honesty, which led Hopkins to place
them in local CWA offices formerly headed by civilians suspected of lacking
the military "sense of honor." Political scientists have shown, however, that
the Army Corps of Engineers is like any private interest group. Arthur Maass
outlined the Corps' ability to manipulate Congress and local business and political groups to its own advantage in Muddy Waters (Cambridge: Harvard University Press, 1953).

[37]Colonel Sultan organized his office with a nucleus of forty-five persons,
but expanded it to over two hundred within a month's time. Colonel Daniel
Sultan, Report on Cook County; for Los Angeles, see Schwartz, "The Bran-
ion-Williams Case," 62–63; Major General L. H. Bash to Deputy Chief of
Staff, March 31, 1934, and R. E. Callan, Memo on War Department Civil
Works Program for Period February 15 to May 1, 1934, February 12, 1934,
WD 262; Dern to Richberg, August 14, 1934, WD 309.

presumed that Hopkins would have wanted to assign experienced relief personnel to each echelon, but added that this would have depleted Hopkins' own state FERAs, whose activities could not be curtailed. Hopkins preferred to go with his own relief staff, familiar with his policies and with the unemployed. He wanted these people in control rather than subordinate to military commanders or Army engineers.[38]

Hopkins' reliance on state and local civilian talent brought a wide range of interests into the state CWAs. Men like Biddle and Chase provided honest, efficient, and relatively nonpartisan leadership, stimulated a variety of projects, and frequently coopted potential opposition into the agency. They put their personal and professional ties to good use, executed federal orders, and got their states through the winter. As old Bull Moosers or independent Republicans, they shared Roosevelt's and Hopkins' commitment to keep politics out of civil works. Biddle confessed he came "from a long line of hard-shelled Republicans," but he also asserted his "most sincere support of the President's magnificent program." At the close of the CWA, Chase expressed his appreciation for the appointment and characterized his CWA experience as a "glorious adventure."[39]

IV

Hopkins did not have a Biddle or a Chase to mediate local interest-group conflicts and satisfy the claims of hungry political organizations in every state. Even King Solomon could not have settled the venomous battle in California, where petty patronage squabbles ballooned into an ugly confrontation of national dimensions.

The promotion of Captain Edward Macauley to California

[38]The War Department later commented on Colonel Lee's report, saying it "contains little, if any, material of military value from which military lessons might be drawn." Major General R. E. Callan, Memo, June 7, 1934, WD 262; Lt. Colonel John C. Lee, Report, no date, HLH 45.

[39]Biddle to Pinchot, December 7, 1933, GP 1239; Chase to Hopkins, May 14, 1934, CWA 12.

civil works administrator and the subsequent enlistment of Army engineers had failed to pacify Senator McAdoo's Democratic regulars. Since Republican Ray Branion still headed the state FERA, they felt he continued to influence civil works. "It appears we have been given the run-around on the Macauley appointment," complained a party man to McAdoo's secretary. A telegram to the Senator commented that Macauley was a "high class, intelligent but utterly inexperienced civic worker and babe in politics." When McAdoo demanded a detailed statement from Washington explaining the dismissals of some friends, Hopkins blandly replied, "It often becomes necessary to remove certain employees of an organization for the good of the service."[40] McAdoo's cronies also attempted to offset Macauley's military cadre by "bearing down" on the National Reemployment Service, which hired half the CWA workers. By having a friend at that desk, many of the "faithful" could still get rewards.[41]

At the same time, John B. Elliott, head of the State Democratic Committee, formed his own investigation unit to examine CWA "corruption." By January 15, 1934, he had sifted through evidence which he claimed pointed to a "general breakdown, demoralization, and political favoritism," charges which the Republican National Committee regurgitated in a pamphlet called CWA Scandals. Hopkins dismissed the uproar as the work of "disgruntled politicians," but California Democrats hoped their findings could eventually discredit Branion.[42] By the end of January, the U.S. District Attorney

[40]*Los Angeles Times*, January 29, 1934; Joseph J. Freeman to Walter Measday, December 16, 1933, and telegram, John B. Elliott to McAdoo, January 16, 1934, WGM 390; Hopkins to McAdoo, February 12, 1934, CWA 5.

[41]Hamilton H. Cotton to Walter Measday, December 28, 1933, WGM 390. Captain Macauley felt that this agency was responsible for a great part of the inefficiency. Macauley to Hopkins, December 26, 1933, CWA 4.

[42]*Los Angeles Times*, January 11, 12, and 16, 1934; Frederick A. Chase to Joseph Keenan, November 10, 1934, DJ; Republican National Committee, CWA Scandals (February 6, 1934), pp. 8–9; telegram, Elliott to McAdoo, January 16, 1934, WGM 390.

empanelled a Los Angeles grand jury to look into charges of padded CWA payrolls. Two obscure women employed in a branch office were charged with accepting a ten percent kickback from truck owners, enough dirt to subpoena all records of the CWA purchase department and to widen the probe.[43]

In one of the most curious episodes in the formative years of the welfare state, a new federal grand jury heard from over one hundred witnesses, including relief executives and CWA employees, who told how workers were hired to dig ditches, fill them up, and dig over again. They described men lounging around without tools and later lining up for weekly government checks. Captain Macauley, Pierce Williams, and Ray Branion also had an opportunity to testify, as the hearings dragged on into March and the CWA was folding. Branion had had no formal connection with civil works since December 15, and Williams had always divided his attention among several Western states. Convinced they had nothing to hide, they spoke "freely and voluntarily." The Los Angeles Times characterized their statements as "principally informative." Nevertheless, the U.S. Attorney summarized that two conspiracies existed—one to misuse work orders and the other to misapply CWA funds.[44] Anxious to show that Branion was not the only man he was after, the D.A. also focused on Williams, whom he believed "vulnerable" and "alone without friends." He tried to show how Williams as field man gave everyone "carte blanche with-

[43]Cummings to FDR, February 16, 1934, DJ; Los Angeles Times, January 21 and 23, 1934; Peirson Hall to Cummings, June 21, 1934, DJ; H. P. Gardner to Ickes, February 12, 1934, CWA 6.
Some thought Elliott had framed the women to have "something to show" for his trouble. Hickok to Hopkins, June 27, 1934, HLH 51.
[44]Los Angeles Times, February 9 and March 6, 1934; telephone conversation, Branion with Hopkins, June 23, 1934, HLH 65; P. Williams to Joseph B. Keenan, June 23, 1934, DJ (includes itinerary for entire CWA period); Los Angeles Times, March 14 and October 16, 1934; Peirson Hall to Cummings, June 21, 1934, DJ.

out regard to rules and regulations or the law."[45] On June 20, 1934, the grand jury indicted Branion, Williams, and five former county CWA officials on charges that they had knowingly released federal funds to employ men on projects of questionable value and sent them to work without plans or tools. Each stood accused of "fifteen overt acts to wrongfully [sic] expend one-half million dollars of government money."[46]

Social workers in California and across the nation refused to accept the indictment. During the summer of 1934, Branion's California associates organized a committee to solicit financial contributions for his defense and shower Washington with telegrams.[47] The charges against Pierce Williams stirred indignation among intimate friends in the welfare establishment, like Paul Kellogg of *Survey*, C. M. Bookman of the Cincinnati Community Chest, and Hopkins, who refused to suspend Williams as Western field man. Fellow CWA agents Alan Johnstone, Southern representative, and Robert Kelso, his Northeastern counterpart, resigned their positions to act as counsel without pay. Welfare executives left little doubt that they considered the indictment a political challenge to their recently established profession and feared for the future of the entire federal relief

[45]Williams later wrote he believed he was indicted to keep him from testifying in behalf of the others. P. Williams to Hopkins, September 8, 1934, HLH 100.

Joseph B. Keenan to Cummings, June 25, 1934, DJ; Hickok to Hopkins, June 27, 1934, HLH 51; Hugh A. Fisher to Mr. Carusi, June 21, 1934, DJ; *Sacramento Union*, November 22, 1933.

[46]California, U.S. District Court, Indictment for Violation: Section 88, Title 18, U.S. Code, DJ; *Los Angeles Times*, June 21, 1934; telephone conversation, Peirson Hall and Hugh A. Fisher, June 21, 1934; and telegram, Edward J. Hanna to Hopkins, June 27, 1934, DJ.

[47]Telephone conversation, Branion and Hopkins, June 23, 1934, HLH 65; *Los Angeles Times*, June 21, 1934; and *San Francisco Chronicle*, June 22, 1934; Hopkins to Cummings, October 12, 1934, and Wayne McMillen to FDR, October 24, 1934, HLH 45; San Diego Chapter, AASW, to Hopkins, September 16, 1934; and others included Los Angeles Chapter, AASW, to Hopkins, September 16, 1934; and California Executives of Public Welfare to Hopkins, September 16, 1934, DJ.

program. "They are aware of the general partisan political character of Mr. McAdoo's influence in California," wrote Sophonisba Breckenridge of the Chicago School of Social Work to President Roosevelt, "and the situation in which interests of selfish local political partisanship seem able successfully to attack honest and efficient and highly equipped professional civil servants creates in their minds a feeling of great anxiety and increasing alarm."[48]

Hopkins sensed this "disturbing uneasiness" among his fellow social workers, but his position as head of the CWA (as well as the FERA) and his responsibility to the President severely restricted his actions. When some welfare leaders began to question his loyalty, Hopkins confessed that their bitterness had become "distinctly embarrassing." Some wondered if Washington would provide any support for Branion's and Williams' legal defense; and Hopkins offered his encouragement, but made clear that any effort would have to come from outside his office. To raise funds and arouse public sentiment, a volunteer committee of about forty members was organized, headed by Robert P. Lane, director of the New York Welfare Council, with a steering committee that included C. M. Bookman; Dorothy Kahn, president of the American Association of Social Workers; Paul Kellogg; Harry L. Lurie, director of the Bureau of Jewish Social Research; and Linton Swift of the Family Welfare Association. Other names on the letterhead of the Branion-Williams Defense Committee included Edith Abbott of the University of Chicago Graduate School of Social Service Administration; Karl De Schweinitz, Pennsylvania School of Social Work; Homer Folks, secretary of the New York State Charities Aid Association; and other champions of social wel-

[48]Paul Kellogg to Frances Perkins, September 15, 1935, Survey Associates Papers, Box 116, SWHA; "Indicted in Los Angeles," *Survey*, LXX (October, 1934), 318–319; telephone conversation, Hunter and Hopkins, September 8, 1934, HLH 65; "The Branion-Williams Indictment," *Compass*, XIV (September, 1934), 1; Sophonisba Breckenridge to FDR, October 20, 1934, HLH 45.

fare. Hopkins' name also appeared—the only formal association his delicate position would permit.[49]

While the Committee intended to solicit contributions, its
real work was the strong pressure it placed on the Roosevelt
Administration. Some members felt that Hopkins had a "personal responsibility" to defend the accused. Claiming the charges
went beyond mere dereliction of duty, Harry Lurie argued that
these professionals had simply carried out orders from Washington. Lurie wanted Hopkins to testify at the trial to explain
how the circumstances of setting up the CWA in the states
contributed to the relative inefficiency. Dorothy Kahn later
chastised the Roosevelt Administration in the *Compass*, stating
that the CWA's dedicated employees "should not have been
left to be rescued by their own social work colleagues from the
hazards of indictment . . . when their sole offense was the
performance of their duties as directed."[50] But Hopkins felt an
equal responsibility toward the President. Claiming that FDR
wanted the indictments quashed as soon as possible, Hopkins
feared the embarrassment of a trial—for the entire Administration as well as for the federal relief program. He hardly rel-
ished the prospect of taking the stand in court and virtually
pleaded with Attorney General Homer Cummings to rescue
the defendants, the New Deal, and himself. Eventually, Cummings sent in a trouble shooter, who, on November 12, 1934,
asked for dismissal of the indictments on the grounds that "the
sole charge against them seems to be that they were overzeal-

[49]Hopkins to Cummings, October 12, 1934, HLH 45; telephone conversation, Hunter and Hopkins, September 8, 1934, HLH 65; *Los Angeles Times*,
July 6, 1934; "The Branion-Williams Indictment," *Compass*, 1; Paul Kellogg
to C. M. Bookman, September 24, 1934, Survey Associates Papers, Box 55;
Lane to Lurie, October 10, 1934, HLL 2; Lane to all members AASW, no
date, DJ.

[50]Lane to Lurie, October 10 and October 20, 1934, HLL 2.

The estimated cost of the defense was $15,000. Wayne McMillen to FDR,
October 24, 1934, HLH 45; "Branion-Williams Defense Fund," *Compass*,
XIV (November, 1934), 8.

ous in putting men to work." The case was dismissed that afternoon by the federal district judge.[51]

But for nearly four months the defendants had lived under the shadow of scandal, not to mention the cost of their defense. Commenting on the huge financial burden, one FERA field man described how it was "extracted from the pockets of low-salaried social workers." California's little committee continued to solicit funds in December to assist Branion with his debts, citing his personal sacrifice to keep the state relief program free from persons "who would not administer it in accordance with recognized standards of social work."[52]

While the charges against Branion and Williams represented the most brazen attempt of politicians of both parties—McAdoo's machine and California Republicans—to capture work relief programs for patronage, it was far from unique. Charges of favoritism, inefficiency, and corruption were heaped with more or less justification against many CWA officials throughout the country, who tried to set up the emergency employment program during those first hectic weeks. Leading citizens, statisticians, engineers, and welfare executives all confronted state and local politicians, who had a very different approach toward administering federal aid. But social workers reacted to the charges most acutely, and they rallied to the defense of their profession, which had supposedly gained an assured status within the New Deal.

[51]Lurie to Lane, October 16 and October 22, 1934, HLL 2; "Branion-Williams Case Dismissed," *Compass*, XIV (October, 1934), 2; Hopkins to Cummings, October 12, 1934, HLH 45; Forrest A. Walker, "Graft and the Civil Works Administration," *Southwest Social Science Quarterly*, XLVI (September, 1965), 168–169; *Los Angeles Times*, November 6, 9, 14, and 15, 1934; "Branion-Williams Case Dismissed," *Compass*, 2.

[52]Wayne McMillen to FDR, October 24, 1934, HLH 45; California Branion Defense Committee, December 19, 1934, DJ.

CHAPTER FOUR

Civil Works and the AFL

"WE ARE going to have to find some way to secure the approval of organized labor," warned Aubrey Williams, as he and Harry Hopkins began discussing plans for a work relief program in October, 1933. The two social workers knew they had to placate the American Federation of Labor, long opposed to government "made jobs." In hard times, building tradesmen had always favored tax-supported public works as long as they were undertaken by private contractors who were covered by collective bargaining agreements. But "work for relief" schemes smacked of charity, and AFL unions feared relief standards would undercut prevailing wages and hours and threaten gains hard won from management. Before Hopkins presented his proposal for the Civil Works Administration to President Roosevelt, he sent Williams to Madison, Wisconsin, to discuss the idea with Dr. John R. Commons. "If there is any one person in this country who can tell us how to make this thing palatable to organized labor, he is the man," said Williams. Commons dug up an old statement of Samuel Gompers in which the AFL leader had outlined a "Day Labor Plan," similar to Williams' suggestions. Encouraged by this precedent, Hopkins was convinced that he could overcome the unions' initial objections to CWA.[1]

Neither Hopkins nor Williams realized how much they had misgauged the AFL's posture. Four lean years of unemploy-

---

[1]Aubrey Williams, "The New Deal: A Dead Battery," pp. 78–80, AW 44; "Employment Ideas Started by Labor Men," *Federation News*, XXXIII (November 25, 1933), 8; Louis Stark, "Labor on Relief and Insurance," *Survey*, LXVIII (November 15, 1931), 186–187; Robert E. Sherwood, *Roosevelt and Hopkins* (New York: Harper and Brothers, 1948), p. 51.

ment had sharply chastened the Federation. By November, 1933, its membership had dropped to under 3 million, as the building trades reported sixty-five percent of their brethren out of work. But the National Recovery Act, with its wages and hours codes, Section 7(a)'s promise of union recognition, and public works funding, had revived the AFL's prospects and brought its lobbyists into a close association with the New Deal. Organized labor's traditional hostility toward "made work" had been transformed into a willingness to see what Hopkins had to offer, as Federation leaders would come to view the CWA as a public works boon which promised "recovery" for union treasuries as well as for the rank and file. Even though carpentry, masonry, and similar trades would amount to just ten percent of all CWA jobs, craft unions would seek undue influence within the agency. Desperate for members and dues, the AFL would demand priorities in hiring and suggest projects that required skilled crafts. Locals would insist on union rates for skilled jobs. When Washington later ordered state and county boards to determine pay scales and redress grievances with worker participation, the AFL would move to insure that its officers sat as labor representatives. Characterized by one historian as the "sleepy headquarters of the American labor movement," the Federation, as of late 1933, would prove wide awake in its ability to lobby for union interests on federal work relief.[2]

With the labor upheaval all around them in late 1933, CWA administrators inevitably faced the delicate task of applying union gains in private industry to public welfare goals—especially in a work relief agency employing 4 million. While extending "uplift" to "down and outers," who were the traditional wards of social work, Hopkins would have to reckon with thousands of unemployed brothers on the CWA payroll who insisted on their prerogatives as skilled mechanics. To accede to the AFL's

[2]Philip Taft, The AF of L from the Death of Gompers to the Merger (New York: Harper and Brothers, 1959), pp. 46–47; Walter Galenson, The CIO Challenge to the AFL (Cambridge: Harvard University Press, 1960), p. 514; Arthur M. Schlesinger, Jr., The Coming of the New Deal (Cambridge: Houghton Mifflin Company, 1965), p. 385.

demands, however, would clearly look like favoritism, since the Federation barely claimed six percent of the entire work force. Yet, at the same time, Hopkins did not want the CWA to have the image of a union-busting agency, which jeopardized gains previously won in collective bargaining agreements. Although he and Williams had shown greater solicitude than many early New Dealers for organized labor, as social workers, they had little experience in negotiating with trade unions. When they sought out Dr. Commons instead of William Green or another AFL leader, they demonstrated how little the "professional altruists" knew about the world of the "walking delegate." But Hopkins keenly sensed the inadequacy of this approach, and he quickly entrusted all CWA labor policy decisions to John M. Carmody, his chief engineer.[3]

I

Carmody's long record in management and union relations brought a new dimension to the CWA. As a Cleveland business executive during World War I, he had differed from associates on the Chamber of Commerce and supported the War Labor Board. "They were afraid of trade unions," he later recalled. "I dealt directly and frankly with every employee." In

---

[3]The attitude of early New Dealers toward organized labor was, at best, "paternal." James MacGregor Burns wrote of President Roosevelt that "he looked on labor from the viewpoint of a patron and benefactor, not as a political leader building up the labor flank of future political armies." See *Roosevelt: the Lion and the Fox* (New York: Harcourt, Brace and World, 1956), p. 218. Both Hugh Johnson and Donald Richberg of the NRA rejected the right of a union with majority support to speak for all the workers. Neither man favored the use of governmental power to compel business to accept collective bargaining, and they resented usurpation of their authority by the National Labor Board. See William E. Leuchtenburg, *Franklin D. Roosevelt and the New Deal, 1932–1940* (New York: Harper and Row, 1963), p. 108. Secretary of Labor Frances Perkins claimed from her experience that "unions never had any ideas of their own; most labor and welfare legislation in her time had been brought about by middle-class reformers in face of labor indifference." See *The Roosevelt I Knew* (New York: Viking Press, 1946), pp. 303–304, 307–310.

CWA Minutes, November 27, 1933, HLH 45.

1922, he surveyed the bituminous fields of western Pennsylvania and Ohio for the U.S. Coal Commission and supported strong organization for the miners. He kept his contacts with both mine executives and the United Mine Workers, as vice president of merchandising for Davis Coal and Coke Company until 1927 and later as editor of *Coal Age* and *Factory and Industrial Management* for McGraw Hill. Although a Taylorite, Carmody appreciated the active participation of labor groups in the movement for greater industrial efficiency. The next call to Washington came from Senator Robert F. Wagner to serve as a mediator for the National Labor Board of NRA. Thrown into the thick of the recognition strikes touched off by Section 7(a), Carmody traveled throughout the Northeast and Midwest, settling disputes and setting up NRA Regional Boards, until Wagner consented to his going over to CWA as chief engineer. Carmody went reluctantly, for he preferred "labor work," but he soon discovered that his position included the responsibility for crucial labor policies, which had eluded the good intentions of welfare administrators.[4]

In the rush to place 4 million at work, social workers on the CWA had never really stopped to take account of union prerogatives. Rules and regulations announced on November 15, 1933, authorized state and local authorities to transfer persons from FERA projects to civil works, which meant that half the quota had been certified by a welfare investigation, and the other half, after December 1, by the United States Employment Service's rough screening according to skill and training. But state and county officers, anxious to complete their allotment by December 15, lest they lose it to other areas, did not trouble to assign workers according to strict craft lines. The wholesale

[4]The Reminiscences of John Michael Carmody, Vol. I, pp. 140–144, 146, in the Oral History Collection of Columbia University (hereafter cited as Carmody COHC); statement of John M. Carmody, U.S. Congress, Senate, Committee on Education and Labor, *Hearings, To Create A National Labor Board,* on S. 2926, 73rd Cong., 2nd Sess., 1934, pp. 307–312; CWA Reminiscences, April 24, 1958, JMC 73; Carmody to Thomas Baker, November 28, 1933, JMC 50.

transfer of FERA relief recipients had flooded the rosters with the unskilled. "The 40,000 men assigned by the welfare organization were not classified as to occupation," noted a California supervisor. "On work relief projects taken over by the CWA they were carried as laborers at laborers' rates regardless of the class of work they were doing." Both job seekers and interviewers were influenced by openings immediately available on specific projects, and state executives readily admitted that few positions called for special skills. "Having a quota to keep within we soon saw we were filling it with unskilled labor," confessed the DeKalb County, Illinois, head. "To have mechanics available when they would be needed on the projects we sent mechanics out as laborers." Some skilled workers, desperate for any kind of job, went on the CWA in the unskilled category, while others without proper training slipped into skilled positions and even wound up as foremen or supervisors.[5]

This haphazard hiring went against much of what the AFL had held sacred—the work ethic, taking care of their own, and protecting traditional craft union prerogatives. *Federation News* called the FERA relief quota a "deliberate penalization of self-independence and the fostering of a spirit of dependence." They were affronted at the idea that to get on the CWA one had to be on the FERA rolls and accept the dole. "Very few of our men have applied [for] or been on the relief," said a Chicago machinist officer, "as we have been trying to take care of them for the past three years." "Most members of our association have done everything humanly possible to keep off the relief rolls," echoed a plumber. "Now when an opportunity is presented . . . they are deprived of the opportunity of maintain-

[5]Civil Works Administration, *Rules and Regulations, Number 1* (November 15, 1933); Henry E. Walker to Harold English, January 18, 1934, USES 233; Macauley to Hopkins, January 12, 1934, CWA 4; O'Berry to Carmody, December 29, 1933, CWA 33; Illinois CWA, *Final Report* (March, 1934), pp. 46–47; John Charnow, *Work Relief Experience in the United States* (Washington: Committee on Social Security, Social Science Research Council, 1943), pp. 32–33.

ing a livelihood because we have not enrolled for relief." The Galesburg, Illinois, Trades Assembly summed up:

> The rules governing the expenditure of funds in taking men off the relief rolls do not make any provision for a type of people we have in Galesburg who have refrained from asking for charity but who were really more entitled to it than many who are now on the rolls. The people I have reference to are mainly members of the building trades unions who have been unemployed for the past three years, have been too proud to beg, but have borrowed from their friends and neighbors in the hope that work would pick up.[6]

The CWA's failure to place applicants according to craft angered many old-line AFL affiliates. Throughout the open-shop wars of the 1920's, locals had not only claimed the exclusive right to do certain kinds of work in their districts, but they had also tried to regulate the number of persons entering apprenticeships to maintain a closed shop. Each local also asserted its right to classify workers, which in effect meant that its officers customarily did the hiring. CWA executives, oblivious to these craft jurisdictions, encountered objections when they proceeded to offer employment on relief work in the various crafts needed for the CWA's thousands of projects.[7] In a bewildering episode, the carpenters carried an old AFL jurisdictional feud over to the CWA. "No attempt is being made to ascertain an individual's qualifications," wrote the California Brotherhood to Senator William G. McAdoo. The secretary claimed that laborers were sent out as carpenters while first-class carpenters fell into the unskilled category. North Carolina Local 1460 reported to William Green that the Guilford County civil works administrator had assumed "arbitrary powers" in assigning jobs.

---

[6]*Federation News*, XXXIII (November 25, 1933), 4; D. M. Burrows to Olander, November 21, 1933, VAO 73; Frank Murphy to CWA, January 4, 1934, CWA 93; "Unemployment," *American Federationist*, XLI (February, 1934), 196; Thomas Downie to Olander, November 19, 1933, VAO 73.

[7]Nels Anderson, *The Right to Work* (New York: Modern Age Books, 1938), pp. 113–114; Galenson, *CIO Challenge*, p. 515.

Foremen were chosen regardless of previous experience, while thoroughly competent people received a rating of "carpenter's helper." A union official cited a supervisor "who does not know what size opening to cut in [a] wall for a given size window as plainly designated for in the plans." Chief William Hutcheson insisted that "with union skilled mechanics as foremen and supervisors to whom it rightfully belongs, then and only then will the intended results be obtained."[8]

The desire of organized labor to have some control over specific CWA positions was expressed in working-class resentment toward the various professionals who interviewed applicants. *Federation News* had little use for social workers who "pry into personal and private lives." An editorial demanded that "American citizens shall no longer be compelled to live under the auspices of charitable agencies." The AFL also resented USES personnel, whom the union charged with a "white collar complex against skilled labor in the building trades." "The organized labor movement will oppose in every possible way," stated William Green, "any proposal to classify skilled mechanics, men who have devoted all of their years to working at their particular trade, by tests laid down by so-called engineers."[9]

In response to union pressure, as well as out of a desire for more skilled workers on the payroll, CWA officials in Washington changed the federal rules. "If an artisan is acceptable to the union after the tests required by the union—the most practical test that can be applied," Carmody assured Green, "then there should be no question as to his status." On December 13, Hopkins made concrete this basic concession in the hiring procedures. All persons given employment on CWA projects other than those certified through relief rolls were to be as-

[8]George D. Hammond to McAdoo, WGM 390; J. M. Purgason to Green, January 1, 1934, CWA 34; Maxwell C. Raddock, *Portrait of an American Labor Leader* (New York: American Institute of Social Science, Inc., 1955), p. 188.

[9]*Federation News*, XXXIII (November 18, 1933), 4; Green to Carmody, January 9, 1934, CWA 54.

signed through the United States Employment Service *except* members of labor unions, who were cleared through their trade councils. This provision meant that organized labor, skilled and unskilled, was not required to register at designated agencies but would be referred in "customary ways" through recognized union locals. Only if locals did not furnish qualified workers within forty-eight hours could the USES then select applicants. Under Carmody's prompting, the social worker had adopted a virtual union shop for the CWA's skilled trades.[10]

Although the new ruling provided for greater union participation in hiring, the degree to which it went into effect varied, often from sheer local indifference. In rural states, where workers were less organized and less respected as a force in the community, craftsmen failed to benefit substantially. Many county CWAs in the South simply disregarded national regulations, and some employment offices discriminated against union members. "The superintendent in charge of this particular job," grumbled a Greensboro, North Carolina, carpenter, "had firmly maintained his right to judge the qualifications of those under his direction." Carmody received numerous complaints from Alabama that "affiliation with organized labor is tantamount to elimination." Other locals were afraid to challenge county administrators when they flouted federal rules and classified applicants as they chose. North Carolina's *Final Report* explained its few placements through union locals because "only a few such organizations exist in the state outside specialized manufacturing trades." About thirty men were employed through the builders council at Fayetteville and about the same in Wilmington. The account concluded, "There is no agency from which to secure accurate figures concerning placements, but it

[10]*Ibid.*; Civil Works Administration, *Rules and Regulations, Number 10* (December 13, 1933).

The CWA defined a skilled worker as "one who has gone through a number of years apprenticeship required to make him a competent skilled workman under standards usually recognized by organized labor." "Labor Definitions," December 28, 1933, HLH 49.

is well known . . . that such unions are so few as to be negligible."[11]

Such indifference was no longer possible in the Northern industrial states, where the struggle to impose NRA codes and Section 7(a) recognition had revived union consciousness in the leading manufacturing and mining centers. Angered by lackluster civil works practices in Pennsylvania, the state building trades councils and central labor CWA committees notified state administrator Eric Biddle, Governor Gifford Pinchot, William Green, and Washington officials how few unemployed craftsmen were selected from lists furnished by their locals. They charged outright discrimination in some counties and offered statistics to substantiate their case.[12] When these efforts failed, union agents took their grievances to Carmody in Washington. "Your complaint seems to be a just one and must be remedied immediately," he replied, admitting that Pennsylvania had been one of the worst offenders. "I personally wrote paragraph seven in Bulletin 10 [which specified union hiring]," declared the chief engineer, "and it means just what it says and I mean to see to it that it is carried out." Carmody immediately telephoned Harrisburg, and the delegation returned to iron out a settlement with state and county executives.[13]

---

[11]Hopkins to all civil works administrators, December 20, 1933, CWA 92; Baker to all civil works administrators, December 27, 1933, CWA 40; J. M. Purgason to Green, January 1, 1934, CWA 34; United Brotherhood of Carpenters and Joiners, Local 87, to Hopkins, January 1, 1934; and Carmody to Thad Holt, December 27, 1933, CWA 1; Winston-Salem Central Labor Union to Hopkins, March 18, 1934, CWA 34; North Carolina CWA, *Final Report* (March, 1934), p. 25.

[12]*Reading Labor Advocate*, January 19, 1934, pp. 1, 5.

The AFL claimed that of 5,000 men employed in Lancaster County not one was a union mechanic, and only 7 out of 165 painters in Berks County belonged to the local. W. C. Roberts to McClure, January 10, 1934, and Reading Building Trades to Carmody, February 12, 1934, CWA 40.

[13]*Reading Labor Advocate*, January 26, 1934, p. 1; February 16, 1934, p. 2; quote from February 23, 1934, p. 3; R. H. Rothrauff to Frank Connor, February 15, 1934, CWA 40.

In New York, labor's radicalization, which revived the great garment unions and touched off a virtual general strike in early 1934, inevitably spilled over into the civil works program. Entrenched, forceful union leaders had little trouble imposing their priority in filling CWA jobs. But skilled labor was not hired through the locals until February, 1934, when an agreement was reached after several weeks of negotiation by George Meany, vice-president of the state federation, James Quinn, secretary of the Central Trades and Labor Council, Hopkins, and Alfred Schoellkopf of the CWA. The group decided that the selection of men for skilled jobs be left to the unions in the vicinity of the project involved. "It is only just that we help the CWA in picking out the men," commented the president of the Central Trades and Labor Council. "In that way we can be sure they will get honest, capable men." This policy was carried out in New York City after the municipal civil works administrator appointed a committee, including Meany, the chairman of the Building Trades Employers Association, a state employment service "expert," and a Columbia University professor of labor economics, which drew up elaborate instructions for union locals to supply workers. Under these special procedures, each local appointed an "authorized representative" to transact all personnel business for the CWA. He obtained from the CWA a supply of "referral cards." When a project needed workers, the representative received a requisition stating the number of men and other specifications. He then selected candidates and gave each a referral card to present at the civil works office. If any union member believed someone unqualified, he filed a complaint to the representative, who reported to central union headquarters, which in turn presented a written statement to the CWA. A "re-rating board," established by the local CWA, investigated the fitness of any particular man for his position. [14]

Organized labor gained a head start in Illinois by having its

[14]Central Trades and Labor Council of Greater New York, *Union Chronicle,* XV (March, 1934), 4; *New York Times,* February 4, 1934, p. 24, February 6, 1934, p. 2; *New York Herald Tribune,* February 6, 1934, p. 36; statement of James A. Emery, Senate, *Hearings, To Create A National Labor Board,* p. 386.

own officers on state and local branches of the Emergency Relief Commission, which initially ran the CWA.[15] Victor Olander, secretary-treasurer of the state federation, sat on the IERC, while many county committees also had a labor representative. When the CWA went into operation, Olander suggested a list of state union leaders as an advisory board to the Illinois Free Employment Service. He sent copies of all CWA rules and updated regulations for the central labor bodies to insure they had accurate information. When IERC chairman Robert Dunham appointed him to handle registration of the nonrelief unemployed, within a week, Olander set up a bureau in Chicago of forty-one offices with 1,200 clerks! Twenty additional locations outside Cook County went up during the second week, along with arrangements to expand downstate facilities.[16] Nonetheless, Olander expressed disappointment over the limited positions opened to skilled trades; and, with staunch support from the labor community, he lobbied effectively for changes in hiring. Olander visited Hopkins in Washington, having arranged at the same time for county leaders to deluge the Walker-Johnson Building with telegrams of complaints. He notified locals in advance of official guidelines on union participation in hiring, which enabled them to take better advantage before the December 15 deadline.[17] While Pennsylvania craftsmen submitted lists of members to the county employment offices, Cook County unions had their own special recruiting system set up with the aid of the Chicago Building Trades president. Olander assured the state federation that "organized labor has

[15]IERC rules provided for a labor representative on all work relief committees and that trade unions be consulted, but downstate counties did not always comply. Olander to Aurora Building Trades, November 21, 1933, VAO 73.

[16]Olander to Martin Durkin, November 17, 1933, and Olander to Officers of Central Bodies of Organized Labor in Illinois, November 18, 1933, VAO 73; Illinois State Federation of Labor, *Proceedings of Fifty-Second Annual Convention, September 10–15, 1934*, p. 45.

[17]Horner to Olander, November 24, 1933, and Olander to Central Bodies of Organized Labor in Illinois, December 9, 1933, VAO 73; Olander to his secretary, December 15, 1933, VAO 74.

a very definite place in the present reemployment drive," but he cautioned them to sign up at the USES to afford themselves of all available channels. The Illinois CWA later boasted of its "primary value" to the building and structural trades.[18]

As unions achieved greater participation in CWA hiring, however, further questions arose regarding initiation fees and dues. Organized labor reasoned that members in good standing had the first claims on CWA jobs, since they had paid dues to insure this priority. But many had been unemployed for a long time, had fallen behind in dues, and had lost their union standing. When CWA jobs opened, leaders argued that nonpaid members could not step ahead of those who had maintained the union during hard times. "Others would have to pay half their earnings until they squared arrearages and restored their membership," concluded the Pittsburgh Carpenters District Council president. Local CWAs contended as best they could against these iron-clad seniority rules. In New York City, official directives emphasized "the privilege of supplying men to the CWA shall in no case be used to force payment of dues by men delinquent" and forbade discrimination on the basis of union dues owed. The municipal administrator reserved the right to withdraw this privilege if such improprieties occurred. On the other hand, the executive council of the International Hod Carriers, Building, and Common Laborers of Chicago scaled down financial obligations of members who got onto CWA payrolls and reduced the initiation fees and dues for those previously unaffiliated.[19]

In the absence of any national policy, either from union headquarters or the CWA, some locals seized the occasion to

[18]Procedure with Reference to Union Cards, December 10, 1933, VAO 73; *Federation News*, XXXIII (December 16, 1933), 1; Illinois CWA, *Final Report*, pp. 193–194.

[19]Anderson, *Right to Work*, p. 114; *Pittsburgh Post Gazette*, January 14, 1934; Statement of James A. Emery, Senate, *Hearings, To Create A National Labor Board*, p. 386; International Hod Carriers Executive Council of Chicago to Dunham, December 11, 1933, VAO 73.

increase membership.[20] "We men of . . . labor sympathies must take advantage of the situation and get as many of our number as possible into positions where we can build up an organization," wrote a Chicago union attorney. Chapters of the Brotherhood of Painters, Decorators, and Paperhangers of America frankly described the benefits. "CWA [is] now employing a large number of painters and we will be able to take in quite a number of members," predicted one secretary. Another officer reported, "We are making a drive for members and are taking advantage of a large amount of work being done on civil works." This opportunism often led to abuses where some labor leaders were more confident of their new influence. In Chicago, after a carpenter showed his credentials with five years in arrears, a union officer replied that he had hundreds of such requests and could square him for $125. A certain percentage of wages was required as part payment of back dues by local union secretaries in California before they would detail men for CWA jobs. "Most of the men cannot afford to give much," sympathized state CWA administrator Captain Edward Macauley, "and in some cases the demand seems excessive and it is not always the same." Macauley noted that discretion was left to the local secretary, whose salary depended on these dues. The *Pittsburgh Post Gazette* charged that the Cathedral of Learning Project had become a closed shop and wired Hopkins that it had documentary evidence of union officers' deducting "terrific sums" for dues from members on CWA jobs.[21]

---

[20]From August, 1933, to August, 1934, the Federation's organizational expenses tripled, as locals greatly enlarged their staffs in response to the NRA. Edwin Young, "The Split in the Labor Movement," in Milton Derber and Edwin Young, eds., *Labor and the New Deal* (Madison: University of Wisconsin Press, 1957), p. 51.

[21]William H. Seed to Olander, November 27, 1933, VAO 73; "Works Administration Boosts Organization," *Painter and Decorator*, XLVIII (February, 1934), 24–25; Searle F. Charles, *Minister of Relief* (Syracuse: Syracuse University Press, 1963), p. 57; *Chicago Tribune*, December 9, 1933; Macauley to Hopkins, March 7, 1934, CWA 13; telephone conversation, Biddle and A. Williams, January 13, 1934, CWA 39; *Pittsburgh Post Gazette*, January 13, 1934.

Such incidents gave ammunition to critics of organized labor and embarrassed public officials and local CWA administrators. James A. Emery, general counsel of the National Association of Manufacturers, declared, "They have undertaken to collect dues of all the workers and transmit them to any private purse." After he gathered affidavits from men forced to pay large sums for reinstatements, George W. Rosseter, president of the Chicago Association of Commerce, charged that the "building trades unions of Chicago were capitalizing on the opportunity made available to them to fill their war chests." Pennsylvania's CWA chief, Eric Biddle, concluded that "a program of this kind should have no labor preference whatsoever," and he strongly urged that all referrals be confined to the USES. "Unions have a real opportunity to make a gracious gesture," suggested Biddle, "by saying that they will ask union workers to register for the duration of the CWA."[22]

On the basis of these opinions and evidence gathered by the PWA Division of Investigation, CWA administrators in Washington decided that they had to eliminate the worst abuses, while maintaining the policy of union hiring. "It is commonly understood that CWA employees have a right to organize," said Carmody, "but this kind of organization work and dues collection should not be carried on." Various federal agencies helped to clear up violations through their field offices. In Illinois, any workers refused jobs because of nonmembership could appeal to the regional conciliator for the Department of Labor. Also, the state director of the National Emergency Council acted as a "watchdog" against possible "union racketeering." Hopkins dispatched field representative Robert Kelso to Pittsburgh to look at employment files and interview complainants. In a majority of instances, Kelso noted only $10 to $20 owed in back dues, and he smoothed over differences at a

[22]Statement of James A. Emery, Senate, *Hearings, To Create A National Labor Board*, p. 387; George Rosseter to Dunham, no date, CWA 13; Biddle to Hopkins, February 1, 1934, CWA 39.

conference with trade union representatives and CWA officials.[23]

Despite the furor, organized labor may have enjoyed more hiring power on paper than in reality. By the time the ruling to select employees through union locals had filtered down to most counties and labor representatives had negotiated with CWA offices, the December 15 deadline to fill all quotas had passed. Although new projects approved after that date afforded greater opportunities for skilled craftsmen, a large proportion of the more specialized plans failed to get underway since the quotas were already completed. In addition, federal regulations had specified that a "working crew" should have continuous employment. Men assigned from relief lists prior to December 1 were considered "permanent employees," and civil works administrators recognized their first obligation to outline new jobs to absorb these people when they finished their initial assignments. Washington did grant some additional allotments in January, 1934, and unions proposed projects that required more skills. But only a few unemployed members could benefit before demobilization reduced payrolls on February 15. Still, the gains on paper amounted to a significant involvement by organized labor, particularly when the AFL could claim a mere ten percent of CWA job holders. "The government has left the door as wide open as possible for our members to secure work," wrote *Bricklayer, Mason and Plasterer*. Because of the recognition of their "customary ways" of selecting job applicants, the Building Trades president expressed his "highest admiration and confidence in the policies and fair dealing pursued by Harry L. Hopkins and the staff of the CWA."[24]

[23]Carmody to Baker, January 29, 1934, CWA 13; *Chicago Tribune*, January 26, 1934, p. 4; John E. Cassidy to Walker, February 26, 1934, NEC 403; *Pittsburgh Post Gazette*, January 14 and February 1, 1934.

[24]Macauley to Hopkins, January 12, 1934, CWA 4; Illinois CWA, *Final Report*, p. 38; telegram, Baker to all state administrators, December 4, 1933, CWA 73; Green to Olander, December 27, 1933, VAO 74; *Bricklayer, Mason and Plasterer*, XXXVII (January, 1934), 4; M. J. McDonough to FDR, December 27, 1933, CWA 65.

II

The good faith between Hopkins and the AFL leaders stemmed, above all, from CWA wage policies. Labor had traditionally feared that work relief payments would undercut existing scales in private industry. But because civil works appropriations initially came from the Public Works Administration, rates spelled out for that agency applied to the CWA as well. The PWA set hourly minimums of $1.00, $1.10, and $1.20 for skilled labor in the southern, central, and northern zones respectively, with the unskilled receiving $.40, $.45, and $.50 per hour. Each person could work up to thirty hours a week with an eight-hour-day maximum. These rates followed suggested "floors" established by the blanket code of NRA, which stipulated minimums of $.30 or $.40 an hour. The CWA further protected union gains by ordering that where either prevailing rates or union rates (from local collective bargaining agreements before April 10, 1933) exceeded the zone minimum, the higher one should be paid but with fewer hours.[25] While businessmen sharply opposed rates that often exceeded levels in private industry, Hopkins had assured unions that he favored "just and reasonable wages" that provided a "standard of living in decency and comfort." He remained steadfast despite an explosion of complaints from private employers. General Hugh Johnson, too, termed it "a perfectly absurd situation" that civil works paid above the NRA code minimums. Though Hopkins

[25]CWA, *Rules and Regulations, Number 1* (November 15, 1933); Charnow, *Work Relief Experience*, pp. 51, 54, 58; Arthur Edward Burns and Peyton Kerr, "Survey of Work Relief Wage Policies," *AER*, XXVII (December, 1937), 714–715.

Within the skilled category, wages were graded in accordance with the union scales. After a protest by the Washington Building Trades Council, Carmody ordered the following hourly rates: bricklayers, $1.75; carpenters, $1.00; cement finishers, $1.25; electrical workers, $1.65; structural iron workers, $1.65; painters and decorators, $1.37; plasterers, $1.75; plumbers, $1.50; steamfitters, $1.29. "Union Wage Rates Won on Civil Works Jobs," *Paving Cutters Journal*, XXVIII (January, 1934), 1.

Civil Works Administration, *Rules and Regulations, Number 6* (November 27, 1933); Baker to all state administrators, November 27, 1933, CWA 92.

publicly defended his program, for he was determined to keep his pledge to organized labor, he privately confessed doubts to his staff. "I personally thought some of these wage rates were too high, but people approved these rates who were far more conservative than I am," he confided at a meeting. "I am inclined to think no matter what public relations will say to us, we have got to use those rates."[26]

Unions knew full well that the CWA wage scales set an example for private industry, and locals sought to ensure that all administrators complied. The Building Trades commended Hopkins on "the great work" that enabled millions of "worthy" citizens to earn a "decent living wage." "Success of the NRA is dependent upon the establishment of a living wage for workers through the CWA," commented another labor spokesman. Union chiefs feared that state and county executives might not carry out the civil works rates and urged their locals to report violations. *Painter and Decorator* published the names and addresses of all state administrators and exhorted members to deal directly with them. "Every official of every subordinate local union should be on the job to secure and maintain fair conditions on CWA," echoed *Bricklayer, Mason and Plasterer.* "If a private employer were engaged in such tremendous operations, all subordinate unions would be awake day and night, looking after wages and conditions."[27]

Some local CWA executives and union representatives ironed out complaints through friendly negotiation. In Madison County, Illinois, for example, the state federation president secured an

[26]Richard A. Lester, "Emergency Employment in Theory and Practice," *JPE*, XLII (August, 1934), 483–484; M. J. McDonough to FDR, December 27, 1933, CWA 65; Harry Hopkins, *Spending to Save* (New York: W. W. Norton and Company, 1936), p. 117; *New York Times*, December 23, 1933, p. 6, and December 27, 1933, p. 6; CWA Minutes, December 6, 1933, HLH 45.

[27]Building Trades Department to Hopkins, December 28, 1933, and telegram, Trades and Labor Assembly to Hopkins, December 22, 1933, CWA 65; "CWA to Receive All Complaints Directly," *Painter and Decorator*, XLVIII (January, 1934), 30–31; *Bricklayer, Mason and Plasterer*, XXXVII (January, 1934), 3.

interview with the CWA official for Brother M. D. Cox and a group of labor leaders from nearby areas. When the local director explained that a low wage scale was necessary to spread jobs among a larger number of people, the union countered that the prevailing rate simply meant the same number of employees would have work for a shorter time. "Instead of working out people say for a three months' period at a low wage scale they could just as easily work the same number of people for two months at the union level," reasoned Cox. The county CWA agreed and sent copies of the settlement to Springfield as well as union locals.[28]

Other administrators did not prove as amenable. Carmody later recalled:

> Many of the local administrators and other officials that had gotten into the program were anti-union. None of them were accustomed to dealing with a union in the fashion that some of us were. They shied away from meeting with union officials. They were fearful of going into negotiation. They were even, some of them, concerned about the wage scale. They thought that the wage scale that was adopted was too high.

Pennsylvania's Eric Biddle declared, "The perpetuation of the present PWA wage rates and other union exceptions have no place in the civil works program." Illinois relief chairman Dunham expressed open hostility toward union "privileges" on the CWA and permitted rates below those prescribed for the zone in several downstate counties.[29]

Carmody was inclined to intervene personally against recalcitrant state executives, where cordial relations with labor were essential. As a mediator for the National Labor Board, he had negotiated directly with both management and unions, and he continued this approach with Pennsylvania's CWA. Carmody learned that Eric Biddle had rewritten the wage bulletin in his

---

[28]R. G. Soderstrom to Olander, December 7, 1933, VAO 73.

[29]Carmody COHC, Vol. II, pp. 308–309; Biddle to Hopkins, February 1, 1934, CWA 39; Olander to Green, December 13, 1933, VAO 73; *Chicago Tribune*, December 24, 1933, p. 6.

own language, "leaving out some things essential to a correct understanding" of federal rules and regulations. Biddle's version gave counties the impression that local prevailing rates, which were lower than the PWA scales, could be paid instead of the zone minimum. When this action triggered complaints from local union leaders, Carmody stepped in. "We can't have him interpret our official rulings," said the chief engineer, as he ordered the return of all directives sent to the counties and had his own office issue correct ones. He also received several delegations of Pennsylvania trade union representatives and flatly instructed Biddle: "Irrespective of our personal opinions about these various wage scales, we are required to advise you that Bulletin 10 . . . was intended to guide all administrators, state and local, in the application of wage rates to CWA projects." Carmody expected the number of complaints to diminish with the new instructions, but reports kept coming from the Keystone State, leading Washington to suggest "more drastic measures . . . to accomplish an adjustment which will really adjust."[30]

Carmody resorted to other means in Illinois to enforce wage rates, when labor protests broke out in several downstate areas. On December 9, union leaders called a strike on twenty-seven projects in DuPage County and ordered 1,000 men to stop work because the hourly rate fell below prevailing levels. Hod Carriers in St. Clair County threatened a stoppage and charged, "This set up will break down wage standards as well as conditions of employment which the labor movement has consciously and honestly fought for these many years." The Tri-City Trades Council wired Victor Olander that unless an immediate adjustment came, "strike, riot, and general disorder will prevail." In response, Carmody asked Benjamin Marshman, regional commissioner for the Department of Labor Con-

[30]Carmody COHC, Vol. II, p. 317; Joseph Guffey to Hopkins, December 15, 1933, CWA 41; telephone conversation, Carmody and A. Williams, January 10, 1934, CWA 41; Carmody to Biddle, December 21, 1933, FERA 249; Carmody to Biddle, February 2, 1934, CWA 92; Myron Jones to Legislative Committee, AFL, January 26, 1934, CWA 39.

ciliation Service, to visit these "trouble spots" and determine if rates were properly applied.[31]

After conferring with the field representatives, IERC chairman Dunham, and chief engineer Frank Chase, Marshman "arrived at an understanding" that he handle all CWA wage disputes in Illinois and that his recommendations be accepted for the localities affected. Labor representatives had to proceed to Marshman's Chicago office to present their grievances because the large number of complaints made it impossible for him to travel to each community. Marshman stipulated that unions could justify a pay scale higher than the CWA rate by presenting a collective bargaining agreement prior to April 30, 1933, along with sworn affidavits from at least three reputable employers that they had actually paid the higher rate for that type of skilled work. Contracts along with affidavits were then investigated by staff members of the Conciliation Department. They filed a detailed report, from which Marshman made his decision, which he passed on to the state and county CWAs.[32]

Marshman heard 111 cases in Illinois, but ruefully concluded that "CWA cases are not matters in which mediation can be used." He found that in a majority of disputes, local administrators either "willfully ignored" the zone rate or were simply uninformed of the rules. Marshman cited one example where his recommendation just sat on the desk. After he had reached a decision for two other counties, IERC chairman

[31]DuPage Building Trades Council and DuPage Teamsters and Chauffeurs International, Local 673, to Frances Perkins, December 13, 1933, VAO 73; International Hod Carriers to Carmody, December 11, 1933, CWA 13; telegram, H. Pinkerton to Olander, December 8, 1933, VAO 73.

CWA, *Rules and Regulations, Number 10*, provided, "In the event that any question be raised as to what wage rates prevail in any district under agreements and understandings between organized labor and CWA administrators, the U.S. Department of Labor shall determine such rates if and when requested."

Carmody to Reynolds, December 13, 1933, CWA 103.

[32]Marshman to Hugh Kerwin, December 23, 1933, CWA 40; Hunter to Marshman, December 20, 1933, CWA 13; Illinois CWA, *Final Report*, pp. 149–150.

Dunham simply overruled him. The vice-president of the state federation and member of the St. Clair County CWA reported that another of Marshman's wage orders had been disregarded. The Illinois federation president declared, "Federal intervention and the work of conciliators . . . will accomplish nothing unless recommendations made by them are adhered to."[33]

The inability of the CWA in Washington to enforce PWA wage standards forced Hopkins to adjust national policy to conform with local practices. Conscious of organized labor's rock-bottom insistence on maintaining hourly rates, he decided to lower total wages by cutting the work week. He further accommodated unions in the cities by reducing the maximum hours from thirty to only twenty-four per week. For rural areas and towns under 2,500, where union strength was negligible, he set maximum hours at fifteen. In March, 1934, when the CWA was no longer financed by PWA money, Hopkins discarded the zones altogether and returned to the FERA approach. He ordered state and county administrators to pay the prevailing rate in the locality for the type of job performed, but in no instance less than $.30 an hour minimum.[34]

If Hopkins appeared to retreat on federal rules, Carmody and his staff still remained carefully solicitous of organized labor. "We cannot afford to be placed in the position anywhere of pulling down wages," wrote Carmody's assistant Nels Anderson. "We have to be fair in these matters, and one way to do that is to arrive at our rates through the aid of the workers involved, or their elected representatives."[35] Borrowing from the regional labor boards under the NRA, Carmody ordered that county wage committees be set up composed of one representative from organized labor, one from the local relief administration, and one from business or the professions se-

[33]Marshman to Hugh Kerwin, January 17, 1934, and Al Towers to Olander, January 20, 1934, VAO 74; Illinois CWA, *Final Report*, pp. 148–149; R. G. Soderstrom to Hugh Kerwin, no date, CWA 14.

[34]Hopkins to FDR, February 15, 1934, FDR-OF 444; Burns and Kerr, "Survey of Work Relief Wage Policies," 715.

[35]Anderson to Macauley, March 21, 1934, CWA 4.

lected by the first two. Carmody further recommended that local boards consider union rates and public construction project agreements between unions and employer associations within each county unit. Their task was to discover rates already in effect as of 1934 rather than set new ones. Findings had to be unanimous; if not, a new body was appointed.[36]

Unions appreciated these steps to safeguard wage standards, although some leaders feared that drastic cuts in rates as well as total wages would follow. William Green noted approvingly: "This is a great change in the former method of appointing committees and will give labor an opportunity to insist on the prevailing rates." Plasterer president Michael J. Colleran, however, warned his locals that state administrators would immediately set up scales "according to their own ideas" and charged his officers to "take every advantage of securing and holding their present wage rates." Conveying a greater sense of urgency, Bricklayer secretary John J. Gleason suggested "if possible, a member of this International Union as the labor member, and where that is not possible to secure the selection of a member of some other building trades organization." Gleason cautioned his brothers to "be on the job," since he feared these new regulations "will be seized upon by private employers as a means of further attacking our standards and beating down our conditions."[37]

Labor's apprehensions proved justified in North Carolina, when the state administrator Anna O'Berry adopted a state-

[36]Carmody personally set up four regional labor boards for the NLB in 1933. Patterned after the national one, they were composed of an employer chosen from the business leaders of the community, a leader from the local AFL unions, and an "impartial chairman" from among outstanding citizens of the locality, known for their interest in public welfare. Reminiscences, JMC 50; Lewis L. Lorwin and Arthur Wubnig, *Labor Relations Boards* (Washington: The Brookings Institution, 1935), p. 119.

Carmody to all state civil works administrators, March 6, 1934, CWA 73; Burns and Kerr, "Survey of Work Relief Wages," 716–717.

[37]"Changes in Wages and Hours," Illinois State Federation of Labor, *Weekly News Letter*, XIX (March 24, 1934), 2; *Plasterer*, XVIII (March, 1934), 1; *Bricklayer, Mason and Plasterer*, XXVIII (March, 1934), 39.

wide schedule of $.75 an hour for skilled labor and $.30 for unskilled, which she considered "slightly in excess" of the prevailing rate. "How can a fair competitive wage be maintained as is declared for in the NIRA . . . with the CWA paying almost any price a bunch of state contractors and administrators wish?" asked the *Union Record and Carolina Farmer*. Craftsmen went out on strike in Wilmington and Salisbury, and the Winston-Salem Central Labor Union appealed to Washington. Their resolution charged that Mrs. O'Berry had failed to set up wage boards or consult labor and had disregarded regional income variations. "This would set a standard for all types of construction which would tend to pauperize a large and respectable part of the population," wrote the local secretary.[38]

Other states apparently sought to comply with Carmody's orders; but, where they failed, union locals responded vigorously. The Los Angeles Central Labor Council claimed a lack of proper representation on its county committee, while the Pennsylvania federation accused some counties of "hand-picking labor representatives notoriously anti-union." "Boards set up with an eye to fairness have been turned into agencies for the perpetuation of low wages," cried *Bricklayer, Mason and Plasterer*. Although upstate New York committees managed to settle on prevailing rates, county CWAs forced workers to limit weekly hours, thereby cutting wages below the agreement. This decision touched off demonstrations, marches, and strikes over "arbitrary" pay cuts.[39] "The general situation in Pennsylvania has become even more aggravated since the sending out of new

[38]O'Berry to Hopkins, March 8, 1934, CWA 34; *Union Record and Carolina Farmer*, XXV (March 9, 1934), 4; *Raleigh News and Observer*, March 7 and 8, 1934; Resolution of Salisbury Labor Union, April 9, 1934, and Winston-Salem Central Labor Union to Hopkins, March 27, 1934, CWA 34.

[39]Carmody to Macauley, March 31, 1934, CWA 3; *Philadelphia Union Labor Record*, May 4, 1934; telegram, Joseph F. Ryan to Hopkins, March 22, 1934, CWA 32; Carmody to McClure, March 13, 1934, CWA 62; *Bricklayer, Mason and Plasterer*, XXXVII (April, 1934), 55; Schenectady Painters Union, Local 62, to Frances Perkins, April 2, 1934, CWA 32; Alexander Leopold Radomski, *Work Relief in New York State, 1931–1935* (New York: King's Crown Press, 1947), p. 308.

rules," reported Bricklayer secretary John J. Gleason to Hopkins. Craftsmen walked off in Reading and Harrisburg, while 1,000 men laid down their tools in Lancaster. The business agent for the Keystone Building Trades Council called the reductions an "injustice and contrary to the spirit of President Roosevelt's decision to increase purchase power."[40]

CWA officials both in Washington and in the states attempted to resolve these disputes to the satisfaction of all parties. In North Carolina, field representative Alan Johnstone held a conference with union delegates, the governor, and Mrs. O'Berry and arranged for wage boards. He distributed a circular letter to all county executives directing them to disregard Mrs. O'Berry's niggardly rates, call committees to meet, and establish new scales for each locality. Eric Biddle appeased union protests in Pennsylvania by creating a Technical Advisory Board to investigate and mediate complaints. Composed of registered architects (recommended by various chapters of the American Institute of Architects) and union representatives chosen by the state federation president, the board had its members travel in pairs to assigned territories to handle grievances. County CWAs worked out settlements with strikers in New York State, and employees returned to their jobs. In all cases reported, decisions restored the PWA scale.[41]

III

Although wage disputes made up the majority of complaints brought by organized labor, cases also resulted from union protests against arbitrary dismissals. Again, Carmody favored the decentralized handling of such grievances to make adjustments more speedy and effective. At the same time, he sought to

[40]John J. Gleason to Hopkins, March 19, 1934, CWA 40; *Philadelphia Public Ledger*, March 21, 1934, p. 8; *Reading Labor Advocate*, March 23, 1934, p. 1.

[41]Carmody to C. P. Barringer, April 5, 1934; Johnstone to Carmody, April 7, 1934; and William L. Nunn to Building Trades Council, April 18, 1934; all in CWA 34; Biddle to Gill, June 26, 1934, FERA 248; Pennsylvania CWA, *Final Report*, p. 64; *New York Herald Tribune*, March 17, 1934, p. 9.

"regularize the machinery" and began by mailing a question-naire to all state offices on January 2, 1934, asking how they had conducted labor relations. While his aides sorted the re-plies, Carmody ordered all states to outline at least some steps for the right of appeal in case of discharge. "We must not be placed in the position of denying our citizens rights that are normally given them by our courts, nor ought we to make this machinery difficult or complex," wrote the chief engineer, as though he were still a trouble-shooter for the NRA. On Jan-uary 17, preliminary instructions emphasized that every dis-missed worker had the right to a hearing before the local CWA and have representation by a person of his own choosing, which, in effect, meant a spokesman from the union district council. State and federal offices were to be informed of all final deci-sions.[42]

Illinois announced the creation of appeals boards on January 26, 1934, and notified every employee of his right to use this facility. In down-state counties, IERC committees frequently acted as the agency, but Chicago set up a separate body, con-sisting of a chairman, two members, and an attorney. Each petitioner had a private interview with a member, who had the authority to render a decision immediately. If the member de-cided on a general hearing or if the complainant insisted, the case was docketed, for the worker to appear with supporting affidavits and witnesses. Foremen, timekeepers, and other CWA officials also testified. Wherever further investigation proved necessary, the legal department assisted. To have a permanent record available of all proceedings, the hearings were taken in shorthand, and the board filed its verdict and distributed cop-ies to concerned parties. Orders for demobilization of the CWA brought an onslaught of petitioners, charging discrimination in layoffs. When the investigation showed that orders were not

[42]Myron Jones to Hunter, March 5, 1934, CWA 81; Carmody to Gill, March 20, 1934, CWA 62; Hopkins to all state administrators, January 2, 1934, CWA 65; Carmody to all state administrators, January 16, 1934, JMC 73; Doris Carothers, *Chronology of the FERA* (Washington: United States Gov-ernment Printing Office, 1937), p. 17.

properly complied with, the board adjudicated the case to prevent injustice. Illinois also created a state board to consider appeals after the county hearing.[43]

Other states followed with slight variations. On February 2, Pennsylvania organized county grievance committees, made up of one building tradesman, one architect, and one "nonpolitical property owner." The number of complaints had diminished by then, and adjustments were reported as amicably settled in all cases. New York had boards of four members—two from the business community and two from the workers, with at least one of the latter from organized labor.[44]

*   *   *

By early April, 1934, Carmody's vision of square, frank relations between labor and management had its impact on civil works labor policies. State and county CWA executives across the nation came to recognize the right of the AFL to select skilled job applicants, sit on committees to determine wages and hours, and appeal grievances to boards with union representation. Social workers could no longer regard work relief recipients as submissive clients. Conservative corporate managers, like Biddle and Dunham, who had shied away from direct dealings with unions, now met face to face with labor spokesmen to iron out hiring procedures, set prevailing wage rates, and resolve disputes. The AFL had been able to bring such pressure in behalf of its members, particularly when they knew that Federation leaders could always directly approach the chief engineer. Having traveled to the scene of innumerable strikes for Senator Wagner, Carmody believed in bringing

[43]Colonel Daniel Sultan, Report on Cook County, no date, pp. 20–21, Illinois State Library, Springfield; *Chicago Tribune*, February 8, 1934, p. 3; Illinois CWA, *Final Report*, pp. 153–154.

Only one man appeared before the state board, and the decision upheld the local action. Illinois CWA, *Final Report*, p. 155.

[44]*Philadelphia Record*, February 2, 1934, p. 5; Pennsylvania CWA, *Final Report*, pp. 63–64; Fred Daniels to William Nunn, April 30, 1934, CWA 32.

management and labor together. With this spirit, he forced many state and local civil works officials with traditional attitudes toward relief and labor to recognize the AFL's role in the CWA.[45]

The impact of these labor policies remains an elusive, though suggestive, question. While CWA wage rates and concessions to unions helped to restore thousands of building tradesmen in good standing with their brotherhoods, there is little doubt that both the AFL and its local councils were less preoccupied with the civil works effort than with the far more crucial question of establishing labor's role with the NRA and the Public Works Administration. By the winter of 1933, the AFL was much too caught up with Section 7(a) organization duties and the pay and jurisdictional squabbles of National Recovery to give more than secondary attention to the CWA as a distinctly supportive agency. But supportive it was. Four million briefly passed through its ranks to be exposed to yet another aspect of the labor upheaval of 1933–1934, with its appeal boards, grievance committees, and job actions. These 4 million also were removed from the ranks of Marx's "reserve army of the unemployed," which had an incalculable effect on the success of union organization drives that winter. Because of CWA quotas, this federal absorption of potential scabs occurred in precisely those Northern and Midwestern industrial centers which had the greatest pool of idle men. While Carmody's conception of labor's role was confirmed by the CWA experience, thousands of civil works employees also found their faith in collective action strengthened by this New Deal program.

[45]Carmody COHC, Vol. II, p. 327; Schlesinger, *Coming of the New Deal*, p. 385.

CHAPTER FIVE

Civil Works for the White Collar and Professional

THE GREAT Depression remorselessly decimated the ranks of America's 14 million white collar and professional employees. By 1932, one third of the nation's clerical workers had no jobs, and a Columbia University study revealed ninety percent of all architects idle. Two thirds of the American Federation of Musicians reported "at liberty," and New York City alone counted 15,000 teachers waiting for appointments. "Not many of us wear white collars anymore," commented a journalist. "We wear blue, green, tan, gray, checked, dotted, striped and a lot of them are badly frayed."[1] Although the depression had slashed salaries, erased fringe benefits, and destroyed familiar routines, still millions of the white collar and professional unemployed clung to their pride and spurned the dole. They first fell back on personal savings or more fortunate relatives. When these resources dried up, some turned to their affiliations or private agencies.[2]

From the outset, many professional societies took heroic, if hopelessly inadequate, steps to aid their fellow jobless. Musicians raised cash through benefit concerts and also formed un-

[1] Alba M. Edwards, "The White Collar Workers," *MLR*, XXXVIII (March, 1934), 501–505; "Relief for White Collar Workers," FERA, *Monthly Report* (December, 1935), pp. 59–60; Harry W. Laidler, "The White Collar Workers," *American Socialist Quarterly*, III (Autumn, 1934), 53–58; Gove Hambridge, "Wake Up, White Collar!" *Today*, I (December 16, 1933), 17.

[2] C. Wright Mills, *White Collar* (New York: Oxford University Press, 1956), pp. 303–320; Albion A. Hartwell and Caroline Whitney, "Professional Workers in Labor Action," *SWT*, III (March, 1936), 13; Gertrude Springer, "White Collar Temperament," *Survey*, LXX (December, 1934), 374–375.

employed cooperative orchestras. In November, 1930, the American Institute of Architects in New York City set up the Architects Emergency Committee and collected $100,000 in prize money for monthly competitions among the unemployed. By 1932, other technical groups undertook to register members out of work in a vain attempt to place them. With the advent of local relief programs, particularly in large cities, these societies cooperated with public officials to propose projects and select candidates for temporary work. Philadelphia's engineering societies put together a Technical Services Committee which placed 100 people in varied tasks, from drawing blueprints for the Franklin Institute to tabulating statistics for the Housing Authority. In New York City, they managed to put 500 architects, 500 engineers, and 200 chemists on such projects.[3] The College Art Association petitioned for emergency funds and assisted the Emergency Work Bureau of the Gibson Committee in "keeping alive" over 100 painters by having them redecorate schools and settlements and teach over 750 youngsters.[4] These voluntary efforts proved severely limited, however, by the lack of local resources.

Only as a last, bitter resort, did the white collar and professional unemployed turn to relief. A "veneer of false academic pride" kept them from seeking the aid they desperately needed, concluded the New York Unemployed Teachers Association; they had an obsession with appearing well dressed, "even if they haven't a nickel in their pockets." Hopkins' roving reporter Lorena Hickok found an aversion toward applying for

[3] I. A. Hirschman, "The Musician and the Depression," *Nation*, CXXXVII (November 15, 1933), 565–566; Grace Overmyer, "The Musician Starves," *American Mercury*, XXXII (June 1, 1934), 224–231; "Work Relief for Professionals," *Survey*, LXIX (December, 1933), 424; Talbot Faulkner Hamlin, "The Architect and the Depression," *Nation*, CXXXVII (August 9, 1933), 152–154; Simon Breines, "Making Work for Technicians," *SWT*, I (October, 1934), 22; *New York Herald Tribune*, December 22, 1933, p. 5.

[4] Rhoda Hellman, "Art for Bread—and for Art's Sake," *Better Times*, XV (January 1, 1934), 10–11, 14; Audrey McMahon, "May the Artist Live?" *Parnassus*, V (October, 1933), 1–4; "Millions for Laborers, Not One Cent for Artists," *American Magazine of Art*, XXVI (December, 1933), 521–522.

aid in Birmingham, Alabama. "I simply had to murder my pride," confessed an engineer. "We'd lived on bread and water three weeks before I could make myself do it," admitted an insurance salesman. A case investigator described for Miss Hickok her first visit to a salesman's home in Atlanta, Georgia: "When she was getting the family background, this man's wife suddenly burst into tears and left the room. You can see how they felt. . . . It's awfully hard." Dread of that strange place, the relief office or even the employment exchange, appeared the major stumbling block in helping these middle-class jobless. "So reluctant were the white collar workers to reveal their need," commented a settlement volunteer, "that even those who finally brought themselves to approach the private agency usually tried to disguise their plight by applying for work in the agency or simply asking for advice."[5]

In the fall of 1933, when Harry Hopkins undertook the first federal work relief program and wanted to extend its benefits to the white collar and professional unemployed, he, too, turned to the professional societies. These national organizations, with their state and local chapters, had the bureaucratic reach to match the federal scope of the CWA. In addition, their specialized knowledge enabled them to propose and administer sophisticated projects necessary to furnish jobs for the highly trained. Their limited but prior experience with those out of work and connections with local relief agencies gave them a head start. And by serving in a voluntary capacity, these groups could also profit from the image of public service. For his part, Hopkins understood that many of these unemployed might be willing to approach private associations long before they would ever venture into a public relief office or even the United States Employment Service. Furthermore, this close involvement with the professional groups would help to allay fears that work relief would lower standards or somehow threaten established

[5]*New York Times*, February 4, 1932, p. 4; Hickok to Hopkins, January 11, 1934, and April 2, 1934, HLH 68; quoted in William F. McDonald, *Federal Relief Administration and the Arts* (Columbus: Ohio State University Press, 1969), pp. 16–17.

business practices and particularly aided Hopkins to fend off criticisms of inefficiency and waste.

For the unemployed white collar and professional workers on the federal payroll, the experience not only sustained them through the winter but also stimulated a new group-consciousness apart from the societies. Ten percent of the CWA's ranks—over 400,000 white collar and professional people—eventually labored together on public projects. Applying a lesson from the AFL building trades or inspired by protests among relief recipients, many organized and demanded the right to collective bargaining with representation on CWA hiring agencies, wage boards, and grievance committees. They were drawn to new occupational groups, like the Federation of Architects, Engineers, Chemists, and Technicians, and radical "industrial" collectives, like the Associated Office and Professional Emergency Employees, which included social workers as well as the clerical and manual staff. New York City, with the largest white collar and professional population, and over 40,000 such employees on the CWA, set the example for smaller communities across the nation.

But this new consciousness also struck a responsive chord among Hopkins, chief engineer John Carmody, and their associates, who were aware that only special programs could meet the needs of the white collar and professional unemployed. Hopkins realized that the highly innovative and experimental aspect of this type of work relief would require outside experts to create a broad range of specialized jobs. Hiring procedures would have to insure applicants' qualifications, meet the relief requirement of need, and yet somehow appeal to this "psychologically sensitive" class. Labor policies would have to be ironed out for employees who still clung to their professional image and yet, after four years of depression, had come to develop a proletarian consciousness. To resolve these delicate issues in the face of the oncoming winter, Hopkins willingly waived federal rules and regulations to allow the broad participation of interest groups at the administrative and employee levels.

I

For the CWA to provide extensive help for the white collar and professional unemployed, Hopkins had to create a special Civil Works Service. The CWA's initial funds came from the National Industrial Recovery Act, which called for projects in public works construction "or leading directly or indirectly to construction." Theoretically, this rubric allowed for the employment of a small clerical staff and some professional supervisors, but hardly the scale that Hopkins and his aide Jacob Baker now envisioned. "We ought to bring Civil Works into a slightly different category than Public Works so as to include . . . a comprehensive plan of public work and work done in the public interest," suggested Baker. Civil Works Service, as he called it, would allow for the CWA to engage in projects outside the realm of those covered by NIRA money. He urged that the Federal Emergency Relief Administration be tapped for the funds, which presumably would be available since civil works would now employ many who had previously relied on direct aid. Following usual CWA procedures, CWS projects could be proposed by any local group as long as they were sponsored by a public tax-supported institution willing to supply materials. County CWA officials would approve proposals and oversee the execution of projects, a procedure that would enable the CWA to absorb white collar and professional work relief done under local or state auspices prior to the CWA, especially in New York and other urban centers.[6]

Hopkins acted quickly in mid-December to implement Baker's suggestions, but he insisted on going beyond local initiative to create the means for employing white collars and professionals. Outside large metropolitan areas, relief officials lacked the experience and imagination to get these people at work on suitable projects before the winter deadline. As a result, Hopkins

[6]Civil Works Administration, *Rules and Regulations, Number 10* (December 13, 1933); Baker to A. Williams and Hopkins, December 11, 1933, CWA 92; Joanna C. Colcord and Russell M. Kurtz, "Unemployment and Community Action," *Survey*, LXX (January, 1934), 22–24.

withheld 1 million jobs from local quotas and set aside $100 million to finance projects that originated with and were executed for branches of the federal government. He frantically made the rounds of all government agencies and solicited ideas for projects, while these bureaus cooperated with the CWA in directing operations through their own regional, state, or local authorities. Sponsored by various executive departments and forwarded to the CWA for approval (and funding), these "federal projects" were handled through their own individual administrations, which meant that the CWA served as the technical authority for other government agencies to undertake white collar and professional work relief.[7] This organizational flexibility allowed for relatively sophisticated programs to get underway rapidly in areas where the unemployed were concentrated and their services could benefit the communities. In urban centers, like New York, Philadelphia, Chicago, and Los Angeles, many CWS projects were developed through local initiative, but federal projects also reached far beyond the major cities to towns and rural communities with no prior experience in this type of relief. At the same time, they proved invaluable to the federal agencies, who could not otherwise have undertaken them because of budget reductions. The projects included: public health, pest control, public property improvement, conservation, and preservation of public records. These imaginative undertakings were made possible because of the close rapport between Hopkins' staff and professional organizations.[8]

[7]Baker to Stone, November 17, 1933, CWA 92; CWA Minutes, December 4, 1933, HLH 45; "Report of the Federal Civil Works Administration, November 16, 1933, to December 31, 1933," FERA, *Monthly Report* (December, 1933), pp. 13–37; Edward Ainsworth Williams, *Federal Aid for Relief* (New York: Columbia University Press, 1939), pp. 116–117.

[8]Roger F. Evans, "Unemployment in Urban Centers," *Annals*, CLXXVI (November, 1934), 86–88; Walter Wilbur, "Special Problems of the South," *ibid.*, 49–56; Josephine C. Brown, "Rural Families on Relief," *ibid.*, 93; Stone to Hunter, February 20, 1934, CWA 81; testimony of Harry Hopkins, U.S. Congress, House of Representatives, Committee on Appropriations, *Hearings, Federal Emergency Relief and Civil Works Program*, HR. 7527, 73rd Cong., 2nd Sess., 1934, pp. 91–103.

The American Institute of Architects played a major role in one of the most impressive of the federal projects, the Historic American Buildings Survey. In early December, 1933, an executive in the Office of National Parks, Buildings, and Reservations replied to Hopkins' request by proposing that the CWA study buildings of historic value and employ 1,200 draftsmen for at least two months. They would measure, draw plans and elevations, and note details of significant structures to secure an adequate record of America's fast-disappearing landmarks, from the colonial remains in Eastern cities to Spanish missions in California and Texas. Begun under the auspices of the National Parks Service, the project soon received the cooperation of the Library of Congress and the AIA. Interior Secretary Harold Ickes appointed a national advisory committee of seven, four named by the Institute and the others by the Office of National Parks. The committee divided the country into forty districts, each with a central office having a paid director and a volunteer committee of five. District supervisors were also named from recommendations by the AIA, local architectural and historical societies, and curators.[9]

Engineering societies participated in the CWA's triangulation and mapping for the U.S. Coast and Geodetic Survey. As part of an ongoing project with the Department of Commerce, the Survey undertook supplemental activities under civil works auspices and became the first CWA federal project for engineers. The Survey had its own long-established organization in each state, and representatives for the civil works project could easily be designated from local chapters of the American Engineering Council and the American Society of Civil Engineers, as well as from engineering departments of colleges and universities. The national director of the Survey acknowledged how these groups "took the jobs in order that they might aid their less fortunate fellows and they have given unreservedly

[9]Alexander Carl Guth, "Historic American Buildings Survey," *Pencil Points*, XV (June, 1934), 271–272; "Architects Participate in Historical Buildings Survey," *Architect and Engineer*, CXVI (February, 1934), 31–32; *New York Times*, December 14, 1933, p. 6; *Los Angeles Times*, December 19, 1933.

of themselves in order to make the project a success." State representatives sent out "survey parties" and set up central offices where the results of the field work were computed and prepared for publication. Since instruments and tools had to be furnished locally, they also secured the cooperation of private firms who loaned extra equipment. Through these efforts over 15,000 men were employed.[10]

To find suitable projects for unemployed schoolteachers and yet avoid duplication of public education systems, Hopkins called on the United States Office of Education as well as state and local associations and school boards. Although the "Emergency Education Program" had actually begun a month prior to the CWA, with FERA, it reached fruition under civil works. Carefully designed to supplement what the public schools could not provide, these projects employed over 33,000 teachers in adult education, literacy classes, vocational training, vocational rehabilitation, and nursery schools.[11] In New York City, many projects were suggested and approved locally under the CWS. A special committee of superintendents outlined sixteen different activities conducted through the public schools, with salaries coming from relief funds. A committee of the local American Federation of Teachers also made suggestions to this body. Illinois CWS projects were in the hands of an advisory board composed of the Chicago superintendent of schools, a dean from the University of Chicago, and the head resident of Chicago Commons. Organizations that submitted ideas included Northwestern University Settlement, the YM and YWCA, PTAs, and the Illinois Institute for Juvenile Research.[12]

[10]"Work Undertaken by Geodetic Survey as Relief Project," ENR, CXI (December 7, 1933), 694; Illinois CWA, Final Report (March, 1934), p. 72; New York Times, November 23, 1933, p. 15; R. S. Patton, Director of Coast and Geodetic Survey, to Editor, ENR, CXII (February 15, 1934), 237–238.

[11]"Educational Work Relief for Jobless Teachers," MLR, XXXVII (October, 1933), 810–811; L. R. Alderman, "Emergency Relief and Adult Education," School and Society, XXXVIII (December, 1933), 717–719; "Emergency Education Program," FERA, Monthly Report (June, 1935), pp. 16–19.

[12]"Report of the Committee on Unemployment," Union Teacher, XI (March,

The Public Works of Art Project began under the CWA on December 8, 1933, as a federal project in cooperation with the Treasury Department. Hopkins, in a conscious effort to gain respect for a program which might draw jibes from New Deal critics, created a national coordinating committee for the PWAP that included Charles Moore, chairman of the Fine Arts Commission; Rexford G. Tugwell; Henry T. Hunt, general counsel for the Public Works Administration; and President Roosevelt's uncle, Frederic A. Delano, director of the National Planning Commission. A later gathering of American art leaders, particularly museum directors, met in the home of Edward Bruce and was honored by the presence of the First Lady. These esteemed people outlined the eventual setup of the PWAP, with Forbes Watson, noted writer and art critic, as technical director, and Edward Bruce as secretary of the advisory committee and chief executive responsible for the administration, distribution of funds, and planning. Bruce was a shrewd choice. A Hoover Republican and alternate at the London Economic Conference, he also had canvasses on display in New York's Whitney Museum and could bridge the worlds of institutional patrons and the avant garde.[13] With the utmost concern to avoid any charges of a federal dictum on aesthetics, Bruce decentralized the PWAP into sixteen regional units presided over by some 600 local volunteers interested in fine arts. Regional chairmen, who were primarily museum directors or distinguished community leaders active in the advancement of art, had the power to authorize local commissions which, when completed, became the property of the federal government. This mass of advisors—the largest ratio of administrators to employees (one to five) in any CWA

1934), 7–8; *New York Sun*, December 21, 1933, p. 34; *Chicago Daily News*, December 12, 1933, p. 4; IERC, Press Release, December 20, 1933, VAO 74.

[13]"Federal Art Plan to Provide Funds for Needy Artists," *Art News*, XXX (December 16, 1933), 3–4; Forbes Watson, "The U.S.A. Challenges the Artists," *Parnassus*, VI (January, 1934), 1–2; "Jobs for Artists," *Art Digest*, VII (December 15, 1933), 5.

program—helps to explain the remarkable initial reception which this first federal venture in the arts received across the country.[14]

The New Deal's uneasy relationship with the theater grew out of a proposal by Actors Equity Association and got underway as a CWS project in New York City. Preparations for twelve shows began when the CWA meted out $28,000 to employ 150 actors for thirty-four days. Emily Holt, associate counsel to Equity, arranged with local CWA executives and public institutions (schools, hospitals, libraries) for the dramas to be staged free of charge in their facilities. Equity selected the plays, preferably classics to avoid royalties, and works that could be produced on simple sets.[15]

Statistical surveys of all kinds absorbed the great bulk of white collar and professional employees on the CWA. Not only unemployed statisticians, but also accountants, clerks, and many others struggled with Hollerith cards and long columns of figures. The American Statistical Association assumed an advisory role along with aid from university professors and municipal department heads in cities where studies were conducted. The

[14]Florence Loeb Kellogg, "Art Becomes Public Works," *Survey Graphic*, XXIII (June, 1934), 279, 282; Bruce to Margaret Breuning, November 25, 1933, EB 83; Forbes Watson, "The Public Works of Art Project: Federal, Republican, or Democratic?" *American Magazine of Art*, XXVII (January, 1934), 6–9; Edward Bruce, "Implications of the PWAP," *ibid.* (March, 1934), 113–114.

The Philadelphia committee included Mrs. Samuel Fels, J. Stogdell Stokes, Ellis Gimbel, and Francis Biddle. *Philadelphia Public Ledger*, December 14, 1933, Sec. II, p. 1. The New York City members were Juliana Force of the Whitney Museum; Alfred M. Barr, Jr., director of the Museum of Modern Art; Edward M. Warburg, trustee of the Museum of Modern Art; William Henry Fox, director of the Brooklyn Museum; Gertrude Vanderbilt Whitney, founder of the Whitney Museum; Lloyd Goodrich, a writer on art; James Rosenberg, lawyer and art connoisseur; and Major C. M. Penfield, "layman." *New York Herald Tribune*, December 13, 1931, p. 14.

[15]"Equity and the Government Productions," *Equity*, XIX (September, 1934), 7–8, 16; Emil Nalence, "Uncle Sam—Producer," *ibid.* (February, 1934), 5–6; *New York Times*, January 15, 1934, p. 13; Sadie Belgrade to Hopkins, January 26, 1934, CWA 32; Jane DeHart Mathews, *The Federal Theatre, 1935–1939: Plays, Relief, and Politics* (Princeton: Princeton University Press, 1967).

ASA recommended supervisors and also gave quick courses to canvassers who fanned out on survey work, like the unemployment census and slum clearance studies for the New York City Housing Authority.[16]

This wide array of projects brought together strikingly diverse and heretofore isolated groups into a cooperative public effort. For a brief moment, the American Federation of Teachers, state education associations, and superintendents joined to outline projects. Architects of varied schools came together on the Historic American Buildings Survey. "Modernists, secessionists, plagiarists all for once laid down their cudgels," wrote one journalist. Artists were drawn out from their solitary studios, free to express their styles as long as they adhered to the theme of Americana. In New York City, an initial objection to the appointment of Mrs. Juliana Force of the Whitney Museum was raised by "conservative" societies, but representatives of various groups conferred and came out "glad to join the common effort." Prestigious engineers got their colleagues who headed private firms to donate extra instruments to the surveys. Hopkins' flexible policies, especially his willingness to delegate responsibility, proved a shrewd catalyst behind the success of many projects, but also sanctioned the most blatant exploitation of federal emergency authority by private groups anxious to take care of their own.[17]

---

[16]Hopkins to Central Statistical Board, November 23, 1933, CWA 53; telegram, Baker to all state administrators, December 15, 1933, CWA 73; Emerson Ross, "Research and Statistical Programs of the Federal Emergency Relief Administration," *Journal of the American Statistical Association*, XXIX (September, 1934), 288–294; Stuart Rice, "Statistical Opportunities and Responsibilities," *ibid.* (March, 1934), 1–10; Frederick P. Stephan, "State and Local Statistical Studies Conducted as Work Relief Projects," *Social Forces*, XIII (May, 1935), 485–490.

[17]Guth, "Historic American Buildings Survey," 271; "Emergency Education Program," FERA, *Monthly Report*, pp. 16–19; Forbes Watson, "The Artist Becomes a Citizen," *Forum*, XC (May, 1934), 277–279; *New York Evening Post*, December 16, 1933, p. 13; *New York Herald Tribune*, December 13, 1933, p. 14; Hickok to Hopkins, December 29, 1933, FERA 69.

II

Hiring the white collar and professional unemployed on the CWA posed the complicated task of helping the genuinely needy while not offending the "psychologically sensitive" middle class. Hopkins was caught in a dilemma. Since CWS money came from Federal Emergency Relief funds, the program had to offer jobs to those who, according to FERA procedures, had undergone a social work investigation of family circumstances to determine eligibility—a process which white collars and professionals deeply resented. To break through this barrier of pride, Hopkins stretched the rules and allowed the first widespread relaxation of the FERA "means" requirement for the CWS. Although these applicants still had to show definite evidence of need, Hopkins ordered only a minimum of individual investigation and follow-up into the homes. In addition, he authorized professional associations and extant unions to recommend candidates with virtually no further check into their finances. Nonprofessionals such as sales and office personnel could be referred by the United States Employment Service, business colleges, high school counsellors, and private relief agencies, which simultaneously set up separate facilities to handle these people.[18]

As one of the few established professional unions, Actors Equity Association enjoyed the same preference given all recognized labor organizations, to select employees from their crafts. On January 15, 1934, when the theater project was officially announced in the press, the unemployed were instructed to sign up at Equity headquarters. Over 1,000 stood in a line that went down three flights of stairs from the office of Margaret Smith, who registered each one. "One cannot just requisition

[18]Gertrude Springer, "Ragged White Collars," *Survey*, LXVII (November 15, 1931), 183–184; "Relief for White Collar Workers," FERA, *Monthly Report*, pp. 59–66; John Charnow, *Work Relief Experience in the United States* (Washington: Committee on Social Security, Social Science Research Council, 1943), pp. 36–37; Colcord and Kurtz, "Unemployment and Community Action," 22–23; CWA, *Rules and Regulations, Number 10* (December 13, 1933).

150 assorted actors," she noted. "Choosing among hundreds of applicants those whose need was greatest and yet who fitted the parts" proved difficult. Equity applauded itself, however, when all but two of the roles were filled within the week.[19]

Since 1930, the professional societies among technicians had registered their fellow unemployed and had cooperated with whatever local relief agencies existed, but with limited success. In November, 1930, the AIA chapter in New York City signed up some 3,000 and managed to place only 522, many in non-professional slots (like chauffeur). The Chemists Unemployment Committee was formed in the winter of 1931 to list the jobless, find openings, and raise funds; and the American Society of Civil Engineers established an employment service, which referred only 100 by 1932.[20]

Still, these associations had the prior experience and advanced registration to help the CWA get more professionals on the payroll. On November 30, 1933, New York's Mayor Fiorello H. La Guardia urged the societies to refer lists of unemployed to the USES and appoint committees to confer with local civil works officials. The New York State Employment Service director had previously cooperated with the Architects Emergency Committee, the Engineering Societies Employment Service, and the Chemists Unemployment Committee under the Temporary Emergency Relief Administration; and this practice continued under the CWA. In San Francisco, the Engineering Societies Employment Service provided a clearing house for all unemployed technicians, and the Chicago chapter took pride in having registered 3,911 and placed 1,136 on the CWA.[21]

[19]"Rush for Jobs as CWA Opens Relief Plan," *Zit's*, XXVII (January 20, 1934), 1; Nalence, "Uncle Sam—Producer," 5–6; Emily Holt, "The Actors and the CWA Audience," *Equity*, XIX (March, 1934), 7, 12.

[20]American Society of Civil Engineers to Pinchot, May 6, 1932, GP 322; Hamlin, "The Architect and the Depression," 152–153; "Work of the Committee on Unemployment and Relief for Chemists and Chemical Engineers," *Science*, LXXXIII (March 13, 1936), 253–254; W. A. Shoudy, "The Engineer and the Depression," *Nation*, CXXXVII (September 13, 1933), 296–298.

[21]*New York Times*, December 9, 1933, p. 7; *New York Sun*, December 9,

The National Advisory Committee of the Public Works of Art Project stressed talent, not need, as the first requirement in hiring 2,500 unemployed artists across the country. Forbes Watson hoped to "secure for the public a large number of works of art, some of which in due time will have a value far in excess of the money spent." Edward Bruce shared Harold Ickes' Public Works approach of creating monuments to the New Deal and insisted that talent had to come first and need second.[22] One of Bruce's assistants was quoted, saying, "We do not want the image of Bohemians who failed to make good," a message that came across quite clearly to the regional chairmen.[23] In New York City, Juliana Force attempted to comply with these national goals. "Quality is of first importance," explained Mrs. Force, "and the major consideration in selecting which unemployed artists shall be employed." Mrs. Force wrote to art organizations for potential candidates. The College Art Association alone classified over 1,400 in need, while the PWAP had allotted only 1,000 positions for the entire region. As a result, the committee could impose rigorous standards, including a competitive trial for 722. After 208 were eliminated, those remaining were classified A, B, and C, depending on creative and technical ability, and wages varied accordingly.[24]

1933; telegram, W. H. Lange to USES, New York State, December 1, 1933, CWA 31; *San Francisco Chronicle*, January 4, 1934, p. 6; American Engineering Council, Conference of Secretaries of Engineering Societies (January 10 and 11, 1935), "Relief Activities for Local Societies," American Engineering Council Papers, Engineering Societies Library, New York. Philadelphia's Engineers Club provided a similar agency. *Philadelphia Public Ledger*, December 6, 1933, p. 1; S. Williams to Fellows, April 23, 1934, CWA 72.

[22]Watson, "The U.S.A. Challenges the Artists," 1; Arthur M. Schlesinger, Jr., *The Coming of the New Deal* (Boston: Houghton Mifflin Company, 1965), pp. 282–289; Bruce to Henry Morganthau, Jr., January 3, 1934, EB 87; Bruce to Leon Kroll, April 24, 1934, EB 83.

[23]Bruce to Levi, January 18, 1934, JL; Edward B. Rowan, "Will Plumbers' Wages Turn the Trick?" *American Magazine of Art*, XXVII (February, 1934), 80.

[24]Quoted in Belesario Ramon Contreras, "The New Deal Treasury Department Art Programs and the American Artist, 1933–1943" (unpublished Ph.D. dissertation, American University, 1967), p. 59; Force to Levi, January

Limited quotas and an insistence on standards resulted in equally rigorous requirements for choosing unemployed teachers. Despite the existence of education associations and several chapters of the AFT, workers for these CWS projects were generally picked by local boards of education. In New York City, for example, where 15,000 teachers had no jobs, applicants had to be on the "eligible list" for License Number 1, have 90 days' experience in teaching, diagnostic, or remedial work, have completed at least 30 hours in diagnostic or remedial courses, and satisfy the state relief requirement of need.[25]

Although these hiring procedures maintained high standards for the CWA, such practices, which bordered on professional exclusiveness, aroused opposition from new, radical organizations among the white collar and professional unemployed. Many had developed out of local work relief programs prior to the New Deal, from an insecurity and fear that their temporary "jobs" would end before they found permanent employment in private industry. Some were old professionals, including a few Taylorites, who had spoken out during the drafting of NRA codes. Most, however, were young, recent college graduates, without much attachment to the established associations. New York City, with the largest white collar and professional population, as well as the most extensive work program under the Emergency Work Bureau and the state TERA, had emerged as the center for such groups among the unemployed.[26]

23, 1934, and March 7, 1934, JL; Joseph Solman, "The Easel Division of the WPA Federal Art Project," in Francis V. O'Connor, ed., *The New Deal Art Projects* (Washington: Smithsonian Institution Press, 1972), pp. 115–116; Richard D. McKinzie, "The New Deal for Artists" (unpublished Ph.D. dissertation, Indiana University, 1969), pp. 19–21.

[25]*New York Sun*, December 18, 1933, p. 38.

[26]"Organizing the Professional Employees," Association of Federation Workers, *Bulletin*, II (January, 1934), 4; Helen Seymour, "The Organized Unemployed" (unpublished M.A. thesis, University of Chicago, 1937), pp. 14–15; Nels Anderson, "Organized Unemployed," in Russell H. Kurtz, ed., *Social Work Yearbook, 1937* (New York: Russell Sage Foundation, 1937), pp. 320–323; William H. and Kathryn Coe Cordell, "Unions among the Unemployed," *North American Review*, CCXL (December, 1935), 498–510.

The Federation of Architects, Engineers, Chemists, and Technicians began in Manhattan as an independent union "to unite technicians in all fields." Its founders mostly unemployed, FAECT sprung up in the fall of 1933 out of dissatisfaction with the NRA construction code.[27] When the CWA began hiring, however, the Federation demanded "equal professional status" in screening applicants and the right to submit members' names for possible jobs. By that time, it claimed to speak for 5,000 members, 1,000 in New York. A committee met with local civil works executives and charged that the city USES director had cooperated only with organizations of his own choosing. One FAECT spokesman claimed that these "older organizations" were interested only in finding work for their registrants for which they charged a fee. "We are today pressing for the right that is accorded all unions under the CWA and the PWA, the right to register the unemployed for jobs and to ask their appointment on the basis of ability and need," stated a Federation *Bulletin* editorial. The Chicago chapter also visited local CWA headquarters to request a Federation representative on the board which hired technicians. "Engineers are now forced to register for jobs with the Engineering Societies Employment Service, a fee-charging agency under employer control," declared a FAECT spokesman.[28]

The Artists' Union in New York City insisted on need as the first criterion for selecting PWAP employees and challenged Juliana Force's emphasis on talent. Formed out of economic necessity, the "Unemployed Artists Group" had initially organized to protest the discontinuance of the first white collar and professional projects under the city's Emergency Work Bureau. With the inauguration of the CWA's Public Works of

[27]Henry Sasch, "The Draftsmen Organize!" *Pencil Points*, XIV (October, 1933), 429–430; "Unions for Technicians," *New Republic*, LXXVII (January 24, 1934), 295–296.

[28]"The Federation in Action," FAECT, *Bulletin*, I (February, 1934), 4–5; "Committee Reports," *ibid.*, 10–11; "News from the Locals—Chicago," *ibid.*, 12; *New York Evening Post*, December 9, 1933, p. 4.

Art Project, it protested the limited number employed and Mrs. Force's merit system. A delegation of fifty jobless appeared outside the Whitney Museum on December 28, 1933, and demanded to know why artists who had registered first remained uncalled while some who had never registered received commissions. Mrs. Force explained that decorations for public buildings had to meet the exact standards of the New York City Art Commission and other municipal agencies. "Need," she added, "is not in my vocabulary." Two weeks later the Artists' Union staged a march 100 strong from Washington Square to the Whitney, where their leader Phil Bard demanded that the Union be part of the selection committee. Mrs. Force refused, stating that the public would prefer quality over the number of artists saved. She did, however, speed up the hiring and henceforth called candidates in order of registration.[29]

Unemployed schoolteachers also resorted to radical pressure groups. In 1933, the American Federation of Teachers represented those in regular appointments and had little relevance for new graduates from college or normal school without permanent assignments. They turned to their own organizations, like the New York State Association of Unappointed Teachers and the Unemployed Teachers Association, centered in Manhattan. When local school authorities set down strict qualifications for civil works appointments, both groups reacted immediately. The State Association adopted a resolution opposing any requirements other than placement on the eligibility list. "The setting up of special rules for eligibility tends to defeat the entire stated purpose of the CWA," declared the UTA. "The necessity for . . . meeting certain requirements over and above those for a regular teaching position leads to abuses in selection and closes the door to many teachers in dire need."

[29]"History of the Artists' Union," *Art Front*, I (November, 1934), 5–6; Lincoln Rothschild, "Artists' Organizations of the Depression Decade," in O'Connor, *New Deal Art Projects*, p. 200; *New York Times*, January 10, 1934, p. 19.

These rules, the UTA pointed out, were more difficult than those for permanent teachers' assignments.[30]

Although hiring procedures stirred some reaction from white collar and professional groups, wage policies aroused even greater protest. Controversy centered on the embarrassing disparity between CWA and CWS hourly rates: the former were governed by PWA minimums and based on collective bargaining in private industry, while CWS levels were pegged to the FERA minimum of $.30 per hour.[31] On December 10, 1933, a delegation of four representatives of the Associated Office and Professional Emergency Employees of New York City arrived in Washington. The group, consisting of a researcher, an artist, an adult education teacher, and a newspaper reporter, charged "gross discrimination against the white collar classes." They protested how their present CWA wage scale of $.35 to $.75 an hour compared with a minimum of $.50 for manual labor and $1.20 for skilled. The committee contended they were entitled, "as skilled professional men and women," to a higher rate. They also insisted on the right of white collar organizations to bargain collectively on all matters pertaining to wages, hours, conditions, and dismissals, especially since AFL craft unions already enjoyed such representation on state CWA boards.[32]

The Federation of Architects, Engineers, Chemists, and

[30]Eunice Langdon, "The Teacher Faces the Depression," *Nation*, CXXXVII (August 16, 1933), 182–185; Celia Lewis Zitron, *The New York City Teachers Union, 1916–1964* (New York: Humanities Press, 1968), pp. 130–131; *Union Teacher*, XI (September-December, 1933); *New York Sun*, November 15, 1933, p. 29; December 23, 1933, p. 32; January 11, 1934, p. 34; January 15, 1934, p. 30.

[31]CWA Minutes, November 22, 1933, "Wage Rates for Work for Which Public Works Funds Cannot Be Used," HLH 45; Arthur Edward Burns and Peyton Kerr, "Survey of Work Relief Wage Policies," *AER*, XXVII (December, 1937), 711–724.

[32]Alfred Schoellkopf to Hopkins, December 2, 1933, CWA 31; AOPEE to Hopkins, December 18, 1933, CWA 32; *New York Times*, December 3, 1933, Sec. II, p. 1; December 9, 1933, p. 16; December 10, 1933, p. 12; *New York Herald Tribune*, December 3, 1933, p. 3.

Technicians quickly echoed the demand for prevailing rates for their professions. "Under the guise of a limited appropriation and the desire to spread work, the threat of a lower living standard for the architectural draftsman, as well as all other white collar employees, had been carried out," wrote a FAECT leader. "On CWA work where the building mechanics and other workers of established unions were paid their regular union scales why must the draftsman requiring far more training and study be forced to accept a pauper's salary?" questioned *Pencil Points*.[33]

Teachers organizations raised similar cries. The AFT feared that relief wages would "create a new class of teachers working at less than regular scale," and the AFL recommended that standard wages for teachers in the Emergency Education Program be at least the scale received by skilled labor. In New York City, the Emergency Teachers in Adult Education, organized during the TERA work relief program, petitioned the state CWA against the present $15 weekly earnings and managed to collect signatures from professors at City College and Columbia University Teachers College.[34]

These demands reached a sympathetic John Carmody, head of CWA labor relations, who was ironing out wages for skilled workers by referring to collective bargaining agreements and prevailing rates. He realized, of course, that no comparable organizations or agreements existed for white collar employees, but he appreciated the need for all workers to organize and negotiate through unions of their own choosing. In the absence of prior contracts, Carmody sent out new rules and regulations

[33]FAECT to Hopkins, January 3, 1934, CWA 32; "The Technician and Skilled Labor," FAECT, *Bulletin*, I (February, 1934), 7–8; Jules Korchein, "The Federation of Architects, Engineers, Chemists and Technicians and the CWA," *Pencil Points*, XV (January, 1934), 43; "Federation of Architects, Engineers, Chemists and Technicians Report," *ibid.* (March, 1934), 154.

[34]American Federation of Labor, *Report of Proceedings of the Fifty-Fourth Annual Convention, San Francisco, 1934* (Washington: Judd and Detweiler, 1934), p. 462; *New York Sun*, November 14, 1933, p. 34, and December 26, 1933, p. 25.

in mid-December, 1933, which instructed that CWS wages (even those funded by FERA) be the prevailing rate for the type of work done but not less than $.30 an hour. Clerical workers were permitted a maximum of thirty-nine hours to allow them to boost total wages by putting in more time. In no case were weekly earnings to fall below $18, $15, and $12 for the northern, central, and southern zones.[35] Furthermore, Carmody encouraged state and local CWAs to deal with *ad hoc* white collar and professional representative groups, and he urged cooperation with whatever organizations arose to speak for these CWA employees. Carmody set an example by receiving the New York delegation of AOPEE and agreeing to their demands. "We must not curtail the right of groups to organize in their own way," he told his associates. Nels Anderson, one of Carmody's chief assistants for labor relations, later stated: "I see no reason why a pressure group should not use every legitimate means for accomplishing its ends. That is the essence of competitive democracy."[36]

Within a week, CWA administrators in New York City began to receive representatives of various white collar and professional organizations. AOPEE requested the right of collective bargaining on questions pertaining to wages, hours, and working conditions without discrimination or intimidation and proposed revised salary scales. The state CWA administrator agreed to the pay increase and guaranteed the Association recognition. This initial victory encouraged other groups to petition, including FAECT and the Association of Emergency Workers in Adult Education. Over 200 workers assembled at CWA headquarters on December 19, 1933, while officials received a delegation of fifteen. Ultimately an entire new wage scale was drawn up for New York State clerical, technical, and professional employees. An official bulletin established minimum,

[35]CWA Minutes, November 22, 1933, and November 27, 1933, HLH 45; Civil Works Administration, *Rules and Regulations, Number 10* (December 13, 1933).

[36]Minutes, no date, JMC 73; Nels Anderson, "Pressure Groups," *Survey Graphic*, XXV (March, 1936), 170.

average, and maximum rates for specific jobs; the gradations attempted to account for differences between Manhattan, rural upstate counties, and middle-sized communities.[37]

Once these groups succeeded in lifting wage rates, they proceeded to consider other grievances. Copying the craft union model, the Federation of Architects, Engineers, Chemists, and Technicians organized CWA employees on a project basis and elected grievance committees to consider complaints and mimeograph papers discussing workers' concerns. At times, these committees took up grievances of individual workers—sometimes all the way to Washington. Appearing in behalf of engineers and architects on the Bear Mountain, New York, Project, for example, FAECT succeeded in reducing the work week from six to five days without a salary decrease.[38] The Unemployed Teachers Association spoke out for CWS reading coaches who complained that supervisors were foisting regular classroom duties upon them. A committee of four met with a CWA executive and had the work relief tutors reassigned.[39] The Artists' Union brought pressure to end the A-B-C classification of painters and demanded representation on all bodies elected by the workers. After demonstrating eight separate times before the Whitney in March, the New York union was granted recognition by Edward Bruce, who admitted that their activities had justification.[40] Even dentists, organized into the Allied Dental Council (with a membership of 3,500), peti-

[37]FAECT to Hopkins, January 3, 1934, CWA 32; Joseph B. Shaw to Carmody, January 10, 1934, CWA 92; New York State TERA, Official Bulletin Number 16 (January 8, 1934), *Rules and Regulations for Clerical, Technical, and Professional Employees on CWA and CWS; New York Times*, December 19, 1933, p. 4.

[38]Simon Breines, "The Federation of Architects, Engineers, Chemists and Technicians," *Architectural Record*, LXXVI (July, 1934), 59–60; "FAECT Report," *Pencil Points*, 154; Jules Korchein, "Report on the Bear Mountain Projects," March 30, 1934, FERA 195; Goldschmidt to Joseph McGoldrick, February 7, 1934, CWA 31.

[39]*Unemployed Teacher*, II (March, 1934), 4; *New York Sun*, January 11, 1934, p. 34.

[40]"For Jobs and Adequate Relief," *Art Front*, I (November, 1934), 5.

tioned the New York State and local CWA for representation in setting fees for those on work-relief payrolls. "CWA bricklayers get from $12 to $14 a day while dentists receive only $18 a week," charged a speaker before the Bronx Allied Dental Economic Chapter.[41]

The ferment, particularly the impact of the Artists' Union, aroused hundreds of writers, who saw projects for artists and musicians and organized to demand work in their field. "Unemployed writers of New York City do not intend to continue under semi-starvation conditions," wrote Robert Whitcomb, secretary of the Unemployed Writers Association in February, 1934. Although a few states had set up local CWA projects for writers, in general, most found employment as "clerks" or other nondescript jobs. Whitcomb's UWA, however, set ambitious goals. In mid-February, forty staged a demonstration at CWA headquarters, while a delegation of three conferred with the local administrator. They demanded that writing be recognized as a profession worthy of public support, the right to a secure existence, wages or relief for all unemployed writers, and complete literary freedom and artistic integrity. They also suggested projects and advocated that the government subsidize publication and sell works at cost to schools, libraries, and other public institutions.[42]

This group consciousness among "clients" touched many social workers and added to their own "rank-and-file" restlessness, which eventually matured into "unions" of relief employees on the CWA. The creation of large emergency relief offices under the FERA in 1933 had, of course, led to grievances among home visitors, interviewers, and clerks, complaints which included "primitive conditions" in cramped, dismal offices, low salaries, heavy case loads, and no job security.

[41]Harry Strusser, "Dental Relief—for the Dentist and the Public," *Better Times,* XV (November 6, 1933), 12–13; *New York Times,* March 1, 1934, p. 3, and March 27, 1934, p. 19.

[42]Quoted in Jerre Mangione, *The Dream and the Deal* (Boston: Little, Brown, 1972), pp. 35–36; "Are Writers Clerks?" *Nation,* CXXXVIII (February 14, 1934), 171; Robert Whitcomb, "Jobs, or Cash!" *New Masses,* X (February 13, 1934), 12–13; *New York Sun,* February 15, 1934, p. 1.

This "crisis" in the administration of relief combined with the NRA's stimulus of organizations in the professions to galvanize young social workers and the agency staffs, who identified particularly with the white collar jobless and their new pressure groups.[43]

One of the first significant rank-and-file social workers' organizations was the New York Relief Bureau Employees Association, set up in December, 1933, among investigators, typists, and clerks. The CWA, under whose jurisdiction the EHRB workers fell, recognized the Association as the group's spokesman and enjoined the Bureau from "any attempt at intimidation." Their organ, the *EHRB Employee*, printed a list of demands: a wage increase, elimination of overtime, a thirty-hour week, reduced case loads, decent sanitary equipment in the office, and the right to bargain collectively through the Association. After negotiation with CWA officials, EHRBA leaders announced a wage increase of $33\frac{1}{3}$ percent and other tangible victories. Recognizing a common interest with workers on the CWA, the Association quickly amalgamated with the AOPEE and promised to be a "potent force in raising living standards for white collar and professional workers in New York." This success prompted similar efforts at organizing the social work rank-and-file in other cities. In early 1934, unions were formed in relief agencies in Newark, Philadelphia, Chicago, and other metropolitan areas.[44]

III

The white collar and professional organizations, which had brought some measure of security and identity on the CWA,

[43]"Organizing the Professional Employee," Association of Federation Workers, *Bulletin*, II (January, 1934), 4; Joseph H. Levy, "New Forms of Organization Among Social Workers," *SWT*, I (October, 1934), 10–12, 30; Jacob Fisher, *The Rank and File Movement in Social Work* (New York: New York School of Social Work, 1936).

[44]"Rank and File," *SWT*, I (May-June, 1934), 23; Marvin Slater, "Personnel Practices in the NYHRB," *ibid.*, II (May, 1935), 13–14; *New York Times*, December 19, 1933, p. 4.

fomented the closest thing to a white collar "united front" when wage cuts and reduced hours warned of the imminent curtailment of civil works. This group consciousness was reflected in the appearance of new periodicals. The first issue of *Social Work Today*, a journal of the "rank-and-file," came out in March, 1934, and the Federation of Architects, Engineers, Chemists, and Technicians *Bulletin* began in February. *Art Front*, a magazine of the Artists' Union, appeared in the fall of 1934, with a detailed account of the group's activities during the CWA period. Although some of these organizations started on exclusive professional lines, others cut across occupational barriers. The Unemployed Teachers Association cooperated with the Association of Office and Professional Emergency Employees, while FAECT reached out to the Architectural Guild, asking it to affiliate on general policy questions.[45]

Some white collar militants also gravitated to the Socialist Party's Workers' Committee on Unemployment, led by an impetuous visionary, David Lasser. A graduate of Massachusetts Institute of Technology in 1924, Lasser had edited *Technocracy Review* and had voted for Herbert Hoover in 1928. His turning point came after he had been laid off by the New York Edison Company and he got involved in an unemployed group on Manhattan's Lower West Side. With the coming of the federal work program, Lasser created what eventually became the Association of Civil Works Employees, which included "teachers, stenographers, file clerks," and others employed in CWA offices and on the projects. After setting up a headquarters at 22 East 22nd Street, the Association in early February started a publication entitled *The CWA Employee*, whose first headline, "Tenth Floor Employees Organizing: Demand Continuation of Job," referred to the proletarian anger among the CWA file clerks at administrative headquarters. Their demands included a five-day week of six hours a day, no discrimination or favoritism, higher wages and proper job classification, and

[45]*New York Herald Tribune*, February 5, 1934, p. 14; *Unemployed Teacher*, II (March, 1934), 1, 4; "FAECT Report," *Pencil Points*, 154.

no overtime. These activities encouraged similar movements in Philadelphia, Chicago, and West Coast cities.[46]

A dramatic confrontation occurred in mid-March in New York City, when the CWA announced its first layoffs and municipal officials stated that all employees would have to fill out a detailed social work questionnaire to help determine need among those who would remain. "We are going to have to go back to a relief wage instead of a working wage," declared the New York City welfare commissioner, who warned that failure to fill out the form would result in immediate dismissal. "We expect that a new large number, particularly of white collar people, will decline to put themselves in the charity class," ventured the head of the city CWA office. Such statements incensed white collars and professionals. Workers from twelve projects representing 10,000 employees descended on the state CWA headquarters to protest the questionnaire, while city civil works executives met with AOPEE officers. A FAECT rally of 3,000 resolved "to turn all questionnaires to the hands of our elected committees and authorize these to represent us in the fight to rescind questionnaires." FAECT also sent delegates to Albany with more than 2,000 copies of the form, having written across the face:

I protest this questionnaire procedure as unwarranted and unjustified and declare my employment on the CWA at present is an indication of my need. . . . I demand that my employment be continued until the day on which the PWA or another agency will employ me with at least the present salary.

Over a third of the city's CWS employees refused to sign, as telegrams flooded Hopkins' desk in Washington.[47] Some civil

[46]Stanley High, "Who Organized the Unemployed?" *Saturday Evening Post,* CCXI (December 10, 1938), 8–9, 30; Selden Rodman, "Lasser and the Workers Alliance," *Nation,* CXLVII (September 10, 1938), 242–244; David Lasser, "Socialists and the Unemployed," *American Socialist Quarterly,* V (June, 1936), 10–14; *New York Herald Tribune,* February 5, 1934, p. 14.

[47]*New York Herald Tribune,* March 9, 1934, p. 18; March 10, 1934, p. 5;

works executives supported these objections, like Grace Gosselin, head of CWA white collar projects in New York City, who condemned the form when a delegation of the Unemployed Teachers Association visited her office. But Hopkins' aide Aubrey Williams explained to local leaders that states had to reduce their quotas by first laying off persons who had more than one family member working. "To accomplish this," said Williams, "it is obviously necessary that a thoroughgoing inquiry be made of those who are at present employed on Civil Works. The action of the authorities in New York City is in keeping with the requirements of this Administration."[48]

Increased layoffs brought more demonstrations, which further reinforced the sense of collective identity among these white collar New Yorkers. Seven hundred men and women from the Association of Civil Works Employees, the Associated Office and Professional Emergency Employees, Emergency Teachers in Adult Education, and Tenement House CWA Workers constituted the major elements of the unemployed's March 24th "Easter Parade" in Washington to protest the demobilization of the CWA. They returned home to stage a one-hour strike of 20,000, under the auspices of the New York Committee for United Action on CWA and Unemployment, sponsored by FAECT.[49]

---

and March 12, 1934, p. 4; "The CWA Inquisition," *New Masses*, X (March 20, 1934), 9; "Jobless to Make Demands on CWA in March on City Hall," *New Leader*, XVII (February 10, 1934), 2A; *New York Times*, March 11, 1934, p. 16; "CWA Summary," FAECT, *Bulletin*, I (April, 1934), 6–8; Association of Federation Workers to Hopkins, March 29, 1934, CWA 32.

[48]*New York Herald Tribune*, March 13, 1934, p. 18; and March 14, 1934, p. 7; "Miss Gosselin Joins Objections to CWA Questionnaire," *Better Times*, XV (March 19, 1934), 1; A. Williams to I. Bagun, March 13, 1934, CWA 32.

[49]"Workers to Protest CWA Stoppage in Washington," *New Leader*, XVII (March 17, 1934), 1, 4; "Easter Parade to Stress Desperate Need of CWA Workers and Jobless," *ibid.* (March 31, 1934), 3–4; *New York Times*, March 25, 1934, Sec. II, p. 1; "Wholesale Dismissals," *Nation*, CXXXVIII (April 25, 1934), 456; "CWA Workers Resist Layoffs," *Unemployed Teacher*, II (April, 1934), 4.

The CWA's transformation from work relief to public employment had generated a particular group consciousness among white collar and professional employees. "The professional, technical, and white collar workers have united in fighting for the abolition of the pauper's oath as the basis for relief jobs, the setting up of trade union wage standards, and the establishment of a workers' commission to take care of workers' grievances," wrote the executive secretary of AOPEE. "It is hoped in time to revive or institute the economic functions of the old vested professional societies to the end that all white collar, professional, and technical workers in New York City when not absorbed in private industry shall be assured government jobs." Such organizations of civil works employees would mature by 1935, when the Workers Alliance developed into a bargaining agent for those on the Works Progress Administration.[50]

[50]O. R. Fuss, "Bad News for White Collar Workers," *New Republic*, LXXXIII (July 10, 1935), 253; Beulah Amidon, "WPA—Wages and Workers," *Survey Graphic*, XXIV (October, 1935), 493–497, 504–505.

CHAPTER SIX

Civil Works for the "Forgotten Woman"

ON NOVEMBER 20, 1933, Eleanor Roosevelt called a White House Conference on the Emergency Needs of Women. Over forty representatives from settlement work, education, government service, and social clubs attended. They listened to the First Lady decry how American women "have been neglected in comparison with others, and throughout this depression have had the hardest time of all." The only man present, Harry Hopkins, head of the Federal Emergency Relief Administration, admitted that unemployed and destitute women had received little attention. Assuring his audience, however, that women would get a fair shake in the future, he estimated that 400,000 could receive aid through the civil works program just getting underway.[1]

This meeting underscored the "double burden" that women had carried from the outset of the depression. Not only confronting them with a decrease of income or loss of position, hard times also revived prejudices which struck at the status that women had recently achieved.[2] Men demanded that since not enough jobs existed for all, women should return to their

[1] Federal Emergency Relief Administration, *Proceedings of the Conference on Emergency Needs of Women*, November 20, 1933, FERA 85; *New York Times*, November 21, 1933, p. 1; Tamara K. Hareven, *Eleanor Roosevelt* (Chicago: Quadrangle Books, 1968), p. 64.

[2] A January, 1931, census showed 18.8 percent of women normally employed out of work. In the nation as a whole, this amounted to 2 million. Amy G. Maher, "Unemployed Women," *SSR*, VIII (December, 1934), 773; Mary Elizabeth Pidgeon, *Trends in the Employment of Women, 1928–1936* (Washington: U.S. Department of Labor, Women's Bureau Bulletin 159, 1938), p. 3; "Unemployment among Women in the Early Years of the Depression," *MLR*, XXXVIII (April, 1934), 790.

families. Theorizing that in such emergencies paid positions belonged to men, both government and private employers followed the motto, "Fire the women, especially the married women, and give their jobs to men." The New Deal had initially failed to offer fresh hope. "We have done very little in the way of care for unemployed women," confessed Frederick Daniels, head of FERA in New York State. Mrs. Roosevelt emphasized in a speech before Manhattan's Junior League that the government "has been tremendously unfair to women in a way because most of the re-employment relief measures have been directed toward men." Since men were traditionally regarded as the principal breadwinners, local agencies hesitated to reduce men's job opportunities by hiring women, even though many were widows or single, and often with dependents. In addition, administrators claimed difficulty finding suitable projects for women, particularly for those unskilled and in rural areas. "There is little organized effort to rescue the girl who has lost her job," noted the *Pittsburgh Post Gazette*. "The problem is one that merits national consideration, with perhaps a definite program from the federal government, the same as has been initiated for other groups of depression victims."[3]

In response to such pleas, Harry Hopkins had established a Women's Division within FERA in September, 1933, and appointed Mrs. Ellen S. Woodward its director. Created to take care of women heads of families, widows with no means of support, and single women, the WD began as a welfare program to give direct relief to women as social dependents. Although it sponsored a few sewing rooms as made work, the Division failed to provide a wide range of public jobs, since it did not regard women as unemployed members of the labor force. With the coming of the CWA, however, Hopkins, Eleanor

[3]Helena Hill Weed, "The New Deal that Women Want," *Current History*, XLI (November, 1934), 179; Frederick Daniels to Woodward, November 10, 1933, FERA 204; *New York Times*, November 17, 1933, p. 4; Joanna C. Colcord and Russell H. Kurtz, "FERA Developments," *Survey*, LXIX (November, 1933), 392; *Pittsburgh Post Gazette*, November 21, 1933, p. 10.

Roosevelt, Mrs. Woodward, and leaders of women's groups across the nation saw an opportunity to extend its activities to an unprecedented area. Although the WD would become the largest single employer of women, it would represent the only major part of the CWA outside the provenance of Jacob Baker's and John Carmody's engineers. Galvanized by the spirit of voluntarism rather than a draft of corporate expertise, the Women's Division remained the last refuge where social work values prevailed. Such differences would significantly affect the civil works program for the "forgotten woman."[4]

I

The formidable task of putting 400,000 women on the federal payroll fell to Ellen Woodward, the very embodiment of the social worker's compassion and a politician's vigor. Daughter of Mississippi Senator William V. Sullivan, she was educated in the East, earned a law degree at the University of South Carolina, and married Judge Albert V. Woodward. Upon his death in 1925, she plunged into numerous state activities, ranging from a legislator (only the second woman in Mississippi history) to trustee of its charity hospital and director of a children's home. Mrs. Woodward then became executive director of the Mississippi Board of Development and conducted her own radio program for over four years. These interests continued in the 1930's, when she chaired a local conference of social work, sat on the executive committee of the State Board of Public Welfare, and joined the Democratic National Committee. As head of women's projects for the FERA and the newly created CWA, she mustered this executive experience

[4]"Women's Division," FERA, *Monthly Report* (July, 1935), pp. 43–46; Hopkins to all governors and state emergency relief administrators, October 10, 1933, U.S. Federal Emergency Relief Administration, mimeographed directives, bound in New York Public Library; Joanna C. Colcord and Russell H. Kurtz, "Federal Relief in 1933," *Survey*, LXX (March, 1934), 90; FERA, Women's Division, *Work Relief Sewing Rooms* (Washington: United States Government Printing Office, 1934).

and political savvy to alert the men around her to female aspirations.[5]

But Mrs. Woodward remained an ambivalent voice between federal action and local voluntarism. As the primary force behind the White House Conference, she engineered the support of Mrs. Roosevelt, whose prestige was crucial to encourage the most nationally prominent women leaders to attend. They included Grace Abbott of the Children's Bureau; Mary Anderson, chief of the Women's Bureau; Mrs. August Belmont and Mabel T. Boardman of the American Red Cross; Colonel Martha Hanson from the Salvation Army; Mrs. Russell William Magna, general of the DAR; Mrs. Frederick M. Paist, president of the YWCA; Mary Dabney Davis, president of the National Association of Nursery Education; Jessie Gray, president of the National Education Association; and Belle Sherwin, president of the National League of Women Voters. For this audience, Mrs. Woodward couched the meeting as a prime opportunity to publicize the needs of unemployed women and explain the responsive role of federal agencies. But she worked up enthusiasm trying to enlist their volunteer efforts and those of their friends at home. An active member in the Federated Women's Clubs, Chi Omega Sorority, the DAR, and League of Women Voters, Ellen Woodward appreciated the ability of such groups to awaken their distaff troops to action. With the winter approaching and the CWA quickly going into operation through state and county administrations, she wanted to enlist the talent and organizational network of social and professional associations in her Women's Division. "We *must* capitalize immediately on the interest of these groups in order to . . . carry it [our program] out in the field," she confided. "If we can utilize the suggestions of these national groups they will help us to secure and to hold the intelligent cooperation and good will of the communities." She ended the Conference by charg-

<hr/>

[5]Clipping, *Jackson Daily News*, December 20, 1953, and *Jackson Daily News-Clarion Ledger*, September 26, 1971, EW; Hopkins to all governors and state emergency relief administrators, October 10, 1933, FERA directives.

ing her listeners to report to their affiliates and have them, in turn, contact state civil works authorities. Realizing that women could not be employed as easily as men on mass construction, she also urged the women to draw up suitable projects and propose them. She told the professionals to go home to their organizations, survey their unemployed members, recommend the qualified, and suggest means of returning them to work.[6]

Stirred by Mrs. Roosevelt's special plea to move "away from the glitter of party life," many clubwomen rallied to Washington's call that very afternoon. The American Home Economics Association offered the aid of its state committees, while the General Federation of Women's Clubs planned to send letters to local chapters and publish in its magazine a plan to meet with other organizations and municipal agencies to submit ideas to civil works administrators. The National Council of Federated Church Women pledged the cooperation of its membership, and a representative of the Pan Hellenic Council declared, "The professional fraternities are at your command." Mrs. Woodward adjourned the meeting, saying that with this volunteer corps "we have never had a greater opportunity for women to do something for women."[7]

Returning from Washington, the national president of the Federation of Business and Professional Women's Clubs pledged that her 1,350 chapters would cooperate with local relief agencies by furnishing information to their unemployed members.[8] Former leaders in the suffrage movement and members of the Women's Party had a new cause, "Equal rights for women,

[6]Woodward to Edith Helm, November 11, 1933, and Helm to Woodward, November 14, 1933, ER 991; *Washington Post*, November 21, 1933, p. 10; Women's Division Activities, November 14, 1933, HLH 16; Clipping, *Jackson Daily News-Clarion Ledger*, September 26, 1971, and Woodward to C. M. Bookman, November 7, 1933, EW 5; FERA, *Proceedings of the Conference*, pp. 9–11.

[7]*Ibid.*, pp. 31–38; *New York Times*, December 2, 1933, p. 2; *Charlotte Observer*, December 5, 1933; Dixon Wecter, *The Age of the Great Depression, 1929–1941* (New York: Macmillan Company, 1948), p. 296.

[8]She named ten associates to chair national committees. *Washington Post*, November 28, 1933, p. 9; *Philadelphia Record*, November 30, 1933.

equal pay for women, an equal chance with men!" Two social workers described the scene:

> All over the country the relief offices and administrators of CWA were visited by the leading women of the communities, all of whom insisted that mothers of dependent children be given their choice. If they chose to remain at home, well and good; but if they chose to work, why they would be allowed to, at wages set forth in the act, and their children could go to nursery schools or day nurseries. . . . *All* women in need of relief, they insisted, must be treated administratively and financially in exactly the same way as *all* the men.

Within two weeks, meetings similar to the White House Conference had occurred in fifteen states.[9]

Illinois women responded immediately. Mary Gillette Moon, former director of the Chicago Women's Service Bureau and new head of the state CWA women's division, organized a luncheon meeting within the week.[10] An advisory board of fifteen professionals and social service volunteers was set up to assist on public policy and the coordination of programs, and Mrs. Moon appointed seven technical committees to develop an ambitious range of projects in nursing, library work, home economics, industry, business, and education. She also assigned directors to 69 counties to organize and supervise projects, and they worked in cooperation with the Illinois Free Employment Bureau for Women, which registered the unemployed in each locality. Practically all volunteered their services without remuneration.[11]

[9]Marie Dresden Lane and Francis Steegmuller, *America on Relief* (New York: Harcourt, Brace and Company, 1938), pp. 64–67; *New York Times*, December 5, 1933, p. 2.

[10]Telegram, Reynolds to Hopkins, November 18, 1933, and Woodward to Reynolds, November 30, 1933, FERA 84; *Chicago Tribune*, November 22, 1933; *Chicago Daily Times*, November 23, 1933, p. 2, and November 24, 1933, p. 8.

[11]The advisory board was composed of fifteen, and some of its members included: chairman Mrs. Florence Bocher, head of the McLean County Emergency Relief Commission; Lea Taylor, head resident Chicago Commons; Theresa

North Carolina women launched their program with a special meeting at the House of Representatives in Raleigh. Although 60 prominent clubwomen were expected, over 125 attended. Southern field representative Alan Johnstone addressed the audience about civil works in general, while Mrs. Lula Martin McIver Scott, a native Tarheel, former activist in state women's clubs, and supervisor of women's work for the Southeast, added her prestige to the meeting. The state CWA administrator named Alice Laidlaw, secretary of the Raleigh YWCA, as director of women's projects for North Carolina, and she selected local heads for 43 counties.[12]

Some states, in contrast, did not witness such immediate action. In New York, Mrs. Charles Sabin, a National Republican Committee Woman and founder of the Women's Organization for National Prohibition Repeal, was chosen by Governor Herbert Lehman and Harry Hopkins to head the state women's division. Claiming a lack of time and difficulty in organization, she proved unable to rally a state-wide meeting immediately after the Washington Conference. Mrs. Sabin argued that she could not get cooperation because of local political antagonisms and jealousies resulting from changes in the state and local relief administrations which occurred when the New Deal agencies were created. Certain women, she asserted, "who were very active in the Emergency Work Bureau are not being used under the CWA." Admitting a lack of knowledge for the position, she suggested forming an advisory committee of experts in fields where women could be employed. Mrs. Sabin declined to make the appointments, however, fearing she would arouse charges of political favoritism. Facing increased discontent and

Clow, Mrs. Charles Gilkey, and Mrs. H. T. Morrison, all of the YWCA; Elizabeth Webster, Council of Social Agencies; and Mrs. R. C. Jacobson of the Illinois League of Women Voters. Telegram, Moon to Woodward, November 29, 1933, FERA 84; Illinois CWA, *Final Report* (March 1934), pp. 54–55, 231–232.

[12]Telegram, L. M. Scott to Johnstone, December 2, 1933, and Woodward to Johnstone, December 2, 1933, FERA 213; *Charlotte Observer*, December 6 and 13, 1933; *Raleigh News and Observer*, December 5 and 6, 1933.

criticism, she characterized her position as "merely window-dressing." Discouraged and ill, she resigned in January, 1934.[13]

Pennsylvania appeared equally faulty in getting the women's program underway. Eric Biddle, the state civil works adminis-trator, confessed that "in the rush of other matters we have been unable to locate just the right person" to head the wom-en's division. On December 2, 1933, he notified Washington of the appointment of Miss Anna Owers, a specialist in voca-tional training on loan from the Philadelphia Board of Educa-tion. Miss Owers complained that she could not get any occupational breakdown on the number of women unemployed, and she used this excuse to justify her failure to initiate enough projects. Her advisors concurred that few economically sound plans could be developed to absorb female industrial or house workers. Miss Owers wrote, "We feel that these groups must count upon the buying powers of workers employed in the CWA to create jobs for them in their regular fields." Later admitting that she "personally" did "not believe there are very many projects that can be developed for women alone," Miss Owers was ultimately replaced by her assistant. This change occurred, however, after the CWA folded.[14]

The haphazard early weeks of the Women's Division pro-vided a distinct contrast to the efficient, business-like opera-tions which had characterized CWA projects for men under Baker and Carmody. A confusion of purposes continually per-vaded the WD and puzzled those who looked to it for aid. An unemployed woman in rural North Carolina understandably wrote to President Roosevelt in mid-January "for some advice

[13]*New York Times*, December 5, 1933, p. 2; and *Washington Post*, December 8, 1933; Hickok to Hopkins, December 29, 1933, FERA 10; Mrs. Charles Sabin to Woodward, December 12, 1933, telegram to Chloe Owings, Decem-ber 2, 1933, to Woodward, December 12, 1933, to Alfred Schoellkopf, Jan-uary 3, 1934; and Nancy Cook to Hopkins, January 15, 1934, all in FERA 204; *New York Times*, January 17, 1934, p. 21.

[14]Biddle to Hopkins, November 24, 1933, FERA 255; telegram, Biddle to Woodward, December 2, 1933, FERA 254; *Philadelphia Public Ledger*, Decem-ber 5, 1933; Owers to Woodward, January 18, 1934, and Marie T. Barlow to Woodward, May 3, 1934, FERA 254.

about this C.W.A. work, for unemployed women, tell me what this money was put out for, to give the needy work, or is it for women who can live without it?" Hopkins' omniscient Lorena Hickok was also uncertain about the goals, when she observed:

> Many women got jobs who shouldn't have had them. Widows, for instance, who should have been taken care of by the communities. No doubt plenty of "Nigger washerwomen," as exasperated citizens insist. Not enough unattached "white collar" women. I thought the women's show was set up primarily to take care of unattached women.

The WD remained the CWA's stepchild, left to the good intentions of clubwomen and "ladies bountiful." Although they took a compassionate concern for distressed women around them, their noblesse oblige and sorority ties, however well meant, were not the suitable means to provide jobs for thousands. Certainly Hoover-type voluntarism was never deemed appropriate for the "Men's Division." Many state WD directors revealed conflicting purposes and failed to develop serious projects for women because, deep down, most of these upper- and upper-middle-class clubwomen and professionals in social work and social hygiene shared the prevalent male attitudes that women should follow the dictates of the depression and gracefully withdraw from the labor market back to home and family.[15]

II

The CWA never set down any guidelines for the number of women to be hired. Although the Washington office had assigned each state a maximum that could be employed, it mandated no systematic percentage for females. Mrs. Roosevelt suggested that a certain number of jobs be allotted in each state or that a fixed amount of money be assigned for this purpose. Neither of these options ever materialized. Ellen Woodward

[15]Hattie Kreeger to FDR, January 15, 1934, NCERA 284; Hickok to Hopkins, February 5, 1934, HLH 61.

telegraphed state administrators and women's work directors, reminding them that women had no separate quota and asking them to ensure that girls get a fair share of the jobs. Mary Gillette Moon later lamented:

> We are greatly disappointed that there is no separate quota for women. . . . So many of our best projects have never gotten under way for lack of a quota. . . . A regional conference being held now in Indianapolis regarding future plans for CWA includes all the men but no woman director. I feel very strongly that we will never get anywhere as long as we are part of the man quota that is determined and controlled by men.[16]

To counteract sluggish leadership and to aid those, like Mrs. Moon, battling to employ more women, Ellen Woodward and Harry Hopkins initiated a new strategy from Washington. In late November, the Women's Division disregarded the CWA regulation that a certain number of employees must come from relief rolls. Hopkins charged the states to draw women for all positions from the United States Employment Service lists as long as they qualified for the job. He also urged the transfer of men from positions that could be performed by women to make additional room.[17]

A more significant resource, however, opened up with the creation of the Civil Works Service for white collar personnel. While not earmarked solely for women nor assigning a special quota for them, the CWS did provide work under the rubric of jobs in "relief offices and education," later defined as "sew-

[16]FERA, *Proceedings of the Conference*, p. 15; Hareven, *Eleanor Roosevelt*, p. 65; Woodward to Frederick Daniels, December 13, 1933, FERA 204; Miss Morton to Woodward, January 2, 1934, FERA 254; Woodward to Mary Barnam, January 3, 1934, FERA 31; Moon to Woodward, February 23, 1934, FERA 84; "Samples of Opinions and Requests Concerning Need of Special Quota and Funds for Women's Work," January 15, 1934, ER 615.

[17]Civil Works Administration, *Rules and Regulations, Number 1* (November 15, 1933); Hopkins to all state civil works administrators, November 29, 1933, Women's Division, W-2 and December 1, 1933, Women's Division, W-5; *New York Times*, December 5, 1933, p. 2.

ing, gardening, canning, teaching, and other work in connection with the emergency education programs and personnel service." Because the CWS was funded by local, state, or FERA relief (and not by the NIRA, which financed civil works) hourly wages, as a consequence, were slightly lower than under CWA. The prevailing community rate could determine the scale, as long as it did not fall below a $.30 hourly minimum. Furthermore, under FERA guidelines, CWS employees came from relief rolls, or proved eligible through certification by professional organizations or by makeshift committees from specialized fields.[18]

With this additional resource, Ellen Woodward charged all the states to get more women on the payroll. On December 1, 1933, she sent a directive entitled "A Few Types of Work Projects for Women," with thirty areas for possible employment. This notice was followed by continual announcements of CWA projects where women could find positions with an appropriate local authority for referrals. The Washington office served as a clearing house of ideas, picked up from imaginative leaders and relayed to the others. When some expressed confusion between CWA and CWS, Mrs. Woodward patiently explained. She frequently encouraged women's work directors to increase their CWA payroll, since more funds were available and wages were higher. Urging state administrators to seek out foremen and supervisors willing to give women a chance, Mrs. Woodward admonished: "If you will study carefully the civil works programs now in operation in your state, you will find that women can be put to work on some part of practically any one of them." Still she had to remind women's work directors constantly that they counted as full-fledged members of the staff and cautioned her "sisters" to attend all conferences, voice their grievances, and learn about the entire program. She advised them to see what was being done for men and note how

[18]Civil Works Administration, *Rules and Regulations, Number 10* (December 13, 1933); Harry L. Hopkins, *Spending to Save* (New York: W. W. Norton, 1936), p. 123; Doris Carothers, *Chronology of the FERA* (Washington: U.S. Government Printing Office, 1937), pp. 27–28.

women's activities compared. In return, she demanded bi-
monthly reports showing the number of women employed, descriptions of projects, newspaper clippings of local publicity,
and copies of instructions to county leaders.[19]

First reports to Mrs. Woodward showed mixed results. New
York State boasted 10,743 women in the CWS category and
2,780 on the CWA by December 20. Other states failed to
differentiate between the CWA and CWS. North Carolina had
close to 1,500 women on the payroll, and Illinois at first accounted for 1,000, mostly in Chicago. Some states had no data
at all. Pennsylvania's director Anna Owers confessed that neither the state employment service nor the statistics department
had classified workers by sex. By January 15, 1934, she could
claim only 3,654 women employed by Pennsylvania's CWA.
Mary Gillette Moon had similar difficulty with downstate Illinois; and, by the end of the year, she still had no male-female
breakdown except for Chicago. Other administrators showed
meager efforts and lack of imagination in their projects. Programs meeting the CWA requirement of "social usefulness to
the community" that would employ a large number of women
appeared difficult to find. The "pick and shovel" mentality
proved a great obstacle. Mary Moon described her predicament
with officials outside of Cook County: "They have so formed
the habit of thinking of CWA jobs as building roads . . . it is
going to take a little time." Just as troublesome were the prevailing stereotypes which Lorena Hickok found throughout her
tours. In small cities and towns of Minnesota, "your average
businessmen just won't believe there are any women who are
absolutely self-supporting!" And in upstate New York, the tough

[19]Woodward, "A Few Types of Work Projects for Women," December 1,
1933, Women's Division, W-3; Woodward to all civil works administrators,
December 19, 1933; Woodward to all state directors of women's work, December 15, 1933, and January 11, 1934, all in HLH 16; "More Suggestions
from Alabama," December 22, 1933, Women's Division, W-11; Woodward
to Mrs. F. McEnnis, January 9, 1934, CWA 91; Woodward to all state civil
works administrators, December 21, 1933, HLH 16; Woodward to all state
directors of women's work, December 29, 1933, Women's Division, W-12.

newswoman could barely manage to suppress her defeatism. "In the women's program . . . suggestions are badly needed," she wrote. "Along the Canadian border, a great majority of unemployed women are factory workers, wholly untrained to do anything else. We would like to know what to do with them."[20]

III

Since unemployed women had no time to wait, the most convenient projects to absorb a maximum number were the sewing rooms—which "became for women what ditch digging projects were for men." In the early 1930's, when only local agencies provided aid, women were required to do this kind of work in return for relief. With cotton donated by the Red Cross, women made clothes, which neighborhood centers distributed to the poor. Since the late nineteenth century, clubwomen had also taken an interest in sewing for the needy. Philadelphia's elite New Century Club had always sponsored charitable sewing circles after its weekly luncheon. Mrs. Woodward had sought to enlist these women as volunteer supervisors when such projects had begun in October, 1933, under the FERA. Sewing rooms really proliferated, however, under the civil works program. Large ones, located in urban centers, primarily made clothing and could often draw on a pool of experienced, though unemployed, seamstresses. A rural community might also aim to teach skills. But everywhere the primary motive was didactic and philanthropic with output of secondary importance.[21]

[20]Telegram, Inez D. Ross to Woodward, December 26, 1933, FERA 204; telegram, Alice Laidlaw to Woodward, December 8, 1933, FERA 213; Chloe Owings to Woodward, December 13, 1933, FERA 84; Anna Owers to Woodward, December 2, 1933, and telegram, Anna Owers to Woodward, January 15, 1934, FERA 254; Moon to NRA Compliance Board, Sparta, Illinois, December 31, 1933, FERA 84; Hickok to Hopkins, December 4, 1933, HLH 61, and December 29, 1933, FERA 10.

[21]Lane and Steegmuller, *America on Relief*, pp. 71–73; Ellen Woodward "This New Federal Relief," *Independent Woman*, XIII (April, 1934), 104; *Philadelphia Public Ledger*, November 17, 1933, p. 30; FERA, Women's Division, *Work Relief Sewing Rooms*.

California's sewing projects had operated under a previous state work relief system, and they easily expanded with the CWA. Admitting that "the majority of women should not be engaged in that type of work," a male CWS state administrator explained that these rooms were nevertheless set up in great numbers because most women could qualify for machine or hand work. San Francisco had over 1,000 women gathered in six units, much like garment lofts or old workhouses, while Los Angeles counted over 2,000 employed in 68 small centers scattered across the city and its suburbs. In rural Stanislaus County, small groups cooperated with community relief agencies. Supervised by a woman who had served many years on the local welfare board, projects were guided by women with sewing skills and executive ability. State CWA administrators expressed disappointment, however, with the relatively few numbers on each program. They claimed that distance between localities necessitated small-scale operations hiring four or five each. But men were trucked over the same distances to form large work crews. The conclusion seems inescapable that for women's projects most localities found sewing rooms the cheapest, most expedient alternative.[22]

Sewing and related handicrafts also represented North Carolina's best attempt to find projects for women. "We seem to have to place so many women one or two in a place," explained Alice Laidlaw, also oblivious to the fact that men were just as scattered. Sewing rooms ultimately accounted for one third of the state's CWA and CWS women employees. Mecklenburg County took special pride in its facility, located at the YWCA, where 50 women made clothing. Materials and machines were all provided locally, as the appeal for donations sounded a call for "patriotic service." Garments were turned over to the Family Aid Society and the Salvation Army, which distributed them among relief recipients. County head Mrs. C. T. Wanzer also noted a separate project in a community house where "col-

[22]State Relief Administration of California, *Review of Activities, 1933–1935* (San Francisco: by the author, 1936), p. 108; Director CWS Projects to Woodward, February 6, 1934, FERA 31; California CWA, *Final Report* (March, 1934), p. 114; L. W. Ganyard to Woodward, March 21, 1934, FERA 31.

ored" women renovated old clothes and made quilts. When women from Charlotte visited the White House on January 17, 1934, to present Mrs. Roosevelt with a sample mattress, Ellen Woodward praised this very high type of work under special supervision of these volunteers. As an indication of the sewing room's flexibility in meeting local needs, women made fishermen's nets by tying knots from heavy twine and attaching corks. "It is complicated for those of us who do not know the coast," commented Miss Laidlaw, "but the women of Hyde, Dare, and other coastal counties really do not know how to do anything else."[23]

The Illinois Women's Division put close to thirty percent of its 3,052 women workers in sewing rooms, by far the largest single job category for females. One cavernous center furnished by the Chicago Home for the Friendless provided work space for 553 women. Supervised by the American Red Cross, which also donated materials, workers received various classifications, such as: operator, inspector, cutter, shipping clerk, watchman, foreman, and messenger, although wages were still tightly grouped around the $.30 minimum. On two six-hour shifts this unit alone produced over 10,000 garments a day. Finished articles ranged from nightgowns and playsuits to sheets and pillowcases, which supplied 1,600 families on a daily basis. In sharp contrast to the CWA projects in Chicago that performed vital work for the Sanitary District, real estate interests, and other parts of the city's economic infrastructure, sewing rooms revealed how closely the women's division remained an adjunct of the charity establishment.[24]

[23]Alice Laidlaw to L. M. Scott, January 13, 1934, FERA 213; North Carolina CWA, *Final Report* (March, 1934), p. 73; *Charlotte Observer*, November 25 and December 27, 1933; Mrs. C. T. Wanzer to Cora Annette Harris, December 18, 1933, FERA 213; Woodward to Eleanor Roosevelt, January 17, 1934, ER 639; Alice Laidlaw to Woodward, January 27, 1934, FERA 213.

[24]Illinois CWA, *Final Report*, pp. 58–60; Moon to Woodward, February 3, 1934, and telegram, Reynolds to Hopkins, April 11, 1934, FERA 85; *Chicago Tribune*, December 12, 1933.

Despite their obvious use in creating projects, sewing rooms nevertheless aroused debate in Washington regarding wages. Women had initially received from $.40 to $.50 an hour, but some localities, especially in the South, charged that these rates were excessive because of "inefficiency." Hopkins, Mrs. Woodward, and others wanted to continue sewing without having to set up new rules or weed out unqualified personnel. They chose an easy way out. In distinct contrast to the differential wage policies elaborated by Carmody in response to organized labor's demands on the CWA, they decided to lower the minimum to $.30 an hour, tantamount to a maximum in the rural sewing rooms.[25]

Having set up the sewing projects in the tradition of nineteenth-century workhouses for the poor, some women's division heads then turned around and fretted about their dubious efficiency! In January, 1934, Pennsylvania's Anna Owers wrote that sewing rooms "have not proved to be economically sound." She believed that such projects could not run properly without displacing women employed in the needle trades. The following month, *Women's Democratic News* recommended the continuation of sewing, but insisted on higher standards and stricter qualifications for employees. Its editors suggested that those untrained should go back to direct aid, but still be allowed to attend sewing classes as a "social outlet" rather than a form of work relief. Two social workers later described sewing rooms as an "expensive and unfruitful blind alley . . . a dumping ground for women for whom no other work can be found." They preferred to remove the unemployable women and convert the rooms to community resource centers, devoted to production for use "with methods of scientific management." Mrs. Wooodward and her staff, however, never considered any of these alternatives.[26]

[25]CWA Minutes, November 22, 1933, HLH 45.

[26]Anna Owers to Woodward, January 18, 1934, FERA 254; *Philadelphia Public Ledger*, April 1, 1934, Sec. II, p. 2; "Work for Women," *Women's Democratic News*, IX (February, 1934), 3; Lane and Steegmuller, *America on Relief*, pp. 78 and 81.

In contrast to sewing, clerical jobs did not provoke an adverse response and yet provided the second largest category of employment for women. Some secretarial positions opened as soon as the CWA got underway. Los Angeles County officials explained, "Almost every service project of a technical nature called for office workers to handle necessary clerical work." Projects requiring the distribution of materials employed women to handle office details. State, city, and county governments requested aides to copy all records, update local files, and help departments where an overload of work caused by unemployment could not be handled by regular personnel. School boards asked for office help in elementary and high schools. Under CWS, the application of trained women expanded to preserving historical manuscripts, indexing county records, and speeding up court procedures. A clerical project in Illinois assigned 20 women to the probate court of Cook County, where they expedited the closing of 35,000 old estates.[27]

Library projects also absorbed an additional number of secretaries, along with unskilled women and unemployed professionals. From the Library of Congress to large municipal branches all the way to elementary school book rooms, CWS women could be found working in the stacks. They often enabled public libraries to remain open when tight municipal budgets resulted in layoffs of regular personnel and at a time of rising demand when idle people sought community diversions. Hailed by *Library Journal* as an "unexpected benefit," CWA funds enabled the regular staff to maintain the daily routine and undertake special projects otherwise impossible. Women performed such chores as mending, cataloging, checking inventories, indexing local newspapers and genealogy lists, and decorating. Oakland, California, reported how unemployed professional librarians took inventories and analyzed collections of songs and instrumental pieces for a music division catalog. Another worker

[27]California CWA, *Final Report*, p. 103; Roy W. Pilling to Woodward, January 24, 1934, FERA 31; North Carolina CWA, *Final Report*, p. 70; Joanna C. Colcord to Chloe Owings, December 21, 1933, and Owings to Colcord, January 25, 1934, FERA 204; Moon to Woodward, February 3, 1934, FERA 84; Illinois CWA, *Final Report*, p. 57.

made subject cards for historical articles in unindexed California periodicals, while a clerk typist revised the author entries to conform with the Library of Congress. An administrator noted a constant demand for this type of work throughout the state. In North Carolina, women aided in school libraries. Twenty-five women under Anne Pierce, head of the Charlotte Public Library, worked in schools throughout Mecklenburg County. Some rural areas had not received these services for the past two years. In other localities, women drove bookmobiles, and in a few "remote" places they even rode a pack horse.[28]

Despite the service and community spirit which resulted from these projects, some librarians had mixed feelings, probably related to the local budget cuts, which had already demoralized the profession. While they appreciated the additional help which maintained circulation and also afforded job opportunities to their fellow unemployed, they expressed skepticism that CWS workers could take over important duties. One Brooklyn librarian commented on the "hastily assembled staff" that "makes this type of help less desirable than properly trained employees." A Chicago professional complained that not enough workers were experienced. Wilson Bulletin for Librarians questioned the effect of civil works on the status of trained members still unemployed. The editor felt the emergency program would set back standards and the status of the profession. And in Erie, Pennsylvania, a local librarian noted that CWA wages were higher than her own, but excused it on the grounds that it was temporary.[29]

The nursing profession, on the other hand, looked upon the

[28]Joanna C. Colcord and Russell H. Kurtz, "Civil Works for the Professional," Survey, LXX (February, 1934), 55; "Civil Works Service in the Library," Library Journal, LIX (March 1, 1934), 208; Bonnie Elliott, "A Suburban Library Meets Today's Demands," Wilson Bulletin for Librarians, VIII (April, 1934), 461; Roy Pilling to Woodward, February 6, 1934, FERA 31; Mrs. C. T. Wanzer to Cora Annette Harris, December 18, 1933, FERA 213; Charlotte Observer, December 27, 1933; "Uncle Sam's Libraries Provide Work Relief Projects for Women," School Life, XX (April, 1935), 182.

[29]"CWS in the Library," Library Journal, 212–213; "Librarians and the CWA," Wilson Bulletin for Librarians, VIII (February, 1934), 345–346; "Librarians and the CWA—A Symposium," Ibid. (May, 1934), 530–531.

CWA quite favorably, largely because the relief workers filled distinctly subordinate roles that would never challenge the professionals' hard-won status. Enthusiastic support from the American Nurses Association resulted from the extensive cooperation between its officers and civil works administrators which occurred at all levels. Ellen Woodward conferred with Ethel Swope, head of the ANA, and paid a special tribute to the organization at the White House Conference. Following this initial good will, Mrs. Woodward sent letters to the executive secretaries of state nursing associations, explaining the CWA and recommending projects, while she invited Ethel Swope to Washington to assist at the national office. The ANA encouraged its state affiliates to participate in civil works, with the clear understanding, however, that only certified nurses would recommend projects, insure the qualifications of those employed, and safeguard professional standards. Understandably, Miss Swope was pleased at the "splendid cooperation" displayed between state directors of women's work and ANA committees, which in most areas controlled the appointment of CWS nursing supervisors, and to whom all matters pertaining to nursing were referred before CWA approval. Placement bureaus provided the link between unemployed nurses and civil works by locating those out of work and checking their credentials, giving the ANA a kind of union shop on the CWS.[30]

Over 10,000 registered nurses were ultimately employed in public hospitals, institutions, clinics, public health staffs, bedside nursing, immunization campaigns, and surveys. CWA financed an adult education program, which enabled the Red Cross to report its highest enrollment ever in home hygiene classes. Ellen Woodward hailed the Illinois project, in particular, as a "very splendid job." In cooperation with the state ANA, the Visiting Nurses Association, and the Red Cross,

[30]"Notes from Headquarters," *American Journal of Nursing*, XXIV (January, 1934), 86–87; Editorial, *ibid.*, 55; FERA, *Proceedings of the Conference*, p. 15; Ethel Swope, "The CWS Program and the American Nurses Association," *American Journal of Nursing*, XXXIV (April, 1934), 356–359; and "Notes from Headquarters," *ibid.*, XXXIV (March, 1934), 282–284.

Illinois employed over 100 women to assist more than 10,000 mothers of relief families. The course taught how to follow physicians' instructions, promoted child care and cleanliness, and gave each mother a certificate upon completion. Nurses in Charlotte, North Carolina, also in conjunction with the Red Cross, examined over 2,500 school children in a three-week period. The statistical breakdown indicated that services were provided for both white and black schools, although many more whites benefited. Alma Haupt, assistant director of the National Organization for Public Health Nursing, commented that, thanks to the CWA, "the public taste has been educated to appreciate the value of nursing." And Ethel Swope wrote with satisfaction, "The relief program has shown the soundness of this great nursing organization in assisting in an advisory capacity with projects of federal origin and nation-wide importance."[31]

One special nursing project, a child health study, originated with a national conference called by the Secretary of Labor, Frances Perkins. Attended by Eleanor Roosevelt, state health officers, and child welfare workers, the meeting pointed to increased malnutrition shown in Children's Bureau reports. Harry Hopkins assured the audience that the CWA would cooperate to prevent further incidence, and Grace Abbott shaped the project to provide employment for women. Supervised by state departments of health in consultation with the Children's Bureau, this survey located and examined undernourished children, administered medical examinations, and followed with home visits. Thirty-four states participated, and over 23,000 nurses

[31]"The Biennial," *American Journal of Nursing*, XXXIV (June, 1934), 613; Woodward, Address before the ANA, EW; Portia B. Kernodle, *The Red Cross Nurse in Action, 1882–1948* (New York: Harper and Brothers, 1949), p. 336; Foster Rhea Dulles, *The American Red Cross* (New York: Harper and Brothers, 1950), pp. 318-319; Illinois CWA, *Final Report*, p. 58; *Charlotte Observer*, January 24, 1934; Florence Knight, "Making Work for Nurses," *SWT*, II (May, 1935), 26–27; Swope, "The CWS and the ANA," 359–360; Kendall Emerson, "Maintenance of Mental and Physical Health," NCSW, *Proceedings* (Chicago: University of Chicago Press, 1934), p. 132.

were employed. California reported "exceptional interest," and almost 300 nurses found work in checking over 3,000 children.[32]

This focus on children laid a basis for civil works day nurseries, which offered parent education in child health as well as jobs for unemployed teachers, dietitians, nurses, recreation directors, and domestics. States developed projects through the cooperation of superintendents of public instruction, state emergency education authorities, and civil works administrators, including the women's work directors. Advice also came from the National Association of Nursery Education, the Association for Childhood Education, and the National Council of Parent Education, who stood careful guard over professional standards.[33] The projects proved especially popular in metropolitan centers. New York City alone had 25 units, each with 20 children, attended by staffs that included a supervisor, teacher, nurse, nutritionist, parent educator, cook, cleaning women, and laundress, and part-time pediatrician. The children, between the ages of two and four, came from needy homes found unsuitable for healthy growth. Each one received a uniform, food, and the inevitable dose of cod liver oil.[34] Philadelphia had similar day nurseries, operating through the facilities of established settlement houses. One centered at the Susan Parrish Wharton Settlement in North Philadelphia was described by its head-

[32]Woodward, Address before the ANA, EW; FERA, *Proceedings of the Conference*, p. 27; Woodward to all state directors of women's work, January 4, 1934, W-13; "Nurses Prove Their Way," *Survey*, LXX (May, 1934), 164; Woodward, Address to Federation of Women's Clubs, ER 639.

[33]Hilda Smith to Eleanor Roosevelt, January 6, 1934, ER 632; Women's Division Activities, November 14, 1933, W-1, HLH 16; National Advisory Committee on Emergency Nursery Schools, *Emergency Nursery Schools during the First Year, 1933–1934*, pp. 8–17; Mary Dabney Davis, "Emergency Nursery Schools," *School Life*, XIX (January, 1934), 93.

[34]Grace H. Gosselin to William Hodson, April 4, 1934, FHL 2616; "The CWA and Nursery Schools in New York," *School and Society*, XXXIX (January 20, 1934), 79–80; "CWA Aids Schools," *School Life*, XIX (January, 1934), 101; *New York Times*, February 15, 1934, p. 17.

worker as in a "handicapped area" where in a four-block radius 4,600 families (92 percent black) were on relief. After the CWA folded, the headworker remarked how the project brought insight to community development, and she was pleased and encouraged by its results.[35]

While children's education provided one avenue of jobs, another revolved around classes for adults. Such projects served the dual purpose of providing work for unemployed teachers and fulfilling a need for men and women who had little opportunity for previous schooling.[36] Under the national leadership of Hilda Worthington Smith, director of Affiliated Summer Schools and founder of the Bryn Mawr Summer School for Workers in Industry, a CWA order went out in January, 1934, authorizing states to appoint full-time directors to administer "workers' education." With the advice of professional organizations, Miss Smith prepared a guide to policies on budget, school staffing, courses, and student eligibility.[37] Classes were held in large cities as well as rural outposts, while courses ranged from literacy and citizenship to carpentry and music. The New York effort had some 1,500 unemployed teachers (1,231 women) conducting classes for over 40,000. Professionals claimed that the CWA meant the beginning of a great adult education

[35]Headworker, Wharton Settlement, to Emma Johnson, August 13, 1934; Headworker to Margaret McDonald, June 14, 1934; Headworker to Eleanor Emerson, January 10, 1934; and Requisition to Council of Social Agencies, December 4, 1933, all in Wharton Settlement Papers, Urban Archives, Temple University.

[36]Hilda Smith, "General Plan for Work Relief in the Field of Education," 1933, Hilda Worthington Smith Papers, Schlesinger Library, Radcliffe College; Woodward, Address to Federation of Women's Clubs, ER 639; Woodward to Hopkins, March 3, 1934, ER 615.

[37]A. Williams to all state emergency relief administrators, January 16, 1934, Hilda Worthington Smith Papers, Box 25, FDRL; Hilda Smith to Hopkins, November 14, 1933, Smith Papers, Box 33, FDRL; *Women's Work and Education*, IV (December, 1933), 2; Hilda Smith, *People Come First: A Report on Workers Education in the FERA, CWA, and WPA, 1933–43* (Published for the Adult Education Fund of the Ford Foundation, 1952), pp. 75–76.

movement, a decisive "recognition of education as a life process."[38]

White collar, professional, and unskilled women all found jobs in statistical programs. Although Washington ordered that at least two thirds of the employees on such projects be women, the order had little effect on supervisory positions, which generally went to men. Girls usually worked as canvassers or in the office staff. The largest single endeavor, the Real Property Inventory, studied land vacancy, overcrowding, and real estate finance in 60 cities. In New York alone, 2,000 women found jobs on this study. The Urban Tax Delinquency Survey measured this economic blight in 309 cities of over 30,000 population, and a CWA national relief census provided hard data on the needy to aid the future expansion of federal aid. The unemployment census represented the largest nonmanual project undertaken in Pennsylvania, where over 2,200 women, mostly white collar and professional unemployed, found jobs. Since many had no previous experience, a two-day training course on techniques of interviewing and the use of schedules was offered and followed by an exam. Dr. Louise Stanley of the Bureau of Home Economics, Department of Agriculture, directed the Farm Housing Survey to examine home facilities in rural areas. Mary Louise Chase, of the University of Illinois, headed the state project, and a home economist supervised each county. Field surveyors gathered data on physical dwellings, water supply, lighting, and toilet facilities. Hopkins took special pride in these projects and commented on their satisfactory results.[39]

[38]Lucile Kohn, "Schools for Workers," *School Life*, XIX (May, 1934), 190–191; "Emergency Education Program," *ibid.* (March, 1934), 137; *New York Times*, November 20, 1933, p. 10; Summary of Occupational Analysis of Workers on CWS Projects, March 8, 1934, FHL 2616; *Women's Work and Education*, IV (December, 1933), 2.

[39]Telegram, Baker to all state administrators, December 15, 1933, CWA 73; Woodward to Eleanor Roosevelt, January 18, 1934, ER 639; Travis Whitney to La Guardia, January 5, 1934, FHL 2616; Marie T. Barlow to Woodward, April 4, 1934, FERA 254; *Census of Employable Workers in Urban and Rural Non-Farm Areas of Pennsylvania, 1934* (Harrisburg: State Emergency Relief

*   *   *

Despite the wide variety of projects and social benefits, the CWA did not fulfill all that women had anticipated. Nearly a quarter of the United States work force was female, and women had accounted for 12.4 percent of all CWA applicants. But by the spring of 1934, only 300,000 were on the payroll, a scant 7.5 percent of the 4,000,000 total and well below the goal set by Hopkins in November. "We haven't been particularly successful in work for women," he confessed to the American Association of Social Workers in February, 1934.[40] The lack of a quota proved the most serious handicap to placement, and lower CWS wages also brought charges of discrimination. Mrs. Roosevelt expressed concern and argued that pay differentials should apply, especially to nursing, teaching, and other professional skills. Women also complained that in some cases men received the supervisory positions, which also brought higher pay. But these shortcomings did not diminish the sense of accomplishment held by Ellen Woodward and her network of local volunteers. The only woman within the hierarchy of the CWA, she had built an organization from scratch to lobby for women's needs, developed projects of some versatility, corralled the Red Cross, YWCA, church women, and social clubs to donate materials and oversee activities, and persuaded professional associations to support projects that employed thousands of teachers, nurses, and librarians. Mary Anderson,

---

Administration, 1936): *Philadelphia Public Ledger*, January 15, 1934; Illinois CWA, *Final Report*, p. 69; Hopkins to all state administrators, April 20, 1934, CWA 73.

[40]United States Employment Service, *Twelve and a Half Million Registered for Work, 1934* (Washington: United States Government Printing Office, 1935), p. 30; Woodward, "This New Federal Relief," 104; Jacob Baker, Report on CWA, December 30, 1935, CWA Papers; Harry Hopkins, "Current Relief Problems," Proceedings of Conference on Governmental Objectives for Social Work (February 16, 1934), pp. 111–112, National Association of Social Workers Papers, Box 18, SWHA.

head of the federal Women's Bureau, hailed the whole effort as "a new day of hope for the 'forgotten women.'"[41]

Yet, the overall record suggests one of limited accomplishment for women, even in what could be considered the "woman's sphere," the New Deal social welfare programs, presided over by what one historian has called a "network" of resourceful feminists. In contrast to Hopkins' expeditious draft of public and private agencies and Carmody's insistence on private-sector labor policies to maintain men's morale, Mrs. Woodward's Women's Division seemed little more than a gesture to the delicate sympathies of her upper-class associates. She never could establish a basic priority for women's employment—national or state quotas within the 4 million. She could not break out of FERA guidelines, which imposed upon women alone as a class within the CWA continued applications of the means test and the $.30 minimum wage. Above all, Mrs. Woodward and her set could rarely move beyond those limited domestic sewing and child care jobs, which continued to keep women's work in condescension and subsistence pay. The one major area for women in the CWA's male domain, the Women's Division, in reality represented a throwback to the progressive era's "ladies bountiful." Cut off from the CWA's business of emergency employment, the WD continued in the tradition of sentimental Christian charity.[42]

[41]Eleanor Roosevelt to Woodward, December 7, 1933, ER 1282; *New York Times*, December 5, 1933, p. 2; Anderson, *Women at Work*, pp. 54–55; Weed, "The New Deal that Women Want," 193; Mary Anderson, "Unemployed Women and Public Works," *American Labor Legislation Review*, XXIV (March, 1934), 38.

[42]Susan Ware, *Beyond Suffrage: Women in the New Deal* (Cambridge: Harvard University Press, 1981); William Henry Chafe, *The American Woman* (New York: Oxford University Press, 1972), pp. 38–45.

CHAPTER SEVEN

The Four Million: From Relief Clients to Work Force

ON FEBRUARY 3, 1940, almost six years after the CWA had folded, J. L. Wickkiser of Easton, Pennsylvania, sent a letter to President Roosevelt, enclosing photographs that he had taken as a civil works employee. "In 1933, I was in desperate circumstances," he recalled. When he applied for work at the local USES office, he was assigned to a project at the Schull Junior High School to help lay a concrete driveway so that garbage trucks could have access to the building's incinerator. Wickkiser had the morning shift, doing menial work in the cold. Years later, this man, a prosperous contractor, could still remember that winter of 1933–1934 and the difference the CWA had meant.[1]

Schull Junior High was physically improved, but the less tangible results, the changes in morale, marked the impact of a civil works experiment that had ranged far beyond the bounds of traditional made work. The array of projects, which encompassed the broadest range of skills, liberated an enthusiasm long imprisoned in idleness. CWA wages gave the first real cash—and freedom to spend—that many had in months and even years. Observers saw individuals back on their feet, their families once again secure. But just as significant was the transformation in the consciousness of those on the job. No longer grateful clients, appreciative of the dole and grocery tickets, CWA employees felt they had "earned" their way. They would demand just wages, decent conditions, and respect from their employers. They vowed never to return to their former de-

[1] J. L. Wickkiser to FDR, February 8, 1940, FDR-OF 444B.

pendency. This change in outlook would ultimately affect everyone with whom they came in contact, from neighborhood case workers to county and state relief administrators, to Hopkins' staff in Washington.

I

In mid-January, 1934, the CWA went over the top, as Harry Hopkins proudly announced that 4,265,000 were on the federal payroll. "Well, they're all at work," he reportedly told FDR. "But for God's sake, don't ask me what they're doing." In truth, Hopkins was well aware and very proud of the diversity of talents that civil works projects had incorporated. Just the year before, over 1 million men had aimlessly taken to the roads and railways in search of employment. Now under the CWA twice that number found work on highway projects, which offered jobs in all types of skilled and unskilled labor. Engineers, surveyors, draftsmen, stone masons, bricklayers, carpenters, mechanics, operators of rock-crushing and paving machines, and manual laborers put in eight hours a day in record-breaking cold and were glad for the opportunity. "Lots of enthusiasm" kept the crews going in twenty to thirty below temperatures to complete miles of new streets in Buffalo, New York; and over 11,550 set brick pavements in Chicago. Zero-degree readings did not keep men from ripping out unused trolley tracks and putting down sand and gravel on the avenues of Williamsport, Pennsylvania. CWA teams platted streets from scratch for TVA towns like Norris, Tennessee, and unemployed black hands earned the minimum wage for laying cobblestones along "feeder roads" throughout the South.[2]

---

[2]Quoted in Marquis Childs, "The President's Best Friend," *Saturday Evening Post*, CCXIII (April 19, 1941), 11; John S. Crandall, "Resurfacing Streets and Highways," *Roads and Streets*, LXXVII (February, 1934), 75–77; "Notes from the Road—Winter Construction," *ENR*, CXII (March, 1934), 287–288; Illinois CWA, Press Release, November 29, 1933, VAO 73; Henry G. Alsberg, *America Fights the Depression* (New York: Coward-McCann, 1934), pp. 22–23, 25.

Public buildings and general construction absorbed another thirty percent of the winter work force, as men repaired a variety of structures at institutions, including: agricultural experiment stations, armories, asylums, auditoriums, cemeteries, City Halls, court houses, docks, firehouses, fish hatcheries, homes for the aged, hospitals, heating plants, libraries, police stations, sanitariums, stadiums, and zoos. Over 40,000 schools were rehabilitated or constructed. Rural schools, fallen into decay and forced to close for lack of money, received needed repairs, installations of sanitary and water facilities, ground improvements, and athletic fields. The CWA helped to maintain educational facilities for rural black children in the South at a rate equalled only by the Rosenwald Fund. Civil works jobs on over 1,000 airports included 250 technical experts, draftsmen, supporting personnel, and 40,000 laborers. The bulk of the projects involved clearing, grading, and putting in drain systems at emergency landing fields. To supplement airport construction, 10,000 more were hired for the aerial mapping of hundreds of cities.[3]

A significant portion of CWA activities involved sanitary and public health projects, many undertaken on a regional basis in cooperation with other federal and state agencies. The United States Public Health Service and Department of Agriculture directed nearly 30,000 employees in the drainage of mosquito-breeding swamps. In the Tennessee Valley alone, this small army cleared over 300,000 acres. Civil works engineers fought typhoid throughout the country by constructing 250,000 sanitary privies. The *Raleigh News and Observer* later praised the "contribution to the public of North Carolina" made by 3,600 men who dug the equivalent of 25 miles of privies in the state.

---

[3]"Civil Works Administration Created to Give Employment to 4,000,000," *ENR*, CXI (November 16, 1933), 606–607; Corrington Gill, "The Civil Works Administration," *Municipal Year Book, 1937* (Chicago: International City Managers Association, 1937), p. 425; Forrester B. Washington, "The Negro and Relief," NCSW, *Proceedings* (Chicago: University of Chicago Press, 1934), p. 130; Baker to Henry T. Hunt, December 13, 1933, CWA 92; "Continue Mapping," *ENR*, CXII (March 29, 1934), 424–425.

Another 6,572 found work when the CWA cooperated with state health departments to seal abandoned coal mines in Appalachia to protect local ground water supplies. Over 11,000 men, mostly jobless coal miners in Pennsylvania's Allegheny County, closed out abandoned shafts in the Ohio River Valley and Monongahela basin. Seventy-two thousand CWA workers also took part in a national campaign to eradicate pests: cattle fever and spotted fever along the Gulf Coast, citrus canker in Texas, Dutch elm disease in New York, sweet potato weevil in the South, and gypsy moth in New England. Two hundred and forty men made war on the grapevine leaf hopper in the San Joaquin Valley, California, and another 350 checked the transmission of diseases from rodents, flees, and mice in Los Angeles.[4]

The winter of 1933–1934 brought natural disasters, and civil works troops provided emergency relief to stricken communities. When floods in the Mississippi Valley and Northwest wrought severe damage, gangs of CWA hands were rushed to repair breached levees, clear away debris, and restore vital roads and bridges. After catastrophic floods in LaCrescenta-Montrose (outside Los Angeles) took many lives and destroyed valuable property, a flood-plain project employed over 1,000 local residents. The CWA dispatched squads to strengthen dikes in Oregon menaced by high water. In York County, Pennsylvania, over 3,200 men enlarged the channel of the Codorus River, and 1,000 Alabamians struggled to contain the flood stage along the banks of the Chattahoochee.[5]

[4]C. E. Waller, "A Review of the Federal Civil Works Projects of the Public Health Services," *Public Health Reports*, XLIX (July-December, 1934), 943–964; TVA-CWA Coordinator to O'Berry, February 19, 1934, CWA 34; E. A. Holbrook to Carmody, February 28, 1934, JMC 73; Pennsylvania Secretary of Health to Pinchot, January 9, 1934, GP 2558; "Cattle Tick Eradication," no date, CWA 19; *Los Angeles Times*, February 3 and March 4, 1934.

[5]Macauley to Hopkins, February 2, 1934, CWA 4; telegram, Mrs. Walter D. Thimber to Hopkins, December 9, 1933, CWA 6; "Three Communities Reemploy Labor on PWA and CWA Projects," *Construction Methods*, X (March, 1934), 29–31; *Philadelphia Record*, November 19, 1933, p. 16; J. Smith Lanier to Stone, December 23, 1933, and Thad Holt to Stone, December 7, 1933, CWA 1.

While putting the unemployed back to work, the CWA, at the same time, developed recreational facilities, which most states and localities had slashed as "luxury" budget items with the onset of the depression. Unskilled laborers cleaned and re-graded municipal parks, while professional landscape artists designed new ones. A group of 1,292 Philadelphians found jobs on the first local CWA project in Fairmount Park. In Chicago, 2,500 installed sprinkler pipes in Lincoln Park, while another 9,200 worked for the Cook County Forest Preserves from Skokie to Palos Park. Virtually every municipal playground in Los Angeles was improved in "one of the most comprehensive recreation development programs ever undertaken." But the most massive park project began in mid-January, when New York City park commissioner Robert Moses generated enough proposals to employ over 52,000 in 5 boroughs and another 11,000 in Long Island State Park, more CWA workers than in some states! By May, 1934, 700 renovation projects would be completed—8 antiquated golf courses reshaped, 145 comfort stations renovated, 284 statues refurbished, 678 drinking fountains repaired, 7,000 waste receptacles replaced, 22,500 benches reslatted, 7,000 dead trees removed, 11,000 new ones planted, and 62,000 pruned, 86 miles of fencing torn down and 19 miles newly installed, and every playground resurfaced and reequipped with jungle gyms, slides, and sand boxes![6]

Ten percent of CWA jobs went to white collar and professional workers, including many on remarkably creative projects never before financed by the federal government. Archeologists and anthropologists directed 1,000 laborers on excavations in 5 states, uncovering lost shards of Indian history and the Spanish exploration. Because the CWA could finance unusually large crews, investigators could explore extensive new sites. A "dig" in North Carolina identified "Guasili," one of the villages mentioned by Ferdinand DeSoto; and another in California unearthed the Yokuts Village, visited by Spaniards

[6]*Philadelphia Record*, December 7, 1933, p. 26; Illinois CWA Press Release, November 29, 1933, VAO 73; *Los Angeles Times*, November 24, 1933, and January 2, 1934; *New York Times*, January 20, 1934, p. 4; Robert A. Caro, *The Power Broker* (New York: Alfred A. Knopf, 1974), p. 368.

in 1772. CWA orchestras gave free concerts in New York, Philadelphia, Newark, and Los Angeles; over 150 unemployed actors staged free shows in New York City hospitals and public libraries; and 2,000 artists painted murals in post offices, City Halls, and libraries. The U.S. Coast and Geodetic Survey employed 15,000 idle engineers, while a San Francisco municipal development project hired 400 architects and draftsmen. In all, some 25,000 technical personnel found a use for their skills on civil works projects. Over 12,500 clerks helped to place their fellow unemployed by working for the United States Employment Service. And more the 50,000 teachers participated in the Emergency Education Program, ranging from adult classes for 800,000 to day care for 60,700 toddlers. About 13,000 teachers kept rural schools opened, and literacy classes brought new vistas, especially to thousands of black Americans in the South. "The Adult School here is the grandest thing that had ever happened since the birth of our Lord," wrote a black to President Roosevelt.[7]

In the final accounting, the CWA had built or improved some 500,000 miles of roads, 40,000 schools, over 3,500 parks, playgrounds, and athletic fields, and 1,000 airports—no small addition to the nation's physical plant. One journalist understandably got carried away, declaring that the Egyptian pyramids, the Roman aqueducts, and the fortresses of the Middle Ages could not match "the concrete achievements of the CWA in 136 days!" But the work program's accomplishments were more modest. The CWA showed that the federal government could pursue a fairly effective program of needed public projects without succumbing to the crass pork barrel or garish

[7] M. W. Stirling, "Smithsonian Archeological Projects Conducted under the Federal Emergency Relief Administration, 1933–34," *Annual Report of the Board of Regents of the Smithsonian Institution* (1934) (Washington: United States Government Printing Office, 1935), pp. 371–400; Mary Ross, "White Collar Jobs Once More," *Today*, I (February 3, 1934), 8–9, 20; Joanna C. Colcord and Russell H. Kurtz, "Civil Works for the Professional," *Survey*, LXX (February, 1934), 55; "Work Undertaken by Geodetic Survey as Relief Project," *ENR*, CXI (December 7, 1933), 694; quoted in Washington, "The Negro and Relief," p. 190.

monumentalism that had marred such efforts in the past. Most of the civil works were projects which localities were too strapped to undertake or way down their list of priorities, and they did not unduly crowd out local contractors. Many improvements, like the highways and flood-control levees, were indispensable investments that had an immediate impact on the private sector. Other projects, like the airport redevelopment or the Real Property Inventory, provided crucial "seed money" for extensive public works and commercial expansion in the next decade. And the literacy classes and orchestras gave to the poor some joy, some escape, and some hope to their drab lives—a gesture which a great sovereign government owed to its people.[8]

II

By providing 4 million with real work at real wages, the CWA also injected what columnist Marquis Childs called "a large shot of adrenalin in the economic bloodstream." He did not exaggerate. One hundred and fifty-five thousand New York City dwellers and another 185,000 upstate took home over $41 million in spending money each week. In Chicago, 114,000 had jobs on public projects, with another 110,000 downstate, while Pennsylvania recorded 319,000 at work. Over $33,500 in federal funds poured into "Middletown" that third week of January to pay 1,840 of its residents, as the CWA reached idle hands in typical communities across the nation. Understandably, Hopkins was convinced that civil works had primed the pump of recovery by increasing the purchasing power of its employees, who in turn "brightened the retailers' tills."[9]

[8]Robert E. Sherwood, *Roosevelt and Hopkins* (New York: Harper and Brothers, 1948), p. 57; Wayne W. Parish, "CWA Ends After Brightening Up Nation," *Literary Digest*, CXVII (April 21, 1934), 9, 50.

[9]Childs, "The President's Best Friend," 11; New York State, TERA, "The State in Public Unemployment Relief," March 1, 1934, FERA 196; Pennsylvania CWA, *Final Report* (March, 1934), p. 73; Illinois CWA, *Final Report* (March, 1934), p. 31; Robert S. Lynd and Helen Merrell Lynd, *Middletown in Transition* (New York: Harcourt Brace and Company, 1937), p. 120; Harry Hopkins, *Spending to Save* (New York: W. W. Norton, 1936), p. 124.

That first pay day was a memorable occasion for many Americans after dreary months of food tickets and other "relief in kind." Lorena Hickok observed the scene in Iowa, where 5,000 men who had gone to work with picks and shovels on Monday lined up and got paid at the end of the week. "They took it with wide grins and made bee-lines for the grocery stores, NOT to shove a grocery order across the counter, but to go where they pleased and buy what they pleased with cash." A Chicago case worker described the U family of four on relief since May, 1932, when the father had lost his job as a garment cutter. "I hated going to the store with the ticket. Everybody would look at you. Everyone knew you were on relief right away," recalled his son. "On CWA, there were no tickets to go to the grocery store anymore. My mother bought for cash." Frank Calmers also preferred his civil works assignment on the Dubuque, Iowa, airport project to direct relief because he received more money and he got cash. "By shopping around at different stores and by taking advantage of 'specials,' " he said, "I could buy food much more economically." National Emergency Council Director Frank Walker traveled to his home state, Montana, where he was dismayed to find old school friends in worn-out business suits digging ditches and laying sewer pipes. Then he discovered why they were smiling. "Do you know, Frank," said one, "this is the first money I've had in my pockets in a year and a half?" And a Fairmont, Minnesota, coal dealer remarked, "They've been a pretty gloomy crowd there last two or three years, but—say, you should have seen 'em last Saturday! Laughing and joking—why, I hadn't seen so much fun in years! They all had a little money in their pockets."[10]

From all contemporary accounts, CWA workers spent this

[10]Hickok to Hopkins, November 25, 1933, HLH 61; Dorothy Mack, "Psychological and Emotional Values in C.W.A. Assignments: A Study of Sixty-one Families on Relief before and after C.W.A.," *SSR*, IX (June, 1935), 265, 267; Jessie A. Bloodworth and Elizabeth J. Greenwood, *The Personal Side* (Washington: Works Progress Administration, 1939), p. 149; Sherwood, *Roosevelt and Hopkins*, p. 54.

money immediately, propelled by that large "marginal propensity to consume," which economists believe motivated those long unemployed. Some were a little giddy. "The first thing I did was to go out and buy a dozen oranges," said the wife of a CWA employee. "I hadn't tasted any for so long that I had forgotten what they were like!" "They got their first checks last Saturday night, and they came in here and ordered steaks," noted a butcher. "I have talked with people on relief who said they hadn't tasted meat in six months!" Many reacted solemnly and repaid old debts that had nagged at their pride. Columbia University Professor James T. Shotwell had "never seen anything so striking as the effect of the CWA" in Woodstock, New York. When local artists were given a chance to earn $34 a week, the first thing they did was to pay their grocery bills and meet their past obligations—"the kind of thing one does not ordinarily credit artists with doing." A country doctor in Jackson County, Georgia, told Lorena Hickok that he was "actually beginning to collect a little on back bills." And in Charles City, Iowa, even though the first check was for only part of a week, quite a few CWA workers made small payments on bills they had accumulated. [11]

But most CWA workers spent their pay on consumer nondurables, claims economist Jeffrey Williamson, particularly those goods manufactured by low-wage, labor-intensive industries. In Columbus, Ohio, the shelves of shoestores were swept bare by midnight of the first pay day. Two weeks later at the St. Louis Annual Shoe Fair, buyers placed orders in a volume not experienced in the previous three years. A furniture store in a South Carolina town ordered fifty mattresses in 1932, but recently the manager put in the sixth order of fifty mattresses each. The California Chamber of Commerce hailed the CWA for "relieving unemployment, putting money in circulation, reviving manufacturing plants, and providing worthwhile public improvements"; and the NRA office in Buffalo, New York,

[11]Hickok to Hopkins, December 4, 1933, HLH 61; James T. Shotwell to Wagner, January 12, 1934, RFW-H2.

wrote that "the general business indices showed an advance of at least ten points over the prior years." "The benefits of CWA are acclaimed universally," wrote the Pennsylvania National Emergency Council director, "especially among merchants and trades people."[12]

CWA wages boosted Christmas sales, and the sharp improvement spilled over into the new year. Sears, Roebuck and Montgomery Ward reported receipts significantly above the year before, as the Chicago Daily Times credited the CWA for the stimulation in sales. The secretary of the Sacramento Retail Merchants Association rejoiced that business appeared as good as the hectic holiday rushes of 1927 and 1928. F. W. Woolworth noted a 10.8 percent increase in gross receipts over December, 1932, and S. S. Kresge and W. T. Grant showed similar gains, with certain lines sold out and others reduced to extremely low inventories. "All sections of the country are participating in the recovery of buying power," reported the Wall Street Journal, with the South and Southwest particular bright spots. The credit manager of Rich's, the largest department store in Atlanta, Georgia, said that whereas the Christmas business a year ago had been forty percent cash and sixty percent credit, this year it had been reversed. "My store has always been crowded at Christmas time," added a rural Georgia merchant, "but the difference this year was that people were buying, instead of standing around looking at things they'd like to buy if they had some money." Lorena Hickok noted that shopkeepers in all the little towns in Minnesota had gotten out their tree decorations and strung them across Main Street. In Minneapolis, she found department stores "jammed—as crowded

[12]Jonathan R. Kesselman, "Work Relief Programs in the Great Depression," in John L. Palmer, ed., Creating Jobs: Public Employment Programs and Wage Subsidies (Washington: Brookings Institution, 1978), pp. 174–175; Louis Brownlow, A Passion for Anonymity (Chicago: University of Chicago Press, 1958), p. 288; Hickok to Hopkins, January 11, 1934, HLH 61; John Smiley to Marvin McIntyre, February 2, 1934, CWA 6; R. M. Rayburn to State Director, NEC, March 14, 1934, NEC 248; State Director for Pennsylvania to Executive Director, NEC, March 14, 1934, NEC 435.

as they used to be when I lived here, back in the 'boom days.' "
New York City's prestige marts, Macy's, Gimbels, and Bloom-
ingdale's, were all mobbed just before Christmas, and even after
the new year sales remained high. The *Wall Street Journal* recorded the largest percentage upturn for January receipts since
the depression had begun, as the surge of consumer buying
during the two closing months of 1933 continued unabated.
Business Week also called attention to the "sharp improvement"
and "the influence of CWA expenditures now being felt
throughout the country."[13]

III

The most significant, yet intangible, effect was the psychological lift, the sheer happiness, which the CWA brought to millions. "I have seen men laugh who had not done so for a long
time," wrote an assistant disburser in Union County, Illinois.
"We were so 'broke' and unhappy two months ago when along
came a job for me as an interviewer in the CWA employment
office," wrote a Pittsfield, Massachusetts, man to Mrs. Roosevelt, "giving this ordinary family . . . so much happiness that
I am unable to describe." "I got a new lease on life!" exclaimed
Mr. V, a sixty-four-year-old foreman, who had grown extremely depressed until the CWA helped prove to him that he
could still do physical labor. And Mr. and Mrs. P looked back
longingly on the days of the CWA: "You don't know how
much happier we were."[14]

The CWA reconditioned those who had grown despondent
and lost all confidence in themselves. Even a common labor

[13]*Chicago Daily Times*, December 11, 1933, p. 8; *Sacramento Union*, December 10, 1933; *Wall Street Journal*, January 5, 1934, p. 1, and January 27, 1934,
p. 1; Hickok to Hopkins, January 11 and January 24, 1934, HLH 61; "Retail
Sales—Hopes," *Business Week*, January 20, 1934, p. 3; "The Business Outlook," *ibid.*, January 27, 1934, p. 3.

[14]Edward L. Karraker to Dunham, December 29, 1933, CWA 13; William
F. Daley to Eleanor Roosevelt, February 9, 1934, FDR-OF 444B; Mack,
"Psychological Values in C.W.A.," 266, 264.

job seemed to restore that self-respect. Three hundred sixty-eight men working on West Side Multonomah (Oregon) CWA projects wrote the President and characterized themselves as "former unemployed who through your help are now working steady again, feeling that we are earning our daily bread instead of living on doles." And Claude Park, who "never felt right about accepting the relief slip," was delighted with a CWA road construction job because he "didn't feel that he was getting something for nothing." From his studies of the unemployed worker, Yale University economist E. Wight Bakke confirmed the different perception of work relief particularly among those on the CWA. "The worker has an employer. . . . He is a producer," wrote Bakke. "As far as the neighbors are concerned, he is a working man." Most CWA hands would have heartily agreed with Bakke's conclusion that employment is the "foundation of the social status in community relationships." "I was working," Mr. W proudly told the case worker, "and I could again hold my head up when I met people." Mr. R not only got a CWA job, but was later promoted to foreman on the project. "His self-respect and confidence in himself soared," noted the investigator. "He spoke with pride and confidence of what he had achieved."[15]

Exhilarated by the return to work routines, CWA employees took pride in a job well done, no matter what their assignment. "After sitting in my office for three consecutive years playing checkers with a lot of indigent Master Painters," wrote a union secretary to President Roosevelt, "we are the happiest group of painters you ever saw. We are all working on school houses under the CWA and wish to thank you for salvaging the human element in all of us." Plasterers at the Sunbeam School for crippled children in Cleveland, Ohio, assured FDR, "We have the honor of working here and are trying to turn out the best

[15]Three-hundred Sixty-eight Men Working on West Side Multonomah CWA Projects to FDR, December 6, 1933, FDR-OF 444B; Bloodworth and Green, *The Personal Side*, p. 16; E. Wight Bakke, *The Unemployed Worker* (New Haven: Yale University Press, 1940), pp. 395–396; Mack, "Psychological Values in C.W.A.," 266, 264.

job in the city." After months of idleness, job-seeking and mental anguish, a nurse on a CWS project was glad to be back in a hospital atmosphere. "At first I felt frightened and doubtful of my ability," she confessed, "but within a few days my confidence returned and my hands became deft servants in carrying out nursing procedures." And Lorena Hickok toured Sioux City, Iowa, where thousands of men were at work on roads, sewers, and building a public swimming pool. "You just can't believe these are the same men who were listlessly and unwillingly doing their time a week ago on work relief projects to get their grocery orders," said a city engineer. When Miss Hickok asked an old fellow busy with a shovel leveling off a site for a water tower if it seemed good to be back at work, he simply replied, "Gosh, Yes!"[16]

A civil works job also eased domestic friction in countless families by restoring financial security and re-establishing the father's position in the household. E. Wight Bakke was not only bowing to convention but to bitter depression reality when he emphasized the value of work relief in giving the head of the family an opportunity to "approximate the normal schedule of the chief bread winner." Cash relief alone could not remove this potent source of family discord. An unemployed structural engineer in Michigan with a wife, mother, and six children to support was grateful even for a common labor job. When he brought home his first CWA check for $15, he felt compelled to write to Washington, "Dear President, how I wish you could have seen the smiles of joy on the faces of my loved ones when 'daddy' came home with the first real money in three years." William Croce, a thirty-four-year-old man with two children and no job since 1928, told the *Chicago Daily Times*: "My wife, she didn't say anything—but she got me up at five o'clock this morning. You know darned well she was glad I was going back to work." Since September, 1932, Mr. O had sat around, mo-

---

[16]William Downie to FDR, December 13, 1933, CWA 65; Walter B. Stoner to FDR, December 29, 1933, FDR-OF 444B; Florence Knight, "Making Work for Nurses," *SWT*, II (May, 1935), 26; Hickok to Hopkins, November 25, 1933, HLH 61.

rose and worried, a source of irritation to his wife. "You know, whether the man is working or not, the woman has her work to do," confided Mrs. O to the social worker. "He is a nuisance in the kitchen all the time, and always under foot." But the CWA helped with the family's bills, and Mr. O was also gone all day, working. His wife reported that he came home "tired but happy. He had been busy. His nervous pacings of the floor at night ceased. His moodiness disappeared, and he was once more able to play and laugh with his children." Mr. Cassella of New Haven, Connecticut, put it best when he told one of Bakke's research assistants, "You're damned glad when C.W.A. gives you a chance because then it keeps you away from home and your money is your own and you don't have time to think about things. . . . And the old woman isn't jumping on your neck all the time."[17]

Although the CWA helped to calm the worries of economic insecurity, many social workers were quick to point out that other causes of family tension, such as alcoholism and incompatibility, were not significantly affected by civil works employment. When Mr. A, a chronic drunkard known to the United Charities of Chicago since 1929, had taken a CWA job, he actually worked and was rarely intoxicated during the first few weeks. But when the novelty of work wore off, Mr. A never came home sober from his job. "It was much harder than relief," stated Mrs. A. "At least on relief we were sure of eating." Mr. Jordan, a case with the St. Louis Relief Committee, was preoccupied over some unhappy occurrence in his past. Even when he went to the project site, he continued to worry and drink heavily. "The treatment was a failure," concluded the investigator, referring to his CWA experience. The E family, while on relief, had "serious problems of family interrelationship." Although fewer quarrels took place after the son got

[17]Bakke, The Unemployed Worker, pp. 396–397; Vernon B. Davis to FDR, November 28, 1933, FDR-OF 444B; Chicago Daily Times, November 20, 1933, p. 4; Mack, "Psychological Values in C.W.A.," 263; quoted in E. Wight Bakke, Citizens Without Work (New Haven: Yale University Press, 1940), p. 148.

a CWA assignment, when the family reapplied for assistance and was budgeted for income, violent outbursts occurred even worse than before. Civil works jobs could not seem to make much difference for breadwinners with severe psychological problems. Although Mr. C had quieted down and became less restless while on the CWA, he remained a pathetic figure, "quite dependent on his wife." Then there was Mr. F, who could not find enough security from his CWA position to return to his old neighborhood. He continued to live in a frowzy Chicago tenement, where his family remained completely anonymous.[18]

Although social workers conceded that domestic and psychological difficulties had diminished when some member of the family had a CWA job, they deeply regretted that "arrangements were not made by which case work could be done with regard to these problems while the economic problem was less acute." The D family of six, for example, first became known to Chicago social service agencies when they applied for assistance in May, 1933. A visiting case worker discovered that Mrs. D had a nervous breakdown and lost all interest in her home. While figuring the budget and relief needs, the investigator also made some attempt to understand and discuss Mrs. D's problems. Then Mr. D got a CWA job, and the family broke off contact with the agency. "Obviously further help was needed," concluded the report. "Possibly if case work treatment could have been continued when the family felt independent economically, greater change might have been effected."[19]

Social workers not only regarded the CWA as an unfortunate interruption of case-work counseling, but they also charged that the short duration of the program hampered its effectiveness as "therapy" for their clients. A survey of 100 St. Louis relief families revealed that one-fifth neither understood its purposes nor could they discuss "the C.W.A. situation in any

[18]Mack, "Psychological Values in C.W.A.," 256–257, 258–259, 260; Marian Lindsey, "Casework Values of the C.W.A.," *The Family*, XV (February, 1935), 326.

[19]Mack, "Psychological Values in C.W.A.," 258–259.

manner." Only five stated they liked this method of getting aid, while *none* seemed to think of the program as real or lasting and knew it to be only a temporary measure. Cases in Chicago were also cited to prove how the brief CWA experience had little effect on clients and their dependents, who simply reverted back to old ways in the spring. Mr. Y had lost all desire to work since he went on relief in 1931, but he accepted the CWA assignment enthusiastically and supported his family of six for three months. Yet when the family returned to the relief agency, no change had occurred in his attitude. "Mr. Y again made no attempt to find employment, but spent his days, as before, sitting in the neighborhood saloon," concluded the report. The improvement in the G family was also short-lived. While the father had a CWA job, the daughter returned to school and seemed happy. A few months after the family was back on relief, she was expelled and home again, "unhappy and disturbed as before." Although traditional social workers granted "some therapeutic value" in a CWA assignment, they also emphasized the other cases where civil works jobs did not offset personality difficulties and the valuable counseling was lost. "Not too much should be expected for four months' relief from worry," concluded Marian Lindsey of the St. Louis Relief Committee in *The Family*, the preeminent case-work journal, "if it proves to be an oasis in a great arid waste."[20]

IV

The CWA had forged a "new consciousness" on the part of its employees. Many living in idleness or on relief had become detached from the camaraderie of the work place; and, as Bar-

[20]Interruptions in cases are vividly documented in Eli Ginzburg, *The Unemployed* (New York: Harper and Brothers, 1943), pp. 201–418, and Bloodworth and Green, *The Personal Side*.

Flora Slocum and Charlotte Ring, "Industry's Discarded Workers: A Study of One-hundred St. Louis Relief Families," *Sociology and Social Research*, XIX (July-August, 1935), 525; Mack, "Psychological Values in C.W.A.," 267, 260; Lindsey, "Case Work Values," 325, 327.

nard College sociologist Mirra Komarovsky found, they were cruelly cut off from neighbors, the church, and society. Once returned to the job on civil works projects, they found a new "group life," as noted by a New York State TERA field reporter. Organizations among the ranks included all classes of workers, from manual labor to professionals. "This expression is certainly all to the good," the observer continued; "in my opinion, it indicates a pickup in morale and attitude of participation and non-acceptance of conditions which have been in the past."[21]

CWA employees gained a sense of collective identity on the projects. "I am working in the CWA gang in Milford [New Hampshire]," wrote Charles O. Brown to President Roosevelt, "and what I want you to know is this that I have Never before Worked With a Gang that Walk right out and go to Work Without some one Using a Drag Net." "The Gang" of CWA Workers of Project 83, Richmond, Indiana, stopped for a minute to pose on a cold winter day on (Theodore) Roosevelt Hill for a picture to send the President as a token of their "heartfelt thanks . . . for the work they are now receiving." In Tulare County, California, two unskilled laborers on a civil works flood control project began a weekly mimeographed news sheet which proved popular with their "brothers" throughout the county. Designed to promote "friendship among men of the CWA— America's Great Project," the CWA Booster (Volume 1, Number 13, which they sent to the White House) sported a jaunty Blue Eagle on the front page, with a pick and shovel in each claw. Other communities witnessed the formation of CWA clubs. In Pomona, California, Leota Hale organized a group of 100 called the CWA Social Club. "We have no dues," she assured the President. "It is absolutely free, just a little pleasure for we poor who love our country." A year after the CWA had begun, on November 28, 1934, the CWA Club of Winthrop,

---

[21]Report on Conditions in New York State as of March 31, 1934, HLH 56; Mirra Komarovsky, The Unemployed Man and His Family (New York: Dryden Press, Inc., 1940), pp. 122–126.

Massachusetts, held a reunion and telegraphed FDR of how the anniversary reminded them of the "new day dawned to thousands of unemployed" by the Civil Works Administration.[22]

The winter holidays accentuated this conviviality, as grateful CWA workers took time to convey greetings to the President. The CWA Employees of Project No. 86 of the Sanitary District of Chicago sent a picture and Christmas greetings, while women of the Pasadena Women's Sewing Program No. 72 expressed their deep appreciation for the work. One hundred and forty-two workers on the LaCrosse County Project 1, State Truck Highway 35, afternoon shift, personally signed in pencil to offer their gratitude to Roosevelt for the Executive Order that they be paid the Saturday before Christmas. During the next weeks came best wishes and even gifts to FDR on the occasion of his fifty-fourth birthday. The women of Local Project 154 of Hatfield, Massachusetts, sent a sample of their output, a pair of pajamas. From the CWA Workers of Bessemer, Alabama, came a thirty-two pound turkey, and from CWA Workers on Project 1, Hennepin County, Minnesota, a marble clock. The CWS Women of Jackson County, Missouri, embroidered a rug with the coat of arms and crest of the Roosevelt family. Birthday greetings in behalf of CWA Gang No. 16, Sacramento, California, accompanied a piece of gold quartz. The most spectacular gift, however, was a crated alligator sent by the CWA Workers of Clearwater, Florida. This "native son," explained the men, retires in winter and gets renewed life in the spring. "Our forced retirement has come to an end," they wrote, "and our new lease on life brings with it a vigorous sense of appreciation."[23]

[22]Charles O. Brown to FDR, December 10, 1933; "The Gang" to FDR, January 15, 1934; CWA *Booster*, I (March 22, 1934); Carney Chess to FDR, March 21, 1934; E. R. Howard to FDR, February 10, 1934; Leota Hale to FDR, no date; Board of Directors, CWA Club of Winthrop, Massachusetts, to FDR, November 28, 1934; all in FDR-OF 444B.

[23]CWA Employees of Project No. 86 of the Sanitary District of Chicago to FDR, December 21, 1933; Employees on Civil Works Project F-1-3, Pasa-

At first the back-slapping jubilation on the work shifts and projects gangs enabled the newly employed to put aside old resentments. The Tulare County, California, CWA administrator believed the CWA *Booster* was "doing a world of good in holding down Communism." Social workers commented how steady work on the CWA had sapped much of the "antagonism and rebellion" from their clients and appeared to draw some away from the lure of radical unemployed unions. Mr. P, who had quarreled with his case worker and punched a gas bill collector, had joined the Unemployed Council, finding "satisfaction in their aggressive demands on the relief organization." Once employed as a foreman on the CWA, however, he regained his confidence and no longer resorted to violent outbreaks.[24]

Inevitably, specific grievances among workers also fostered a spontaneous joining together. Local No. 7 CW Employees of Gresham Township, Montgomery County, Illinois, opposed a cut in wages for the "common labor employees" on all road work. CWA asphalt pavers in Buffalo, New York, walked out when they were docked pay because of a work stoppage when the temperature fell to fourteen below zero. Laborers in East Moline, Illinois, collected enough money to put through a telephone call to President Roosevelt. Their spokesman chatted with White House aide Marvin McIntyre long enough to complain that the new county director had reduced pay by $.10 per hour and lengthened the work day. Pennsylvanians on four CWA projects in Woodward Township, Clearfield County, held a mass meeting and resolved to continue work under protest. CWA was paying them $.40 an hour, while men alongside them on "borough projects" got $.50, all for the same type of

---

dena, California, to FDR, December 6, 1933; One-hundred Forty-two Workers on LaCrosse County Project 1, State Truck Highway 35, Afternoon Shift, to FDR, December 20, 1933; W. H. Nixon to FDR, January 18, 1934; Elmer N. Kelly to FDR, January 24, 1934; and CWA Workers of Clearwater, Florida, to FDR, January 6, 1934; all in FDR-OF 444B.

[24]Carney Chess to FDR, March 21, 1934, FDR-OF 444B; Mack, "Psychological Values in C.W.A.," 264.

road construction. A "Colored CWA Committee" in Portsmouth, Virginia, appealed to Hopkins to appoint a new local civil works administrator because of the present one's "indifference to the suffering of Negroes in the city." About 250 CWA employees in Birmingham, Alabama, met every Friday evening in the court house with an attorney to take action against political favoritism in the county office.[25]

A remarkable outbreak of civil works populism occurred throughout California, where laborers developed a proprietary, conservative interest in their new routines. Establishing a vigilante guard against corruption and political favoritism in job assignments in the Oakland and Alameda County CWA, the rank-and-file organized the Alameda County Road Workers Association, describing themselves as follows:

> The present membership is more than 2,500. They are bound by obligation to "Support the President's intent and wishes, to carry out his program on all CWA projects. To stamp out Communist activities wherever found among the workers, and to help avoid Radical demonstrations of any kind among the workers. To do their utmost to rehabilitate the men given a chance to earn an honest dollar, for an honest return in labor, in lieu of the dole that charity formerly gave them— as the price of their American spirits."

The California CWA *Final Report* counted no less than twelve "labor organizations" in Los Angeles County. Those "voluntary, informal groups of workers on numerous projects banded together to instill more patriotism on the job, to thrash out alleged inequities in pay, and to add to the morale of the mem-

[25]Nels Anderson notes this spontaneity in "Organized Unemployed," in Russell H. Kurtz, ed., *Social Work Yearbook* (1937) (New York: Russell Sage Foundation, 1937), p. 321. Paul Spensberger to Hopkins, January 8, 1934, CWA 14; "Notes from the Road," *ENR*, 287–288; Marvin McIntyre to Hopkins, March 18, 1934, CWA 13; William Bishop to Hopkins, January 12, 1934, CWA 40; Colored CWA Committee, Portsmouth, Virginia, to Hopkins, March 23, 1934, CWA 83; C. D. Comstock to George Huddleston, February 10, 1934, CWA 1.

bers." All twelve continually requested information on hiring and payroll schedules, so that the Sacramento office had to set up a special bureau of information, complete with speakers to attend local meetings and soothe grievances. This response "had a pronounced effect in eliminating considerable labor dissatisfaction," claimed the state CWA administrator.[26]

While some CWA workers spontaneously joined together in response to a particular grievance, project "unions" were also encouraged by radical groups, who had attempted to mobilize the unemployed from the outset of the depression. In the early 1930's Communist Unemployed Councils had grown in the big cities out of rent riots, hunger marches, and protests against chaotic local relief. Their leaflets, sit-ins, and street demonstrations had built a cooperative neighborhood solidarity which forced occasional increases in relief appropriations. Although the National Executive Committee of the Socialist Party opposed deliberate organization of the jobless, local Workers' Committees on Unemployment began to take action, with particular effectiveness in Chicago and New York. At the same time, a third movement led by Reverend A. J. Muste and his Conference for Progressive Labor Action pursued the formation of Unemployed Leagues. Working closely at first with self-help groups, which devised practical barter and exchange services among the unemployed, they built a following in the small industrial and mining towns of Ohio, the anthracite fields of eastern Pennsylvania, and soft-coal counties of West Virginia, where Communists and Socialists had failed to make much headway. More often than they would have cared to admit, these radical groups' activities adapted to the very relief administrations which they claimed to despise. With the establishment of FERA state and county offices, the Communists, in particular, curtailed the street demonstrations to concentrate on formal negotiations with relief officials. All three move-

[26]Walter R. Bethel to Frances Perkins, January 11, 1934, CWA 4; George P. Miller to Hiram Johnson, January 20, 1934, CWA 5; California CWA, *Final Report*, p. 108.

ments soon developed interest-group routines, complete with regular meetings, speeches, and grievance committees, and relegated the abrasive confrontations and sit-ins to last-resort tactics.[27]

Radicals had grown accustomed to conferences with local relief administrators, when the CWA got underway in November, 1933, and presented the greatest chance yet to attract new followers, particularly among the common laborers. Although some historians and sociologists have argued that the New Deal relief and work programs pacified the jobless and made them less likely recruits for these militant organizers, there is no doubt, as one contemporary observer stated, that the CWA "hastened once again organizational attempts of the unemployed." The Communist *Party Organizer* correctly pointed to the CWA as an "opportunity to organize large bodies of workers," since the projects had conveniently gathered the jobless and made them far more accessible than scattered individuals sitting idle at home. The President of the National Unemployed League, Anthony Ramuglia, claimed that "the CWA drew into the Leagues hundreds," while a teacher in West Virginia described how "almost overnight League membership and activity in the state increased." Nevertheless, despite their boasts and the splendid opportunity presented by the CWA's rank-and-file, radical groups never constituted more than five percent of all the unemployed at any one time. They did manage,

[27]Roy Rosenzweig, "Organizing the Unemployed: the Early Years of the Great Depression, 1929–1933," *Radical America*, X (July-August, 1976), 37–62, and "Radicals and the Jobless; the Musteites and the Unemployed Leagues, 1932–1936," *Labor History*, XVI (Winter, 1975), 52–77; Daniel J. Leab, " 'United We Eat': The Creation and Organization of Unemployed Councils in 1930," *ibid.*, VIII (Fall, 1967), 300–315; Helen Seymour, "The Organized Unemployed" (unpublished M.A. thesis, University of Chicago, 1937), pp. 17–19, 61; Irene B. Oppenheimer, "The Organizations of the Unemployed" (unpublished M.A. thesis, Columbia University, 1940), pp. 14–23; Thomas to Fred Daniels, December 28, 1933, NT 7; for the Chicago Workers Committee on Unemployment, see Judith Ann Trolander, *Settlement Houses and the Great Depression* (Detroit: Wayne State University Press, 1975), pp. 92–102; William H. and Kathryn Coe Cordell, "Unions among the Unemployed," *North American Review*, CCXL (December, 1935), 506.

however, to generate an inordinate amount of publicity as well as become a focus of analysis for future scholars to warrant an assessment of their relationship to the CWA.[28]

No sooner had the civil works program gotten off the ground than radicals looked for possible issues to exploit in mobilizing CWA employees. The Communist *Party Organizer* had a laundry list of obvious grievances: low wages, long hours, costly transportation to the project site, unsanitary or unsafe conditions, abusive foremen and county administrators, delayed pay, and loss of pay due to the wintry weather. Following these guidelines, on November 27, 1933, the Unemployed Councils of Cook County called on all CWA workers "to organize and fight" for union scale, adequate clothing on outdoor jobs, and no pay reductions due to the weather. They also demanded that blacks, singles, and women be hired on the same basis as married white males, and called for supplementary relief in case of layoffs. In New York City, the Association of Unemployed Single Women, an affiliate of the Socialist Workers' Committee, was created on November 9—two days after the CWA—and wired Mrs. Roosevelt urging federal funds for work relief for women as well as for men. On December 8, a delegation of five met with the head of the New York State women's division and presented a list of recommendations, while 150 members marched outside, carrying placards, saying, "What's to become of forgotten women?"[29]

[28]Rosenzweig, "Radicals and the Jobless," 63; Nathan Rogg, "The Unemployed Unite," *SWT*, III (June, 1936), 14; "Editorial," *New Masses*, X (February 6, 1934), 4–5; "Some Suggestions on Organization for Relief (C.W.A.) Workers," *Party Organizer*, VI (December, 1933), 26–28; Anthony Ramuglia, "The Unemployed Incorporate," *New Republic*, LXXVII (January 10, 1934), 246; Kay Lascelle, "Stranded Folks," *SWT*, II (January, 1935), 15; Sarah Limbach, "The Tactics of the CPLA," *World Tomorrow*, XVII (February 15, 1934), 90–91.

[29]"Some Suggestions on Organization," *Party Organizer*, 26–28; Unemployed Councils of Cook County, *Hunger Fighter*, November 27, 1933, p. 1; *New York Times*, November 9, 1933, p. 6, and December 8, 1933, p. 8; Association of Unemployed Single Women to Eleanor Roosevelt, November 20, 1933, FERA 204; "Unemployed Single Women Organizing," *New Leader*, XVI (November 25, 1933), 2a.

Militant groups tried to take advantage of CWA provisions for union hiring which the AFL building trades had enjoyed. A small faction of Chicago painters and paperhangers who belonged to the Communist Trade Union Unity League challenged the AFL local's exclusive right to select applicants for CWA jobs. Admitting that their members were also called for civil works assignments, TUUL organizers used the occasion to call attention to AFL abuses in collecting back dues and initiation fees from CWA workers. In the end, the rival unions reached a compromise, and they all joined the AFL, leaving the radicals to claim they would "fight from the inside!" In New York City, the Socialist Workers' Committee also tried to expedite placements for Party members, with limited success.[30]

Radicals attracted more attention, however, when they tried to exploit the wage issue and similar complaints. As Ramuglia put it, "Workers taken on CWA jobs found themselves immediately up against grievances requiring adjustment and have joined the Leagues as one organization they knew which seemed capable of handling miscellaneous unskilled workers." By defending the laborers' interests, Communists sought to mobilize CWA employees into what they liked to call a "Relief Workers Protective Association" that would eventually become the militant voice for the CWA masses. In reality, however, the wage boards and grievance committees devised by John Carmody quietly absorbed the radical leaders into the CWA structure and soothed many disagreements. These mechanisms, combined with the receptive climate for friendly negotiation with labor spokesmen, which pervaded the CWA from Carmody's staff down to the county offices, served to settle most disruptive issues and enabled the workers to continue on the job, forcing the militants to look elsewhere.[31]

[30]"Chicago Painters Win a Victory," *Labor Unity*, IX (March, 1934), 13–15; Thomas to Morris Feldman, December 28, 1933, NT 7; see also Chapter Four.

[31]Ramuglia, "The Unemployed Incorporate," 246; "What's Behind Civil Works," *Labor Unity*, IX (January, 1934), 24–26; see also Chapter Four.

In Pennsylvania, radicals took advantage of local grievances to influence small CWA "unions," although such inroads occurred in towns with long-standing Socialist or United Mine Workers traditions. The "CWA Workers and Unemployed Men" in the Bloomsburg-Columbia County area in January, 1934, charged political control of jobs. After their leader, Reverend E.C.V. Hunter, and a committee of five went to Harrisburg and achieved redress, their activities expanded with suggestions for projects and a grievance committee to settle disputes. When a labor board was chosen, the group's treasurer became one of three members, and he stood fast for the $.50 rate. A mass meeting at the local armory attracted 1,000, as leaders boasted how wages never fell below $.50 "due to the fact that the county is organized."[32] The Slate Belt CWA workers formed an organization of 450 in Northampton County and met at the Union Hall. "There are millions of CWA workers for whom industry in their community offers no prospect of employment even if prosperity returns," warned the speaker; "only permanent organization by these victims of our system will enable them to survive." On February 23 they drew up a constitution and protested the delay in starting a CWA post-office project. Their efforts were not completely successful, however, since the wage committee was "handpicked" by the county administrator.[33] In Socialist Reading, the "United CWA-PWA Workers of Berks County and America" distributed leaflets and formed committees to report on projects. By mid-February, the union claimed 446 members paying monthly dues of $.10 and demanding a restoration of hourly rates equal to the building trades' schedules. They eventually extracted a promise

[32]Bernard Karsh and Phillips L. Garman, "The Impact of the Political Left," in Milton Derber and Edwin Young, eds., *Labor and the New Deal* (Madison: University of Wisconsin Press, 1957), pp. 91–92; (Philadelphia) *Union Labor Record*, May 4, 1934, p. 8.; Reverend E.C.V. Hunter to Hopkins, February 17, 1934, CWA 40.

[33](Philadelphia) *Union Labor Record*, February 9, 1934, p. 3; February 23, 1934, p. 7; and May 4, 1934, p. 9.

from county CWA officials that wages would be maintained and no one laid off unless absolutely necessary.[34]

The most interesting pacification of militance occurred in the anthracite fields around Mt. Carmel and Shamokin, where Lorena Hickok had reported large numbers of jobless and widespread unrest back in August, 1933. A mass meeting in December, sponsored by the local unemployed union, resulted in a "severe heckling" of the CWA engineer. But the civil works administrator for the five counties followed Carmody's example and extended an invitation to meet with a committee of three representatives. Impressed by the sincerity of the man, the unions proceeded to cooperate in ironing out grievances. The administrator was so pleased that he wrote a long letter to President Roosevelt about his reconciliation with the "radical elements."[35]

In West Virginia, another stronghold of the Unemployed League, members on a CWA project struck in November for $.45 an hour, followed by a mass demonstration. League grievance committees invaded the relief office with demands for more aid and evidence of graft. An ugly confrontation seemed likely, but in December the leadership failed to follow through on plans for more protests. In a state notorious for brazen political deals, the local (Republican) CWA administrator simply went with tradition and named all the League leaders—the past president, his brother, the new president, and two "trouble makers" in the Charlestown locals—to supervisory positions on civil works projects. "The Holly Grove local was destroyed," wrote a bitter observer, "and by this time, mud, snow, cold and flooded creeks had isolated Holly Grove. The rest of

[34]*Reading Labor Advocate*, March 16, 1934, p. 1; (Philadelphia) *Union Labor Record*, May 4, 1934, p. 5; United CWA and PWA Workers of Berks County to Hopkins, February 26, 1934, CWA 40; Kenneth E. Hendrickson, Jr., "Triumph and Disaster: the Reading Socialists in Power and Decline, 1932–1939—Part II," *Pennsylvania History*, XL (October, 1973), 385.

[35]Hickok to Hopkins, August 6, 1933, HLH 61; W. Edwin Druckemiller to FDR, December 14, 1933, FDR-OF 444B; S. Williams to Carmody, January 8, 1934, CWA 92.

the mining town locals were similarly isolated and bewildered, and the League died as a rank-and-file organization."[36]

At a Communist-sponsored National Convention Against Unemployment, held in Washington, February 3 to 5, local organizers boasted of their "victories" on the CWA, but their details rang hollow. A New Orleans, Louisiana, delegate related how a Relief Workers Protective Union had marched to the capital, demanding $.90 daily carfare to a military barracks project. The state administrator responded instead with open-air busses and silenced the commotion. Making the best of the situation, the radical sighed, "Still, it was transportation!" An Illinois delegate recounted how the Unemployed Council leafletted, calling the $.40 per hour rate a "swindle," and the administrator quickly raised the pay to $.50. A black youth from Detroit told how his crew had no pay for two weeks. When the men proceeded to unbolt the flange plates for the trolley tracks they were supposed to be laying, the foreman ran to CWA headquarters and returned with the checks. Although radicals interpreted these incidents as triumphs, in reality they were quick, effective settlements that permitted little follow-through on the Councils' part.[37]

Radicals undoubtedly had more success among New York City's working-class ranks, just as they had appealed to the city's white collar and professional employees on the CWA. Communist involvement helped to spark the first strike of CWA workers on December 5, when a reported 2,700 laborers refused to go to the Bear Mountain project site unless demands on hours and wages were granted. As the men assembled at the train station, agitators urged them not to report for the job unless concessions were granted. After fist fights and police intervention restored order, the strikers elected a delegation to confer with the state CWA administrator, who agreed to a wage

[36]Lascelle, "Stranded Populations," 13–14.

[37]I. Amter, "The Unemployed Plan for Battle," *Labor Unity*, IX (March, 1934), 6–7; Robert Whitcomb, "Delegate to Washington," *The Commonweal*, XIX (April 6, 1934), 627–628; Charles Emmett, "The Unemployed Propose Action," *SWT*, I (March-April, 1934), 6–7.

increase as well as half pay for each rainy day, with the opportunity to make up time. With this victory, the Communists went on to set up the first manual relief workers organization, the Relief Workers League, on January 6, 1934, and demanded $5 a day and four days a week minimum.[38]

At the same time, David Lasser's Association of Civil Works Employees was attempting to reach beyond its white collar core to "other classes of labor employed in the CWA." Lasser drew national attention when he and Julius Bertman were arrested on December 21, 1933, in Brooklyn, at the Dyker Beach Park Development project, for disorderly conduct and inciting to riot. They were distributing leaflets to a pick-and-shovel crew to demand full pay before Christmas, since the men had put in three weeks with no compensation. The magistrate dismissed the case, a decision which brought praise from the American Civil Liberties Union and *Upton Sinclair's National EPIC News*. With this notoriety, Lasser went on to set up offices in the outer-boroughs at the Bronx Labor Center and the Brownsville Labor Lyceum in Brooklyn. These efforts forced staid Socialists, including Norman Thomas, to give the impetuous engineer his due. Nevertheless, despite the receptive political environment and pool of some 200,000 CWA workers and thousands more unemployed, the largest radical group in New York, the Relief Workers League, could claim only 3,000 members at its height.[39]

Significantly, the demobilization of the CWA, with pay cuts, reduced hours, and layoffs, touched off the most genuine rank-and-file upsurge among civil works employees, although the

[38]*New York Times*, December 5, 1933, p. 2; "Relief Workers Fight," *SWT*, I (July-August, 1934), 17; Relief Workers League to FDR, March 10, 1934, CWA 32; Seymour, "The Organized Unemployed," p. 14.

[39]See Chapter Five; David Lasser, "Socialists and the Unemployed," *American Socialist Quarterly*, V (June, 1936), 10–14; *New York Times*, January 9, 1934, p. 17; "Court Decision Favors CWA Men," *Upton Sinclair's National EPIC News*, March, 1934, p. 3; Thomas to Louis Waldman, January 25, 1934, NT 8; "CWA Organizers Discharged," *New Leader*, XVII (January 13, 1934), 7; *New York Herald Tribune*, February 5, 1934, p. 14.

largest contingent came from the white collar groups. In New York City, a February 15th demonstration in Union Square was acclaimed "unique" by the radical press, since practically all unemployed organizations participated, from professional associations to unskilled manual laborers, from Socialists and Communists to *ad hoc* local groups. They rallied around two demands: continuation of the CWA and opposition to layoffs. While the *New York Herald Tribune* reported 5,000 demonstrators, *Workers Age* boasted that 8,000 attended, still not much of a turnout considering the efforts of a "united front."[40]

On March 15, the United Action Conference on the CWA and Unemployment met in Philadelphia to resist liquidation of the program, maintain wages, and provide relief for those already out of work. This regional gathering sparked a local Philadelphia CWA Workers Union, which called for full-scale wages and a thirty-hour week on all projects. The city's civil works administrator, William Connell, responded by visiting twelve projects and talking with the workers. He reported "no tendency . . . to form a union." Nevertheless, the movement persisted, but could claim only 300. Connell did not attend their meetings, stating "the majority of CWA workers were not in sympathy with this movement."[41]

On March 24, Easter Sunday, a mere 700 paraded in Washington against the demobilization of the CWA. Led by Norman Thomas, the marchers were primarily from Socialist and white collar groups from New York City, although other radical organizations were represented. Harry Hopkins listened to demands for an indefinite continuation of the CWA and a minimum wage of $20 a week. "We want jobs, not charity," read one banner. New Yorkers returned home to stage a march on City Hall under the Greater New York Committee for United

[40]Anderson, "Organized Unemployed," 322; "CWA Workers Demonstrate," (New York City) *Workers Age*, March 1, 1934, p. 7; *New York Herald Tribune*, February 16, 1934, p. 18; *New York Sun*, March 8, 1934, p. 38; "CWA Front," *The Militant*, VII (February 24, 1934), 2.

[41]FAECT, *Bulletin*, I (April, 1934), 10–12; *Philadelphia Public Ledger*, March 16, 1934, p. 2, and March 18, 1934, p. 3.

Action on CWA and Unemployment. Although Mayor Fiorello H. La Guardia was warned of possible violence, only 1,500 showed up for a peaceful, rather limp, demonstration.[42]

With little of substance accomplished, the demobilization outcry did help to lay some significant foundations for the future. In late March, the Chicago Workers' Committee joined with Socialist Party affiliates in downstate mining towns to form the Illinois Workers Alliance. It staged a regional protest against the liquidation of the CWA and along with Lasser's group in New York would form the nucleus of the Workers Alliance of America, the chief employees' union on the Works Progress Administration. Before the marchers departed from Washington, they formed the Eastern Federation of Unemployed and Emergency Workers, and by May the first issue of a bi-weekly publication entitled *Unemployed News Service* appeared, with reports of protests and encouragement of further coordinated action. "Spurred by the current boom in organization of the unemployed," the editors established this publication for "all groups to learn from each other's experience in organizing and building their strength to where it will mean increased relief and employment, but it will also enable all groups to coordinate their activities to an extent never before possible." They pointed out that the "CWA might never have been cut off had the unemployed organizations over the country been aware of the widespread demonstrations that were being planned."[43]

* * *

In retrospect, the radicals had less of an impact on the "transvaluation" of relief workers on the CWA than did the inherent

[42]"Easter Parade to Stress Desperate Need of CWA Workers and Jobless," *New Leader*, XVII (March 31, 1934), 3–4; Clarence Senior to Thomas, April 2, 1934, NT 10; *New York Times*, March 25, 1934, Sec. II, p. 1; Thomas to Stephen S. Wise, March 21, 1934, NT 9; *New York Times*, March 29, 1934, p. 7, and March 30, 1934, p. 1.

[43]Seymour, "The Organized Unemployed," pp. 35–36; Thomas to Stephen S. Wise, May 21, 1934, NT 9; *Unemployed News Service*, May 24, 1934, p. 1.

character of the work program.[44] Within a few weeks, millions of unemployed had acquired a distinct group identity on their shift, their project, or their county CWA. When this temporary public employment took on the characteristics of a regular job, especially with no immediate alternatives in the private sector, workers quickly took a positive interest in their civil works assignments. As their families came to rely upon the size and regularity of their pay checks, many organized to insure a continuity of that work at fair wages. The slight radical inroads were achieved through the wage boards and grievance committees, designed by John Carmody as part of his CWA labor policies. While these institutions provided expedient solutions for a sprawling federal agency, they had little significance in the creation of working-class militancy, where most grievances relate to long-term unremedied abuses on the job. Carmody's conciliatory approach paid off—emergency employment on the CWA had restored the productive, wage-earning role of the American work force and represented one of the most fundamentally conservative investments that the New Deal could make in the early 1930's.[45]

Carmody, Jacob Baker, and other corporate liberals like William Connell in Philadelphia could remain unfazed by all the radical hoopla. As Taylorites and management experts, these men had long conceptualized about the labor force in large collective groups. Carmody, Baker, and their assistant, Arthur Goldschmidt, had first-hand experience with self-help associations on the Emergency Exchange in New York City. Thoroughly acquainted with labor militance with the United Mine

[44]Frances Fox Piven and Richard A. Cloward, *Poor People's Movements* (New York: Vintage Books, 1979), pp. 40–44, 48–49; Bernard Sternsher, "Victims of the Great Depression: Self-blame/Non-self Blame, Radicalism, and Pre-1929 Experiments," *Social Science History*, I (Winter, 1977), 137–177.

[45]Frances Fox Piven and Richard A. Cloward note the restoration of the occupational role in *Regulating the Poor* (New York: Vintage Books, 1972), p. 89. See also David Ziskind, *One Thousand Strikes of Government Employees* (New York: Columbia University Press, 1940), pp. 136–137; Cordell, "Unions among the Unemployed," 510; Anderson, "Organized Unemployed," 322.

Workers' battles in the coal fields, Carmody in particular would hardly be disturbed by the alleged gains of a few agitators on the CWA. His experience at Ryerson Steel, Davis Coal and Coke, and the Wagner Labor Boards would again apply—provide round-table negotiations, fair-wage adjustments, and grievance review boards with worker representation, and rank-and-file discontent would largely merge into an enthusiasm for the job.[46] Nels Anderson, Carmody's aide for labor relations, also understood the perspective of most CWA workers. "They want work and wages where they are and generally when they get fairly decent conditions their organizations languish," he wrote to a social work audience. But not many case workers could accept this insight. They had become that uncomfortable with a work relief program which engineers, technicians, and management experts had transformed into an emergency employment corporation in every sense of the word.[47]

[46]See Chapter Two and Chapter Four.

[47]Anderson, "Organized Unemployed," 322.

Social workers were bothered by organizations of the unemployed, especially the radical tactics of sit-ins in the relief offices and demonstrations in the streets. Seymour discusses this antagonism in "The Organized Unemployed," p. 59. See also Alice Brophy and George Hallowitz, "Pressure Groups and the Relief Administration in New York City" (unpublished professional project, New York School of Social Work, April 8, 1937), p. 77; Nels Anderson, "Pressure Groups," *Survey Graphic*, XXV (March, 1936), 168. Only in New York City and Chicago were settlements receptive toward unemployed organizations, says Trolander, *Settlement Houses*, pp. 91–106.

CHAPTER EIGHT

Demobilization

FEW MEN had a more distasteful task to perform than Harry Hopkins in mid-January, 1934. Just as the CWA had gone over the top, with more than 4 million Americans on the federal payroll, he had to issue orders for retrenchment. The speed and daring with which the CWA had achieved its goals had also ballooned weekly wage totals, pushed material costs far above original estimates, and spread worries of mounting compensation benefits as a permanent expense for the U.S. Treasury. The very policies which had lifted the CWA above traditional made work had forced expenditures beyond the November appropriation from PWA funds and made the civil works budget a concern for Hopkins' staff, the National Emergency Council, President Roosevelt, and the Congress. Afraid he could not meet future payrolls, Hopkins reluctantly ordered a reduction.

On January 18, 1934, Hopkins instructed state CWAs to cut weekly working hours immediately to a new maximum of 15 for small towns and rural districts under 25,000 inhabitants, and from 30 to 24 in more densely populated areas. Although a large protest occurred in Manhattan and New York Governor Herbert H. Lehman and Pennsylvania's Gifford Pinchot sent pleading telegrams to Washington, President Roosevelt declared that the agency would definitely come to an end. The cut in working hours permitted Hopkins to stretch his funds until Congress in mid-February voted several million dollars to "clean up" the program. When full-scale demobilization began, the CWA would discharge crews, slash wage rates, and even scale down compensation benefits until the final demise on Easter weekend.[1]

[1]Hopkins to all civil works administrators, January 15, 1934, CWA 73;

Contemporary observers, like Arthur Krock of the *New York Times* and T.R.B. of the *New Republic*, saw in these events a triumph for fiscal conservatives, like Budget Director Lewis Douglas and Southern Democrats, among the inner councils of the White House. But few could look beyond this liberal-conservative tug of war around Roosevelt and on Capitol Hill to the growing tension *within* the social welfare establishment. The losing struggle to extend the CWA was marked by an abdication of those so committed to the experiment in November, notably Harry Hopkins and the social workers. Hopkins' motives were clear. Loyal to the President and realistic enough to accept budgetary priorities settled in the executive office, he stood ready to impose Roosevelt's wishes on his staff. But Hopkins' acquiescence was also determined by the failure among social work organizations to launch a drive for a substantial appropriation to extend the CWA to 1935 or raise more than *pro forma* objections to demobilization. Throughout its short existence, after all, the CWA had provided the arena for an intense rivalry between social workers and technical experts. At its peak, the civil works organization had been transformed from a social welfare agency to a public employment operation, run by engineers, accountants, and industrial managers. Demobilization revealed the struggle of welfare officials to prevail once again over the administration of aid to the unemployed. By the spring of 1934, social workers would reemerge to take charge of relief and work relief under the Federal Emergency Relief Administration.[2]

I

Despite its enormous popularity with the unemployed and with small retailers, the CWA had aroused opposition from other

New York Times, January 18, 1934, p. 7; Herbert H. Lehman to FDR, January 17, 1934, Herbert H. Lehman Library, Columbia University; Pinchot to FDR, January 24, 1934, GP 867; "Not Back to Hoover, Please," *Nation*, CXXVIII (March 28, 1934), 341.

[2]Arthur Krock, "In Washington," *New York Times*, January 23, 1934, p.

groups, particularly the business community. Private industry had never overcome its objections to work relief and saw even ditch digging as competitive. A large, well-paying, and intrusive public employment program seemed particularly offensive to small industrial managers in thousands of towns across the country. With the bulk of CWA projects in light construction and repairs, complaints came most often from builders, who had been "fighting for and living for a public works program," and found themselves excluded by the CWA force account.[3] "General contractors and subcontractors have had little to do in the past three years and then you set up a construction program which continues to leave them on the outside," cried the Pittsburgh Builders Exchange. The Chicago Plumbing Contractors Association declared that the CWA "had put the master plumber out of business." A paving contractor in Lincoln, Illinois, complained that his work in surrounding townships had been "eliminated by the CWA," and the Johnstown, Pennsylvania, Builders Exchange charged the federal relief program with "discrimination" against private employers. Alarmed by the "scope of projects," the Illinois Builders Institute held an emergency meeting in Springfield. Members feared that Hopkins contemplated the "taking over of potential work that the construction industry must look forward to" and resolved for an end to the CWA at the earliest possible date.[4]

18, and "President's Stand on CWA Has Bearing on Inflation," *ibid.*, January 28, 1934, Sec. IV, p. 1; T.R.B., "Washington Notes," *New Republic*, LXXVIII (February 7, 1934), 361–362; Robert E. Sherwood, *Roosevelt and Hopkins* (New York: Harper and Brothers, 1948), p. 56.

[3]John M. Carmody, "The Relation of General Contractors to the CWA," January 19, 1934, CWA 62; National Association of Builders Exchanges to Hopkins, December 29, 1933, CWA 95; "Codes and Federal Construction Subject of Contractors Meeting," *ENR*, CXII (January 18, 1934), 99; Arthur M. Schlesinger, Jr., *The Coming of the New Deal* (Boston: Houghton Mifflin Company, 1965), p. 274.

[4]Pittsburgh Builders Exchange to Biddle, January 16, 1934, CWA 40; Chicago Plumbing Contractors Association to Hopkins, March 6, 1934; and Harvey K. Rhoades to Hopkins, March 13, 1934, CWA 13; Johnstown Builders Exchange to Hopkins, January 18, 1934, CWA 40; Meeting of Board of Directors of Illinois Builders Institute, Springfield, December 9, 1933, CWA 13.

Besides undertaking projects normally performed by private industry, the CWA, with its high wages, angered employers, particularly in hard-pressed farm communities. Agricultural organizations blamed civil works pay scales for increasing the cost of stoop labor. "Continuation of the CWA might seriously impede the President's program of farm recovery," advised Pierce Williams, Hopkins' field man in the West. CWA wage competition "nullified efforts now being made by the government to obtain for us an approach to the 1910–1914 parity," claimed the Pear Growers Protective League. The California Farm Bureau Federation protested the rate of $.60 per hour as "higher than that which prevailed in the boom days of 1928 and is causing labor to leave essential work on farms for more lucrative civil works jobs." Individual farmers were also incensed, particularly those in the South. "I'm three weeks behind in my work right now because of CWA," complained a Georgia peach grower. "I could have got along if they'd taken half my hands to work on CWA, but I can't get along with ALL of them working on CWA." Afraid that high civil works wages would cause grumbling among his hands, a tobacco grower hesitated to put in a big crop "with the chance of having to use dissatisfied labor." A representative of 500 South Carolina asparagus planters called attention to the seasonal nature of the harvest, from March 1 to May 15, which required 6,000 hands, including women and children. "If the CWA continues, certain asparagus growers will be seriously handicapped," he warned.[5]

The wage issue was compounded in the South by racial tensions, since many of the farm workers were black and rarely enjoyed decent wages or payment in cash. FERA direct relief had seemed bad enough to the Southern gentry, who feared the dole would undermine "self-reliance" and draw the idle away from productive work on the land. But the CWA appeared even worse, since it jeopardized the region's great resource of

[5]P. Williams to Hopkins, February 6, 1934, JMC 73; Pear Growers Protective League to Hiram Johnson, January 11, 1934, CWA 5; *Sacramento Union*, December 24, 1933; Hickok to Hopkins, February 8, 1934, HLH 61.

cheap labor. "You can't hire a nigger to do anything for you," declared a North Carolina landlord; "high wages is ruinin' 'em." "I wouldn't plow nobody's mule from sunrise to sunset for 50 cents per day," wrote an aggrieved planter to Georgia Governor Eugene Talmadge, "when I could get $1.30 for pretending to work a DITCH." Small farmers were furious. "No one to help me as I pick up a hand now and then," scrawled an angry Tarheel grower to Senator Josiah W. Bailey. "The CWA's paying sorry no account negroes 45¢ per hour. . . . I can't get any job—only to farm." Southern cities, too, felt added tension as whites perceived that the CWA had drawn blacks off the land. Lorena Hickok, whom Hopkins trusted to provide an accurate picture of local conditions, visited Savannah, Georgia, where over half the population was black, and she wrote:

SUCH Negroes! Even their lips are black, and the whites of their eyes! They're almost as inarticulate as animals. They ARE animals. Many of them look and talk and act like creatures barely removed from the Ape. . . . For these people to be getting $12 a week—at least twice as much as common labor has ever been paid down there before—is an awfully bitter pill for Savannah people to swallow.[6]

Small manufacturers in industrial states had their own quarrel with CWA wages. Plant owners, forced to cut their work week to a few days, claimed that their hands had left for more steady income offered on civil works. Men left the Beaver Valley Alloy Foundry in Rochester, Pennsylvania, for the CWA because the company president could afford to operate his machines only a few days a month, while Harry Hopkins could guarantee much more. The Dunkirk, New York, Chamber of Commerce called an emergency meeting after local industrial-

[6]Walter Wilbur, "Special Problems of the South," *Annals*, CLXXVI (November, 1934), 53–54; quoted in George Brown Tindall, *The Emergence of the New South, 1913–1946* (Baton Rouge: Louisiana State University Press, 1967), pp. 478–479; quoted in Schlesinger, *Coming of the New Deal*, p. 274; E. W. Riggs to Bailey, January 22, 1934, JWB; Hickok to Hopkins, January 16, 1934, HLH 61.

ists reported having lost employees to the $.50 per hour paid by the CWA against the $.40 rate mandated by various NRA codes. E. Wight Bakke's investigators in New Haven, Connecticut, found two cases where men saw their friends earning more on civil works and were tempted to leave their jobs. A laborer employed by Yale University had witnessed some of his gang quit and join the CWA because they could receive better pay and more regular work. Thinking that only road construction was available, Mr. Fremont first shunned the CWA because of his weak back. But after a man in his sales force got a clerk job, Fremont was envious. "It was hard to take," he admitted, "the knowledge that a friend was getting $25 a week and working in an office at that." The short duration of the program could not have lured many from private-sector jobs which offered any permanency, but this fact hardly consoled manufacturers who imagined great losses to the government. "We have no objection to anyone leaving our employ in order to improve themselves by obtaining higher wages," wrote a Pennsylvania steel executive; "but it does seem unfortunate that we should lose men from industry because they are able to obtain higher hourly rates by working on welfare projects."[7]

While small businessmen voiced personal complaints against the CWA, corporate leaders preferred to dwell on the larger question posed by what they deemed the immense cost of work relief. Winthrop D. Aldrich of Chase National Bank bemoaned "the tremendous additional expense involved in work relief as against home relief for materials, supplies, and supervision." "Direct relief in the form of cash," stated Henry I. Harriman,

[7] Illinois Manufacturers Association to Hopkins, November 17, 1933, CWA 13; Beaver Valley Foundry to Hopkins, January 15, 1934, CWA 40; Dunkirk Chamber of Commerce to Royal S. Copeland, January 9, 1934, CWA 32; Dunkirk Radiator Corporation to Wagner, January 9, 1934, RFW-H2; E. Wight Bakke, The Unemployed Worker (New Haven: Yale University Press, 1940), pp. 208, 215; Jonathan R. Kesselman, "Work Relief Programs in the Great Depression," in John L. Palmer, ed., Creating Jobs: Public Employment Programs and Wage Subsidies (Washington: Brookings Institution, 1978), pp. 201–202; Ludlum Steel Company to Hopkins, January 29, 1934, CWA 32.

president of the U.S. Chamber of Commerce, "is undoubtedly the most economical and the least burdensome to the taxpayer." Robert E. Wood, characterized as the forward-looking executive of Sears, Roebuck, wrote, "We should tighten up relief all along the line and if relief is to be given it must be on a bare subsistence allowance."[8]

Mounting evidence of the CWA's huge expenditures—$200 million per month on civil works as compared to only $60 million for FERA direct and work relief—gave ample ammunition to conservatives around the President who were distressed by the growing federal deficit. Lewis Douglas, director of the Bureau of the Budget, contended that states and localities were imposing a financial burden on the federal government for relief services which they should assume themselves. Douglas was particularly unnerved by the compensation costs. Only three weeks after the CWA began, he warned that opening federal benefits to temporary employees was creating an unknown and lasting drain upon the U.S. Treasury. Harry Hopkins appreciated the force of this argument. "Douglas is very properly worried, about this insurance problem of ours, that the Government is going to be left holding the bag," he confided to his staff. "These claims are not submitted until after we are out of business and out of money, and he is very anxious . . . to make sure that out of the $400 million adequate funds are made available . . . to meet this bill."[9]

Douglas presented these facts in two convincing memos to the President that urged an end to the CWA on February 15, if not before, and for the Administration to revert back to di-

[8]Winthrop D. Aldrich, "The Financing of Unemployment Relief," *Vital Speeches of the Day*, I (December, 1934), 178–179; Henry I. Harriman, *Unemployment Relief and Housing* (Washington: United States Chamber of Commerce, 1934), pp. 9–10; quoted in Schlesinger, *Coming of the New Deal*, pp. 274–275.

[9]Goldschmidt to Hopkins, December 27, 1933, CWA 92; Corrington Gill, *Wasted Manpower* (New York: W. W. Norton and Company, 1939), pp. 167–168; Douglas to FDR, January 24, 1934, FDR-OF 444B; CWA Minutes, December 6, 1933, HLH 45.

rect relief. Predicting that thousands would settle into govern-
ment-made jobs if civil works continued until spring, he insisted
that wage rates be decreased so the unemployed would seek
jobs in private industry. Douglas also insisted on a return to
rigid tests to determine eligibility for relief and suggested that
CWA payrolls be significantly diminished in rural sections first.
He warned that "political forces" generated by a prolonging of
the CWA might become so great that it might be impossible to
end it. All of these arguments influenced the President, who
confided to the National Emergency Council on January 23,
1934, that the CWA "will become a habit with the country.
We want to get away from the CWA as soon as we can."[10]

Aware that conservatives around the White House had made
a compelling case for a quick end to the CWA in mid-February,
Harry Hopkins couched his plea to Roosevelt for more funds
to make "an orderly liquidation" of the program. Stressing that
FERA and Department of Labor estimates of the unemployed
had fallen far too low and that CWA wages were poured immediately into retail sales, he asked for a continuation at least
through the winter. Later, Hopkins took a modest approach in
testimony before the House Appropriations Committee, when
he conceded that civil works was initiated as an emergency
measure and was not intended as a permanent enterprise of the
federal government. "I believe that it should be demobilized,"
he flatly stated, but in the same breath he asked the Congress
for enough money to last until April. Predicting that public
works would pick up in the spring, Hopkins proposed to carry
on CWA projects at maximum level until the first of March,
and thereafter cut back on a geographical basis beginning in
the South until complete termination by May 1.[11]

[10]Douglas to FDR, January 24, 1934, and January 30, 1934, FDR-OF 444B;
Lester G. Seligman and Elmer E. Cornwell, Jr., eds., New Deal Mosaic (Eugene,
Oregon: University of Oregon Press, 1965), p. 76.

[11]Hopkins to Ickes, December 17, 1933, CWA 81; Louis Brownlow Diary,
December 22, 1933, pp. 126–128, University of Chicago; Brownlow to Hopkins, December 27, 1933, CWA 102; Hopkins to FDR, December 29, 1933,
FDR-OF 444; U.S. Congress, House of Representatives, Committee on Appropriations, Hearings, Federal Emergency Relief and Civil Works Program, H.R.
7527, 73rd Cong., 2nd Sess., 1934, pp. 29–30.

II

Hopkins' retreat was made inevitable not only by the formidable opposition from conservatives, but by the disenchantment of some liberals, notably from the social work establishment, who preferred to let the CWA expire. While Hopkins struggled for an acceptable compromise in the growing climate of retrenchment, some of his own field reporters were echoing the same arguments for an abrupt end to civil works. Pierce Williams, his representative in the West, wrote a lengthy memo on February 6, 1934, advocating a speedy shutdown. Bothered by the "tremendous cost," he warned of the "bad effect on private business to continue the expenditure of $40 million a week indefinitely on the CWA." Shaken by the personal attacks from California Democrats that would eventually culminate in an indictment, Williams also sensed the pressure building on other Western civil works officials. He warned Hopkins against continuing through the summer months, making the CWA a campaign issue in the fall. "The sooner the politicians of the country are given evidence that CWA employment will cease, the better it will be for all concerned," he wrote. Lorena Hickok's letters also reiterated the arguments of those conservatives who feared the 4 million might never get off the public payroll. "I guess it's true that the more you do for people, the more they demand," she wrote Hopkins. Though Miss Hickok acknowledged the unfair newspaper publicity given to a few cases of graft, she also conceded that "It's getting a bad name. . . . It's having a bad effect on the 'state of mind' of the public." She believed this partisan influence discouraged good welfare executives and reflected poorly on the FERA too. "Honestly, if I lived down here [North Carolina] and cared about my reputation, I don't think I'd want an administrative job with CWA," she confided.[12]

While social workers were disturbed by the CWA's political

[12]P. Williams to Hopkins, February 6, 1934, JMC 73; Bonnie Fox Schwartz, "Social Workers and New Deal Politicians in Conflict: California's Branion-Williams Case, 1933–1934," *Pacific Historical Review*, XLII (February, 1973), 53–57; Hickok to Hopkins, February 14 and February 18, 1934, HLH 61.

vulnerability, their uneasiness toward federal work relief stemmed from other, more profound, concerns. At the CWA's start in November, 1933, some welfare spokesmen criticized the increased impersonalization of relief-giving. Oriented to the needs of individual clients, some could not overcome their suspicions of massive public aid, and even more of a work program with centralized national controls. Seeking a continued role for the private neighborhood agency, Pierce Atwater of the St. Paul Community Chest saw dangers in a bureaucracy far removed from local citizen participation. "We who believe strongly in independent initiative and personal responsibility for private charity have maintained that our private agencies must be kept alive," declared Edward L. Ryerson, Jr., former chairman of the Illinois Emergency Relief Commission. Alfred H. Schoellkopf, of the New York State Temporary Emergency Relief Administration and a CWA official, saw relief as a community activity to be integrated with local government, where local authorities could design projects best suited to the needs of their idle neighbors.[13]

The CWA's hiring and compensation procedures had also threatened the professional standards that relief administrators had struggled to establish since the progressive era. North Carolina officials claimed that civil works had disrupted the orderly development of the state's social welfare program. "Case records had lapsed and visiting habits suffered," they declared, while others resented "staffing their [work] projects with persons whose need of relief had not been demonstrated." Long advocates of detailed individual investigations, social workers were appalled by the CWA's hasty procedures, which rode

[13]Pierce Atwater, "Reorganizing Local Social Work Programs under Private Auspices," NCSW, *Proceedings* (Chicago: University of Chicago Press, 1934), pp. 446–455; Edward L. Ryerson, Jr., "Out of the Depression," *Survey*, LXX (January, 1934), 4; Alfred H. Schoellkopf, Harold S. Tolley, and John F. Sanderson, "The Effect of the State and Federal Programs on Local Community Organizations," *Quarterly Bulletin of the New York State Conference of Social Work*, VI (August, 1935), 30–37; James T. Patterson, *America's Struggle Against Poverty, 1900–1980* (Cambridge: Harvard University Press, 1981), p. 57.

roughshod over the means test and allowed men to go on the job without a physical examination. "If soldiers had been inducted into the service during the Great War without this precaution," declared the Conference on Governmental Objectives of Social Work, "it is easy to imagine what a free hand would have been given the compensation claims attorneys after their return."[14]

Much of this criticism stemmed from a genuine belief in the primacy of social case work. To many professionals, the CWA had swept away the procedures to investigate and advise relief clients, just when the FERA had finally established them on a nation-wide basis during the summer of 1933. As a result of civil works employment, welfare agencies had to "close" hundreds and even thousands of cases, because families no longer needed relief. Social workers deeply regretted how the CWA, by easing a family's economic burden, had cut off home visitors from further contact with their clients so that they could no longer provide guidance with other problems, like alcoholism and domestic incompatibility. And some could evaluate the civil works experiment only in terms of their own methodology. "Coming when it did and lasting as along as it did, was the [CWA] work valuable as case work treatment?" asked Marian Lindsey of the St. Louis Relief Committee. If the wages were not sufficient to allow a family economic independence or if they were higher than a family could ever reach again, she answered, then "a valuable part of the treatment was lost."[15]

Not only had case-work procedures gone by the boards, but so had much of the welfare administrators' influence over policy decisions. Although Hopkins and his close aides could accept the adverse effect of the civil works program on the role

[14]J. S. Kirk, Walter A. Cutter, and Thomas W. Morse, eds., *Emergency Relief in North Carolina* (n.p.: Edwards Broghton Company, 1936), 111; NASW, Conference on Governmental Objectives of Social Work (February 16–17, 1934), p. 9, NASW, Chicago Chapter Papers, Box 2, Chicago Historical Society.

[15]See Chapter Seven; Marian Lindsey, "Case Work Values of the C.W.A.," *The Family*, XV (February, 1935), 325.

of the welfare worker, others made no bones about how it undermined their newly established positions in the New Deal and state relief administrations. "Will the FERA continue to exercise the leadership it has shown in this field [home relief] to date despite its huge responsibility to direct the CWA program?" asked Russell H. Kurtz:

> Will there be local reaction now that jobs are supplanting doles to a continuation of adequate investigations and service to families left behind on relief? Social workers must concern themselves with these questions at the risk of having their motives questioned.

Some of Hopkins' advisors from the federated charities were so troubled by the shift in emphasis that they suggested a redefinition of professional lines of authority in all subsequent programs for the unemployed. C. M. Bookman, head of the Cincinnati Community Chest and president of the National Conference of Social Work, recommended that any appropriation administered by relief departments after the CWA must be on the basis of need. "Funds that are to be used with the thought of increasing consuming power should be administered through other agencies of the government," he declared. Bookman advised that in the future "we may be wise enough to provide two separate work programs"—public works carried out by the regular departments to employ men on an efficiency basis and work relief under a supervision of case workers primarily designed as social therapy for the client. "The whole concept of work relief should be formulated anew," echoed Pierce Williams, who also suggested that a comprehensive program of public works be carried on jointly but separately from relief. Grace Gosselin, head of white collar projects in New York City, frankly agreed in an article, "If I Were To Do It Over," that the combination of relief and employment had proved unfortunate. "Groups do not work together for an effective plan for all the unemployed because they are too busy in their concern for their own small group," she observed. "The lack of interest these groups have in one another has been a discouraging revelation." A year later, in May, 1935, Paul Benjamin, executive secretary of the Buffalo Council of Social Agencies, looked back and reaffirmed that "work and relief mix no better than do oil and water."[16]

Settlement house workers, federation organizers, and charity officials were conspicuously absent from the struggle to extend the CWA in Washington. Despite formal objections to demobilization from the American Association of Social Workers, the National Federation of Settlements, and similar organizations, these groups sent no lobbies to Capitol Hill and offered no testimony of hardships of the kind that had stirred the LaFollette-Costigan Committee only a year before to allocate funds for the FERA. At the AASW Convention, held in Washington in February, 1934, the CWA provided a major issue, with Hopkins talking for a half hour and giving rationales for the cutback. "The CWA was never anything but a temporary measure," he declared. The audience was abashed, but only followed with "inconsequential questions."[17]

The Congressional debates for additional appropriations, therefore, centered around the precise amount needed to close out the program. In early February, the Administration fashioned a bill, according to Douglas' recommendations, which asked for $950 million for relief, including about $350 million

[16]Edward C. Lindeman, "Social Workers in the Depression," *Nation*, CXXXVIII (March 7, 1934), 274–275; Hopkins, *Spending to Save* (New York: W. W. Norton, 1936), p. 114; Jacob Kepecs, "What Do Social Workers Want?" *Survey*, LXX (December, 1934), 378–380; Russell H. Kurtz, "Relief from Relief," *ibid.*, LXIX (December, 1933), 403–405; Marie Dresden Lane and Francis Steegmuller, *America on Relief* (New York: Harcourt, Brace and Company, 1938), p. 20; C. M. Bookman, "The Federal Emergency Relief Administration: Its Problems and Significance," NCSW, *Proceedings* (Chicago: University of Chicago Press, 1934), pp. 13–31; P. Williams to Hopkins, February 6, 1934, JMC 73; Grace H. Gosselin, "If I Were To Do It Over," *Better Times*, XV (March 12, 1934), 26; Paul L. Benjamin, "Unemployment and Relief," *The Family*, XVI (May, 1935), 67.

[17]*New York Times*, February 19, 1934, p. 11; National Federation of Settlements, Resolution, February 2, 1934, Lea Taylor Papers, Box 3, Chicago Historical Society; Phyllis Lowell, "Social Workers Take Counsel," *SWT*, I (March-April, 1934), 3–4.

for the CWA. In the House of Representatives, Speaker Henry
T. Rainey marshalled forces to block a move by Congressman
Kent Keller of Illinois to increase the sum to $2 billion to keep
the CWA going until 1935. While 1,000 jobless picketed the
White House, leaders on Capitol Hill invoked rigid House rules
to stifle Keller's amendment and limit debate to forty minutes.
A few urban liberals, like Emanuel Celler of Brooklyn, pleaded
for more money and quoted Mayor Fiorello H. La Guardia that
riots would break out on the sidewalks of New York. But the
Appropriations Committee chairman urged members to follow
the Administration's wishes, reminding them that "federal relief is like a rapacious maw." The House passed the bill 382
to 1, with the lone negative vote from George B. Terrell, a
seventy-one-year-old Texan, who maintained that the CWA
was unconstitutional. Liberals, governors, mayors, and the unemployed looked to the Senate as a last hope.[18]

On February 8, the Senate began to consider the appropriation bill, and a small group of liberals planned to ask for a
more substantial amount to carry the CWA to 1935. Bronson
Cutting offered an amendment, calling for $2.5 billion, which
was defeated after several hours of debate by 58 to 10. When
Robert M. La Follette, Jr., sought a $1.5 billion substitute, his
proposal won over only four more votes. Robert F. Wagner
pointed out that at least 10 million were still jobless. "Whether
he [Hopkins] wants more or not, he needs more, if we are to
take care of the unemployed," cried Wagner. "I cannot see any
other answer for it except that he indulges in an optimism I
cannot share." At this point, the White House, fearing that
the rhetoric was getting out of hand, stepped up pressure behind the Administration bill. The President sent for individual
senators, explained personally his budgetary priorities, and asked
them to go along. To ease the pain, Roosevelt mentioned that
if unemployment figures remained high on May 1, Congress

[18]The exact sum for the CWA was not precisely stated in the bill. Douglas
to FDR, January 24, 1934, FDR-OF 444B; Memo for Congress, December
28, 1933, FB 20; *Washington Post*, February 5, 1934, p. 2, and February 6,
1934, p. 2; "Professional Giver," *Time*, XXIII (February 19, 1934), 11–13.

would still be in session and could act. He further hinted that he did not intend to discontinue the CWA abruptly on that date, that relief funds "may be used in CWA fashion but not under the CWA name." On the Senate floor, spokesmen for the Administration beat back the liberals' efforts, and they cited Hopkins' own insistence that the CWA was just a temporary measure.[19]

On February 15, 1934, the fiscal conservatives had their way, when President Roosevelt signed the Appropriation Act, granting $950 million for federal relief and modifying those civil works policies which Congress found most objectionable. Resenting CWA federal projects as a usurpation of its power to stipulate exact expenditures in the Executive Branch, Congress authorized funds only to complete improvements on federal lands or public property, but not on other jobs conducted by federal agencies. The appropriation also drastically scaled down the compensation benefits enjoyed by civil works employees. It amended the Federal Employment Compensation Act of 1916 as applied to CWA workers to provide only for disability or death resulting from injury while on the job, a stipulation the conservatives demanded to prevent spurious claims. Congress also considerably reduced the schedule of payments compared to those provided to regular federal employees. The total could not exceed $3,500, with a monthly maximum of $25, both exclusive of medical costs.[20]

By Executive Order, the same day, President Roosevelt al-

[19]William Hand, "Congress Turns to Civil Works," *Today*, I (February 17, 1934), 6; A. Williams to Edith Foster, February 7, 1934, CWA 1; *Washington Post*, February 7, 1934, p. 1, February 8, 1934, pp. 1, 9, and February 9, 1934, p. 1; telegram, La Guardia to Wagner, January 19, 1934, and Wagner to La Guardia, January 19, 1934, RFW-H2; T.R.B., "Washington Notes," *New Republic*, LXXVIII (February 21, 1934), 46–47.

[20]*New York Times*, February 11, 1934, p. 16; E. Glenn Callan, "Some Workmen's Compensation Problems of Persons on Work Relief," *SSR*, VIII (June, 1934), 222–224; Joanna C. Colcord and Russell H. Kurtz, "Unemployment and Community Action," *Survey*, LXX (March, 1934), 90; Doris Carothers, *Chronology of the FERA* (Washington: United States Government Printing Office, 1937), pp. 43–44.

located $450 million of this appropriation to close out the CWA. Within this budgetary limit, Hopkins and his staff had to outline procedures for an orderly demobilization of their army of 4 million. Although Hopkins had intended the CWA to go on until May 1, his financial advisors quickly realized that the allocation could hardly last beyond the end of March. Facing a deadline once again, Hopkins, his aides, and field men would have to draft orders to dismantle the organization they had worked so hard to create.[21]

III

Demobilization of the CWA also reflected the tension between engineers, accountants, and management experts who had come to run the program and social welfare administrators who would eventually prevail. Technicians insisted on an orderly close-out of projects based on engineering criteria, effective use of remaining tools, and responsible disposition of records. Hopkins' call to cut employees from the payroll, however, brought back the case workers as the most qualified to determine those who could least afford to be laid off. Facing a new deadline, both groups had to compromise. Social workers could not possibly carry out detailed investigations of 4 million people, and engineers could not expect to complete all projects efficiently. Priorities and performances, as usual, varied at the state and local levels. But orders from Washington forced an undeniable return to traditional work relief policies, which Hopkins and Aubrey Williams thought their CWA had left behind.

Official demobilization began on February 15, 1934, with the President's Executive Order, immediately followed by Hopkins' instructions to the states. To keep expenditures within the allotment, the CWA adopted, first of all, a new wage pol-

[21]United States President, Executive Order, "Allocation of Funds to the Federal Civil Works Administration," February 15, 1934, FDR-OF 444B; Hopkins to Douglas, February 16, 1934, CWA 53.

icy. No longer financed by PWA money, the CWA was no longer subject to its hourly minimums. Effective not later than March 2, civil works wages above the national minimum of $.30 an hour would conform to the prevailing rates in each community. A wage board consisting of one representative from labor, business, and the CWA would determine scales for each county. Hours remained shortened at twenty-four per week in urban areas and fifteen in rural districts. But, Hopkins and his staff also acquiesced to proposals to "stagger" workers, particularly in the Southeast where eight states were permitted to cut the time of their present force in half rather than fire half the workers. Hopkins had initially opposed this rotation of crews, siding with aides who argued that the gradual curtailment of hours tended to break down morale more than an immediate separation from the payroll. But others countered by noting that unemployed Southern whites might riot against black CWA jobholders; and the staff, in general, rationalized that, even with less pay, workers would still fare better in that region, where men had often toiled for ten hours a day and brought home a dollar.[22]

Hopkins not only surrendered to the regional prejudices of many CWA critics in the South, but also began to revert back to relief practices rather than maintain standards for efficient public works. On February 16, he directed state administrators to drop employees according to "relative need," first those having another family member at work and then workers with other financial assets. Although Hopkins ordered that women receive equal consideration with men, he failed to set a female quota, as some state women's work directors had requested, leaving the door open to a wholesale scrapping of many women's projects. Demobilization would start in communities with

[22]Plan of Demobilization, February 18, 1934, FDR-OF 444; telegram, Hopkins to Biddle, March 7, 1934, FERA 248; testimony of Harry Hopkins, House of Representatives, Hearings, Federal Emergency Relief and Civil Works Programs, p. 56; CWA Minutes, December 6, 1933, HLH 45; telephone call, A. Williams and O'Berry, January 12, 1934, CWA 33.

seasonal opportunities for rehiring and those least affected by industrial shut-downs.[23]

These general orders pointed to the return to work relief as it had existed before CWA. The drastic scaling down of compensation benefits in the Appropriation Act and subsequent modification of the wage scales reduced all payments close to subsistence levels. Hopkins admitted to the National Association of Social Workers that the introduction of "relative need" and requiring the means test for any future job would reactivate a considerable investigative service. Although he did not expect thorough case work for 4 million people in the brief time that remained, officials in many counties began to dig out records from the early FERA days.[24]

Hopkins' staff divided over the exact method to implement cutbacks as applied to individuals. Aubrey Williams, an outspoken critic of the means test, argued that the United States Employment Service should requisition competent personnel from relief agencies to check files and clear them against case folders. He adamantly opposed, however, the revival of any elaborate investigations. Others considered the use of a questionnaire or health service records. At any rate, the employment policies promulgated by the CWA and implemented through the USES would no longer be taken into consideration. Hopkins and his aides acknowledged that any future relief program would rely on the FERA Social Service Division to check individual needs, but they never set down in CWA *Rules and Regulations* standard procedures and criteria to fire a worker. They left the ultimate decision to the discretion of state and local administrators who had to implement the cuts.[25]

[23]Hopkins to all civil works administrators, February 16, 1934, CWA 53; Baker to all civil works administrators and state emergency relief administrators, March 6, 1934, JB 1.

[24]Harry Hopkins, "Current Relief Problems," Proceedings of Conference on Governmental Objectives for Social Work (February 26, 1934), p. 122, National Association of Social Workers Papers, Box 18, SWHA.

[25]Memo Covering Proceedings of Federal Civil Works Conference for Regional Engineers and Field Men, February 20, 1934, JMC 73; A. Williams to I. Bagun, March 13, 1934, CWA 32; Notes on Conference called by Howard

Just as the CWA meted out job allotments in November, Hopkins now instructed each state to dismiss a given number by February 23. The first mass discharge of some 600,000 workers lowered the national payroll to 3,407,212 employees. Beginning March 1, further reductions would come at the rate of ten percent per week. While the hiring quotas in November and December were based on a ratio of the number of relief cases and the general population, cutbacks depended on seasonal work opportunities and rural-urban densities as perceived by the Washington staff. That last week in February, New York State dropped only 25,000, Pennsylvania fired just 15,000, and California released 20,000. Regardless of their size and unemployment figures, most Southern states had to lop off 20,000 each, about twenty-five percent. The eventual closing of the CWA in North Carolina was equivalent to the dismissal of the entire employed labor force in all the state's large cities, observed the USES state director.[26]

Massive reductions in the South, rationalized by FDR's assumption that "nobody is going to starve during the warm weather" and that spring planting would absorb layoffs, actually plunged thousands back into dire need. All across the region, record-breaking cold in February delayed the opening of farm jobs. The mayor of Winston-Salem, North Carolina, pleaded for a postponement of CWA cutbacks, while another Tarheel official declared, "Washington authorities [are] under the false impression it is balmy and warm." Federal officials also overlooked the inability of depressed family farms to hire additional labor. Far worse, they had underestimated the impact of Agricultural Adjustment Administration commodity schedules. New cotton quotas went into effect on January 1, slashing 580,000 acres in North Carolina alone. "Because of reduced acreage in tobacco, farms cannot absorb vast numbers

Hunter of Relief and Civil Works Administrators, February 23, 1934, HH 92.

[26]*New York Times*, February 18, 1934, p. 15; telegram, Hopkins to Biddle, February 17, 1934, FERA 248; telegram, Hopkins to O'Berry, February 20, 1934, NCERA 78.

of unemployed," wired the Wilson, North Carolina, Chamber of Commerce to President Roosevelt; "East North Carolina major tobacco markets closed now and thousands formerly employed in redry and auction work out of work because of AAA cutback."[27]

In Southern market towns and large cities, early CWA dismissals wreaked great havoc. Factory hands and miners, who had gone on relief rolls, were not farm laborers. The Louisiana Council of Social Agencies confirmed that the approaching farm season would have little effect on CWA employees, since few agricultural workers had registered for such jobs. "They are industrial laborers and should be given work on various projects," declared Southern regional engineer Joseph Hyde Pratt. Senator J. H. Bankhead of Alabama called attention to Walker County, "the second largest coal mining county in Alabama, dotted all over with closed coal mines and the mines that are running on short time." Many local officials asked Washington to reclassify their small communities as "urban" to make their cutbacks less severe. Asheville, North Carolina, a tourist and health resort, saw no way of taking up the 2,479 currently on CWA projects and another 7,000 applicants waiting for jobs. The mayors of Montgomery and Mobile, Alabama, stressed the impossibility of providing alternative work for skilled craftsmen, and the chairman of the Orleans Parish CWA Advisory Committee reported that maritime activity had fallen to the lowest ebb and no private construction of any kind existed; and he asked Hopkins to reconsider his "untimely drastic cut."[28]

[27]Seligman and Cornwell, *New Deal Mosaic*, p. 76; Mayor of Winston-Salem to FDR, February 27, 1934, CWA 34; Thad Page to Bailey, no date, JWB; *Charlotte Observer*, December 17, 1933, and January 1, 1934; Wilson, North Carolina, Chamber of Commerce to FDR, February 22, 1934, JWB.

[28]"Observations on Business, Industry, and Agriculture, and Expected Trends in Public and Private Employment in the State of North Carolina," no date, NCERA 79; Louisiana Council of Social Agencies to Hopkins, February 28, 1934, CWA 19; Senator J. H. Bankhead to Hopkins, February 21, 1934, CWA 2; Mayor of Asheville to Bailey, January 13, 1934, JWB; Mayor of Montgomery to Hopkins, February 20, 1934, CWA 1; telegram, Mayor of Mobile to Hopkins, February 22, 1934, CWA 2; S. Williams to Hopkins, February 27, 1934, CWA 19.

Rural demobilization also stirred reactions from county civil works administrators outside the South. Farming communities in southern California protested against Washington's early discharge of CWA employees. The Lake County CWA office appealed to Senator William G. McAdoo to have Hopkins restore the thirty-hour week. "We have over five hundred needy people for whom we cannot provide work," wired the local administrator. "The present fifteen-hour week is not accomplishing practical or equitable relief. We feel that small communities such as ours should not be discriminated against." The CWA director of Huntingdon County, Pennsylvania, also questioned the shortened work week. "It is more profitable, economical, and easier for a man to go on relief than to get a CWA job where he only gets fifteen hours at $.35," he stated. "Personally I cannot see where the government is going to get ahead."[29]

Cutbacks also generated appeals and protests from the workers, as CWA and relief officials tried to implement their quotas. Pennsylvanians from Mercer and Sandy Lake asked their congressmen to explain "this discrimination" between rural and urban districts. In Allentown, Lancaster, and Reading, workers "struck" against reduced hours. The New York City public welfare commissioner's announcement of a return "to a relief wage instead of a working wage" only for "the destitute" and his resort to the "needs" questionnaire brought defiance from white collar employees, who refused to fill out the detailed four-page form. Reduced time and layoffs caused marches, picketing, and strikes among skilled and manual laborers in Albion, Buffalo, Geneva, Rochester, Schenectady, Syracuse, and Utica. In one week over 50,000 letters and 7,000 telegrams poured into Washington. A laid-off black man, Willie Brown of Abbeville, Georgia, cut from a $.50 a day job on March 10 begged for work to support his wife and two children. "I need work and I need aid," he pleaded to Harry Hopkins. "Your

[29]William Neblett to McAdoo, February 17, 1934, CWA 6; telegram, Lake County CWA to McAdoo, February 3, 1934, CWA 5; telegram, Huntingdon County CWA to Hopkins, January 22, 1934, CWA 40.

honor I do prey you want threw this in the wast basket [sic] . . . please your honor some kind of aid a job any where any kind of work."[30]

While the workers demonstrated, engineers and other technicians lobbied with Washington officials to save the worthy projects. The Salisbury, North Carolina, city manager appealed to Congressman Robert L. Doughton, "We have over one and a half miles of sewer ditches dug which are rapidly caving in and unless something is done in the near future the enormous amount of work already done will be wasted." Southern regional engineer Pratt called attention to Dare County, on the North Carolina coast, where renovation of hurricane-damaged bridges over inlets, the Hatteras ferry piers, and roads had come to a halt since Washington reduced weekly hours and the work force. "We have a large number of projects in various stages of progress and on many of them ditches and trenches have been opened and work partially completed," wrote the Pittsburgh director of public works. "The suspension of work now may result not only in loss due to trenches caving in, but also a very serious hazard to the public." California civil works administrator Captain Edward Macauley predicted that under the present allotment, some airports would remain unfinished, which "would constitute a menace to aviation and cause unwarranted criticism."[31]

Technical experts emphasized the need to hold on to workers whose skill was essential to bring projects to an orderly conclusion. Colonel Pratt and the Eastern regional engineer, Thomas Hibben, insisted on retaining key men, whether or not they

[30]W. J. Gilmore to Congressman T. C. Cochran, January 29, 1934, and Mandel to A. Williams, March 10, 1934, CWA 40; Pennsylvania CWA, *Final Report*, p. 64; Alfred H. Schoellkopf to Hopkins, February 26, 1934, CWA 32; *New York Herald Tribune*, March 13, 1934, p. 4; E. E. Rice to Nathan Straus, Jr., March 13, 1934, and Nathan Straus, Jr., to Walker, April 23, 1934, NEC 428; Willie Brown to Hopkins, March 12, 1934, CWA 10.

[31]H. C. Holmes to Doughton, May 22, 1934, and Pratt to Carmody, March 15, 1934, CWA 34; Pittsburgh director of public works to Hopkins, April 28, 1934, CWA 40; Macauley to Hopkins, March 10, 1934, CWA 3.

could prove need. Colonel Pratt ordered that his supervisors, foremen, skilled craftsmen, and particularly equipment operators, be kept on. "Such positions cannot be filled by men who are on relief rolls," he wrote bluntly. These demands for efficiency won support from the building trades, who wired Hopkins that only skilled craftsmen could finish many jobs. "We cannot locate in the skilled trades sufficient relief clients in many localities," declared an Illinois employment officer. "In many instances the failure to go ahead, for example, with bricklayers on a schoolhouse keeps many other classes of labor, in which relief clients are available, out of employment."[32]

The engineering staff used such evidence to modify demobilization according to need. Technical experts frankly concluded that projects should be completed regardless of the financial status of individuals employed on them, a policy, they added, which would make the most rational use of remaining materials. "This business of bringing these projects to a conclusion is an engineering job that must ultimately . . . be made through the cooperation of local communities, our field representatives, and this office," emphasized chief engineer Carmody. "Unless a thorough analysis is made during the next few weeks with a view to making final and intelligent disposition of the CWA program it may leave a bad taste all around." Regional and state engineers carried this attitude to the counties. Southeastern field engineer Pratt recommended that technical staffs remain for approximately five more weeks (until May) so that administrators could fill out the appropriate forms for each project, particularly S-16, which required details for completion, transfer, or discontinuation. Captain Macauley brought in additional experts to help close out the California programs "with a degree of business-like dispatch." He particularly relied on retired naval engineer Captain Powers Symington, who "straightened everything out in Alameda County

[32]Pratt to O'Berry, March 29, 1934, NCERA 79; Thomas Hibben to Carmody, April 20, 1934, CWA 79; telegram, Building Trades Council, Will County, Illinois, to Hopkins, March 26, 1934, CWA 14; Edward Blair to Hopkins, March 13, 1934, CWA 12.

and produced a condition of order and efficiency from what had been before more or less confusion."[33]

In states with substantial engineering control, public works priorities figured heavily in demobilization. The Illinois CWA chief engineer, in anticipation of successive cutbacks on February 16, ordered counties to conduct a project survey under a joint committee of the local civil works administrator, the re-employment officer, and the district engineer. In Cook County, which took in over half the state payroll, the group analyzed and classified existing projects on technical criteria and disbanded first those that were poorly planned and supervised or that wasted expenditures for material. Project engineers surveyed remaining supplies and sent inventories to the chief, who used the data to set up material depots in central locations in charge of a tool supervisor. While the Cook County USES and Emergency Relief Committee forwarded information on the finances, dependents, and other data on CWA employees, project engineers had the ultimate discretion to retain the neediest workers or those with special skills essential to complete projects. Downstate offices, in contrast, generally reduced the number of workers according to need. Out of 33 local CWA's in Illinois outside of Cook County, 16 relied on this method, while 10 reported a combination of need and project evaluation.[34]

In North Carolina, efficiency criteria also prevailed, largely because of Colonel Pratt's continued prodding. To assure the completion of selected worthy projects, civil works administrator Mrs. Anna O'Berry held a series of conferences with dis-

[33]Carmody to Baker, May 15, 1934, and Hackett to Fellows, February 23, 1934, CWA 92; Fellows to O'Berry, March 1, 1934, CWA 34; Meeting, Regional Engineers and Staff, February 21, 1934, JMC 74; "CWA Reductions Keep Expenditures within Budget," ENR, CXII (January 25, 1934), 124; Pratt to O'Berry, March 29, 1934, NCERA 79; Macauley to Hopkins, May 10, 1934, CWA 3.

[34]Illinois CWA, Press Release, February 18, 1934, VAO 74; Illinois CWA, Final Report, pp. 178–182, 185.

trict engineers to reapportion man-hours. Officials transferred workers from those sites which they judged could be abandoned without waste—like privies, roads, and drains—to jobs of a "permanent nature that would be practically useless unless completed."[35]

In the end, despite Washington's intent to demobilize the CWA on a relief basis, workers' protests and local conditions at project sites kept much of the dismantling operation in the hands of the technical cadre. "Until the last bill is paid, it will be necessary to maintain in each civil works administration an acting administrator, . . . and a sufficient accounting force to keep the accounts and finally close them," wrote Hopkins. "Until the last project record and completion report is submitted, it will be necessary to maintain sufficient engineering staff to make these reports." Often the staff dwindled down to a few disbursing officers and one engineer to "close the books" on the CWA.[36]

*   *   *

The CWA had gotten the country through the winter only to become a victim of the success of its administrators. Engineers and management experts had launched the program with a special dynamism, as they applied techniques from large corporations and municipal and state reform administrations on a nationwide basis. They put over 4 million Americans to work on public projects within a few weeks and at the same time implemented policies in hiring, wages, workmen's compensation, and safety commensurate with the most progressive in private industry. Regarded as nonpartisans or Republican holdovers from

[35]Pratt to O'Berry, March 29, 1934, NCERA 79; *Raleigh News and Observer*, March 2, 1934; J. G. Steed to Walker, May 26, 1934, NEC 429.

[36]Hopkins to state emergency relief administrations and civil works administrations, March 22, 1934, JB 1; Gill to Thomas B. Rhodes, March 23, 1934, CWA 73.

an old regime, estranged from social workers, and aloof from ethnic leaders in the big cities, the managers of the CWA ultimately lost out in the politics of balanced budgets and social welfare legislation that would characterize the New Deal in the years ahead.

CHAPTER NINE

Reconversion to Work Relief: the FERA Work Division and the WPA

On February 28, 1934, the White House issued a press release, announcing a new three-point program under which the Federal Emergency Relief Administration would replace the scrapped CWA. Throughout the winter, FERA grants-in-aid had continued to support direct relief as well as supplementary programs for transients and self-help cooperatives through state and local emergency relief offices. Now, the FERA would take up the great burden, according to an ambitious blueprint. First, rural relief, coordinated with the Department of Agriculture, would provide subsistence homesteads. Second, "stranded populations" in communities dependent upon a single industry, such as miners in the worn-out Appalachian fields, would be transplanted to areas that offered jobs or self-support through farming. The third provision, in response to Senate liberals and the great mass of unemployed in the cities, was the announcement of a new work program.[1]

In truth, the new jobs component was really a return to the FERA Work Division, which had existed prior to the CWA. While the demobilization of civil works proceeded, a few alumni, like Jacob Baker (who headed the Division) tried to maintain much of the technical priorities in administration, project execution, and labor policies. But as control over the program reverted to the states and localities and as social workers took charge of FERA-WD offices, they reintroduced case-

---

[1] Doris Carothers, *Chronology of the FERA* (Washington: United States Government Printing Office, 1937), pp. 46–47; "The President's New Relief Policy," *Survey*, LXX (March, 1934), 72; Aubrey Williams, "The New Relief Program: Three Great Aims," *New York Times*, April 1, 1934, Sec. IX, p. 1.

work investigations and payments based on family budgets, which would eventually restore CWA jobholders to the status of relief recipients.

The plans of early 1934 would prove no more than an unacceptable makeshift amid the clamor of the unemployed and urban liberals for the dignity of real work. Within less than a year, during the Second Hundred Days of 1935, President Roosevelt would be forced to end the FERA and replace it with a more durable social welfare provision. He created Social Security for chronic dependents (widows, orphans, and unemployables) and the widely acclaimed Works Progress Administration for the able-bodied, temporarily out of work. But the WPA would more closely resemble the Work Division than civil works. Despite creative projects in art, music, theater, and writing, employees were selected on the basis of need and paid "security wages" according to means. Roosevelt had quit the "business" of emergency employment, but the federal government would still dispense relief and work relief.

I

While skeleton crews dismantled the CWA, the new "Emergency Work Program" had already begun, designed to occupy 2 million unemployed in urban-industrial communities and still satisfy balanced-budget advocates, business conservatives, and orthodox social workers. It represented a compromise between federal financing and local control. Although FERA monthly grants-in-aid would provide funds and its Work Division would review projects, the program would nevertheless be a state-run operation, carried out by state emergency relief administrations. SERA work divisions would have the total responsibility to plan, organize, and conduct projects by use of the force account. States would have the option to provide accident compensation and safety engineering or to dismiss these CWA features entirely. The White House carefully stipulated that the Work Program would "provide employment only for persons in need of relief," and need would remain the pervasive criterion. The initial ranks would come from those (in theory, among the most distressed) still on the CWA as of March 31, with additional "employees" selected according to FERA case-work procedures. Only one person per family would receive an assignment, which would continue only with periodic proof of destitution through the means test. Hours of work would be limited to twenty-four at the prevailing rate for the locality, with a minimum of $.30. Maximum weekly earnings could not exceed the amount necessary to meet family budgetary requirements, also determined by a local case worker. The program would be as creative or spartan as local opinion would tolerate.[2]

With state emergency relief administrations in control, the FERA Work Division in Washington served, at best, as a "clearing house" and coordinator. Jacob Baker, Perry Fellows, and others from the civil works engineering staff, however, tried to exert some degree of technical influence, while they still possessed the CWA letterhead. Throughout March, they issued a flurry of orders and advance bulletins to maintain civil works engineering guidelines during the transition to the FERA-WD. They channeled whatever remained of the engineering department into a "Civil Works Division of the Relief Administration," with Baker in charge, along with two assistants, also from the CWA. Perry Fellows, former aide to Carmody, became chief administrative officer and directed a planning and advisory staff of respected professionals from engineering, architecture, and construction. Thomas Hibben, former CWA field man, took a desk in Washington as head of regional engineers for the Work Division.[3]

Amid civil works cutbacks, with each state breaking loose

[2]Baker to all civil works administrators and state emergency relief administrators, March 6, 1934, and Baker to all state emergency relief administrators, March 15, 1934, JB 1; Edward Ainsworth Williams, *Federal Aid for Relief* (New York: Columbia University Press, 1939), pp. 124–125.

[3]Jacob Baker, "The Range of Work Relief," *Public Works Engineers Year Book, 1935* (Chicago: Joint Secretariat, American Society of Municipal Engineers and International Association of Public Works Officials, 1935), p. 63; "Work Relief and the Work Division," *Project*, I (January, 1935), 12–14; Baker to Fellows, February 20, 1934, and memo, Baker to all state emergency relief administrators, March 8, 1934, JB 1.

from CWA federal controls, Baker and his assistants tried to maintain "as high a standard of engineering procedure, inspection, . . . as possible." To organize state work divisions within the emergency relief administrations, on March 3, Baker notified all FERA directors and civil works officials to combine their staffs and carry forward all desirable CWA projects still in operation. On March 20, while the CWA still had over 2 million on the federal payroll, Baker issued WD-3, for the planning and coordination of possible Work Division projects. Though Baker acknowledged the states' ultimate authority to approve plans and control operations, he believed his office could "suggest the general policies governing the development of the work program upon which Federal funds are used." He emphasized the need for "efficient planning" and outlined six project areas with a tentative percentage distribution of labor: planning (as a guide for the approval of projects), three percent; public property, resources, and utilities, thirty percent; housing, fifteen percent; production and distribution of goods needed by the unemployed (self-help associations), fifteen percent; public welfare, health, and recreation, seven percent; public education, arts, and research, 10 percent; and twenty percent optional. For each state and the larger cities, Baker recommended that an engineer, with experience in civic or industrial planning, study existing master plans and recommend new proposals consistent with ongoing community development.[4]

Baker's office also put out a volume of "Working Procedures," based on memos used informally to improve CWA project execution. On March 21, he requested each state to outline its operations for one project from each of the six areas and turned to professional associations to generate ideas for white collar jobs. Aides sorted the returns and formulated "standard practice sheets," which Baker intended to distribute

---

[4]Baker to all civil works administrators and state emergency relief administrators, March 3, 1934, JB 1; Baker to all state emergency relief administrators, March 20, 1934, and "Outline for Suggested Projects for Work Divisions," March 20, 1934, CWA 53; "Types of Work for New Urban Works Program Outlined," *ENR*, CXII (March 29, 1934), 424.

on a regular basis so that local work divisions could "build up a manual of standard procedures." This barrage of directives was climaxed by the *Project*, a magazine of civil works ideas, which Baker expected would improve communication between Washington and local offices.[5]

Baker also resorted to outside conferences to stimulate better projects. On March 23, Harry Hopkins called a meeting in Washington to discuss demolition as a possible activity for the fifteen percent of the WD assigned to housing. Builders, wreckers, and city officials heard Baker deliver the keynote address. He described a civil works venture in Chicago, where the Cook County CWA used its Real Property Inventory to locate vacant buildings and enlisted the help of the Metropolitan Housing Council and property owners to authorize large-scale clearance. Although these projects had hardly begun before the CWA tapered off, Baker intended to apply this experience toward WD housing and community improvement, beginning with the systematic demolition of derelict structures. He charged the audience to gather interested civic groups to initiate plans, and he asked a few to summarize rules and regulations for a typical slum clearance project.[6]

To a remarkable degree, the material accomplishments of state and local work divisions resulted from the inheritance of the CWA engineering tradition and Baker's efforts to maintain its integrity. A significant number of CWA projects, incomplete on April 1, were transferred to the WD. They tended to be well planned, sophisticated, and stamped by the imaginative spirit of the CWA. In Charleston, South Carolina, the ERA continued work on a modern incinerator to replace an unsightly garbage dump. A Florida community center, the largest

[5]Baker to all state emergency relief administrators, March 21, 1934, JB 1; "Working Procedures," *Project*, I (January, 1935), 47.

[6]Jacob Baker, "Opening Statement on Demolition," March 23, 1934, CWA 56; "Demolition as Work Relief Project Discussed at Washington Meeting," *ENR*, CXII (March 29, 1934), 424–426; John H. Millar, "How To Start Demolition of Bad Housing," *Public Management*, XVI (February, 1934), 39–41; "Slum Clearance in Chicago," *ENR*, CXII (March 29, 1934), 415.

of its kind built of coquina, would be completed during the summer. Just outside Phoenix, Arizona, an up-to-date tuberculosis hospital for 150 patients was erected, and the Pennsylvania WD carried on the Pittsburgh Cathedral of Learning and the construction of a differential analyzer at the University of Pennsylvania. FERA relief labor completed one of the most modern airport administrative centers begun by the CWA in Newark, New Jersey. Where state directors consented, white collar and professional civil works went on, such as aerial mapping, and even federal projects like the Coast and Geodetic Survey.[7]

In fifteen months following the CWA, the work divisions undertook a variety of projects on their own initiative. Relief workers made or completely reconstructed 44,000 miles of road and repaired over 200,000 more, built nearly 7,000 bridges and more than 10,000 large culverts, dug 2,700 miles of sanitary and storm sewers, piled more than 9,000 miles of river embankments, laid over 1,000 miles of new water mains, and erected 400 pumping stations. The nation could thank the WD for 2,000 children's playgrounds, 800 restored parks, 350 new swimming pools, and 4,000 athletic fields.[8]

These achievements came despite the implementation of traditional social work policies for those "employed" on WD projects. On April 1, the most conservative and bitterly resented feature of the new program—the means test—began with the wholesale reassignment of CWA workers. Most were among the neediest, but a large fraction included technicians and professionals, along with nonrelief cases that had somehow escaped previous investigation. Now, with the White House determined to furnish jobs only to those on relief rolls, the FERA Social Service Division insisted on a "definite distinction re-

[7]Jacob Baker, "Construction in Relief Service," *ENR*, CXIV (February 7, 1935), 255; Hibben to E. M. Shinkle, April 30, 1934, CWA 53; "Continuing of U.S. Mapping Urged by Engineering Council," *ENR*, CXII (March 29, 1934), 424–425; Pratt to O'Berry, March 29, 1934, NCERA 79.

[8]Harry L. Hopkins, *Spending To Save* (New York: W. W. Norton and Company, 1936), pp. 164–165.

garding the economic status of the people employed." State and local relief officials carried out this policy in varied ways, "all of them bad," remarked Gertrude Springer in the *Survey*, "because there was no good way to do it." Some dropped all those on civil works not previously on relief, with orders to reapply and wait for a home visit. Pennsylvania's Allegheny County CWA laid off 23,000 on March 29; and by April 1, social workers on the relief bureau had certified the needs of about 9,000. "The intake waiting rooms in New Orleans were jammed the day I was there—as they are in most places these days," wrote Lorena Hickok. "In any town on this trip I can find the relief office without any trouble at all, by the crowd hanging outside." She noted that the case load on March 31 was 8,708, but by April 9 it had jumped to over 10,000 and was still climbing. A few local offices were reported to have made clients account for their expenditure of CWA earnings and declared them ineligible if they had spent the money "injudiciously." Some rural counties even resorted to a pauper's oath![9]

The impatience of masses of unemployed, along with the need for special skills to carry on projects, however, forced many relief officials to compromise on the rigidities of professional case work. In Minneapolis, 6,000 former CWA jobholders stormed City Hall on April 6 and demanded reinstatement on an "employment basis," to be signed on according to skill and training, regardless of need. The city council, without authorization from the Minnesota Emergency Relief Administration, finally agreed to put thousands back to work on the FERA. The shift of about one quarter of a million to the New York State WD during the first week in April could not have been accomplished without foregoing strict application of the means test. Similar case loads also forced the Philadelphia office to suspend rigid investigations. Following a week's shutdown, the local work division recalled about 22,000 former CWA em-

[9]Williams, *Federal Aid*, pp. 124–125; Mandel to A. Williams, April 9, 1934, HLH 54; Gertrude Springer, "X Equals?" *Survey*, XXIII (May, 1934), 249; Hickok to Hopkins, April 13, 1934, HLH 61.

ployees and put them on a twenty-four-hour week at the prevailing rates. "The present program is practically a continuation of the CWA," remarked Arch Mandel, after a field trip on April 6. During these first hectic weeks, thousands who had not proved their need wound up on the new program. In addition, project requirements dictated exceptions for hundreds more not in dire straits. The WD employed a limited number whose training made them essential to the successful prosecution of projects. And, within the quota for "non-relief" personnel, which could not exceed five percent, professional organizations and unions continued to refer eligible technical and skilled workers.[10]

Though thousands slipped into the WD on an "employment basis," local officials nevertheless bore down on the wage policies, which marked a significant return to old work relief remunerations. Payments were still in cash, and the use of prevailing hourly rates during CWA demobilization continued, but weekly allowances were now severely limited to family budgetary needs as computed by a case worker. In North Carolina, for example, the social service division set weekly hours for each client. Those with large families received more work time than those with few or no dependents, who generally found their schedules limited to a few days or alternate weeks per month. Each locality in every state determined its own rates through a wage board set up by the county relief administration, with representatives from labor, business, and the ERA. While no rate could fall under $.30 per hour, the maximum of twenty-four hours per week brought average earnings to about

[10]Josephine C. Brown, *Public Relief, 1929–1939* (New York: Henry Holt and Company, 1940), pp. 235–236; Carmody to Baker, March 15, 1934, CWA 92; "In the Case of Minneapolis," *New Republic*, LXXVIII (April 18, 1934), 254; Joanna C. Colcord and Russell H. Kurtz, "Unemployment and Community Action," *Survey*, LXX (May, 1934), 169; Nathan Straus, Jr., to Walker, April 23, 1934, NEC 248; David M. Schneider and Albert Deutsch, *The History of Public Welfare in New York State, 1867–1940* (Chicago: University of Chicago Press, 1941), pp. 323–324; *Philadelphia Public Ledger*, April 3, 1934, p. 1; Mandel to A. Williams, April 9, 1934, HLH 54.

$28 a month (as compared with $60 on the CWA). Although the FERA guaranteed at least fifty hours per month, it forbade continuous year-round employment and set a maximum of six months a year, which further reduced annual earnings to between $97 and $187. Even these subsistence levels aroused opposition, until the $.30 minimum was scratched on November 19, 1934, leaving localities free to set their own "prevailing" rates. Progressive social workers, like Aubrey Williams, bitterly denounced this "retreat on work relief caused by a growing conservatism."[11]

Besides imposing drastic wage reductions, the WD also ended federal compensation for injury on the job. No longer classified as federal employees, relief workers on WD projects again became wards of the states, which now had the responsibility to provide accident insurance. Though most governors and legislatures did not recognize WD laborers as public employees, they did offer some assistance in the wake of the CWA precedent. The New York TERA and the state comptroller set up a "disability fund" from appropriations for work relief wages, which carried those temporarily incapacitated on full budgetary relief and medical care, but sharply limited death benefits and permanent disability allowances. Rather than provide insurance, Illinois put up "safety-first" posters on project sites and placed its injured on direct relief. A Workmen's Protection Department coordinated preventive measures, investigated accidents, and handled suits against the IERC. Several states preferred such a special agency within the relief office, while legislatures drew up separate benefit laws to avoid confusion with regular public employees, whom they considered legitimate recipients. This segregation also dampened the fear that

[11]Hopkins to all state emergency relief administrators, March 6, 1934, CWA 73; J. S. Kirk, Walter A. Cutter, and Thomas W. Morse, eds., *Emergency Relief in North Carolina* (n.p.: Edwards Broghton Company, 1936), pp. 158–159; Viola Wyckoff, *The Public Works Wage Rate* (New York: Columbia University Press, 1946), pp. 93–94; Joanna C. Colcord and Russell H. Kurtz, "Unemployment and Community Action," *Survey*, LXX (December, 1934), 391–392.

compensation for relief labor might depress standards for those injured in private industry.[12]

Shortcomings in the states' liability coverage put more emphasis on the maintenance of safety programs, but in the hands of state and local relief administrators they became a mere remnant of the CWA achievement. Hopkins created a safety division in the FERA under W. O. Wheary, a former civil works safety field man. But without the CWA's power to issue federal orders, Wheary could inform only through advisory bulletins. A few state officials and work division engineers, however, took up where the CWA left off. New York's TERA followed civil works regulations and suggested that local units have an inspector check hazards and provide first aid on each project. The TERA took pride in its safety organization's ability to reduce liability suits and increase funds to aid the unemployed. But many other states placed a low priority on industrial safety engineering. Although the Worker Protection Department of the IERC, for example, encouraged safety, it gave more emphasis to restrictive physical examinations. Compared to the CWA's vigorous centralized campaign under engineers, state ERAs reverted to the social work concern for first aid and individual medical checkups.[13]

The transformation of safety, compensation, wages, and hiring policies from CWA public employment back to the traditional orientation of the FERA was accompanied by the reemergence of social workers over technicians. In May, 1934, the FERA regrouped the states into ten relief districts, each handled by a field representative with a social welfare background. Although many had managerial experience, they came

[12]William H. Aicher, "Workmen's Compensation on Work Relief Programs," FERA, *Monthly Report* (July, 1935), pp. 6–10; "Workmen's Compensation," *Survey*, LXX (July, 1934), 224; Alexander Leopold Radomski, *Work Relief in New York State, 1931–1935* (New York: King's Crown Press, 1947), pp. 211–212.

[13]"Safety," *Project*, I (October, 1934), 23; "Safety Conditions under FERA," *Safety Engineering*, LXVIII (September, 1934), 102; R. L. Morrow, "Low Accident Costs Conserve Work Relief Funds," *National Safety News*, XXXI (May, 1935), 17–19, 60; Margaret Cochran Bristol, "Changes in Work Relief in Chicago," *SSR*, IX (June, 1935), 243–255.

largely out of the private charities, with their historic commitment to local responsibility and case work. They included Pierce Atwater, executive secretary of the St. Paul Community Chest; Arch Mandel, executive director of the Dayton Community Chest and Council of Social Agencies; Travers Edmonds, formerly with the Red Cross; and Alan Johnstone, who headed the Baltimore Community Fund and directed the South Carolina Relief Administration, 1932–1933. Each district office had a case worker, engineer, financial examiner, and, where applicable, a rural rehabilitation expert. Although field engineers maintained contact with their technical superior in the Work Division in Washington, they were still accountable, in the first instance, to the district social welfare supervisor.[14]

Throughout the summer and fall of 1934, states followed this national model and took the CWA's closing as the occasion to add new departments (to coincide with new FERA programs) and consolidate rural, urban, and suburban counties. Although this reform made administration more efficient, it also placed social welfare people in charge of the engineers and accountants who remained. Technicians continued to use standardized methods and procedures which the CWA had introduced, but their influence over SERA policies sharply varied. In large industrial states where the social work tradition was strong and charity institutions were entrenched, professional welfare executives regained control over the relief administration. In other areas, particularly in the South, where public relief organizations were relatively new with the depression, engineers seemed to retain more of the influence they had gained under the CWA.[15]

After the CWA demobilization on April 1, the New York

---

[14]Donald Stone, "Reorganizing for Relief," *Public Management*, XVI (September, 1934), 259–262; V. O. Key, Jr., *The Administration of Federal Grants to States* (Chicago: Public Administration Service, 1937), pp. 102–103; Russell H. Kurtz, "Work—and More of It," *Survey*, LXX (September, 1934), 277; Hopkins to all department heads, field representatives, regional examiners, and regional engineers, May 3, 1934, JB 1.

[15]Stone, "Reorganizing for Relief," 259–262; "Reorganization," *Survey*, LXX (July, 1934), 255.

State TERA consolidated and created new divisions. Staff roles were more precisely defined, intra-staff relations became decidedly more formal, and the body of precedents and standard procedures reduced each day's business to a set of routines. Yet alongside this efficient reorganization, TERA regained its social-welfare tone, as engineers were eased out of the "inner circle." They no longer figured in policy-making, nor determined the selection of relief workers, nor set priorities on funding, wages, and materials. With the field staff reduced in November, six of the nine district directorships went to former field representatives with social service training, while only three, including the "special problem district of New York City," went to engineers. The "special problem" was Robert Moses, the "works czar," who preferred to deal with fellow public administrators and engineers. Statewide, the TERA project division remained important, however, because the social workers had to rely on its staff to expedite project approvals and inspections, which continued to follow rigorous CWA practices. TERA took the CWA application form as a model, and in the fall even issued a *Manual of Procedures for Local Relief Administration*.[16]

North Carolina, in contrast, consolidated and reformed its relief administration after the demise of the CWA. The 107 county units were reorganized into 31 relief districts. CWA personnel continued to staff emergency relief offices, while the state work division absorbed the legacy of engineering control. The state WD examined and recommended CWA projects for transfer and approved new ones after a thorough study of their engineering soundness. The Raleigh staff pored over plans, the availability of labor, and details on material and equipment covered in lengthy application forms, accompanied by the usual blueprints and specifications. Supervision descended in a straight

---

[16]New York State Governor's Commission on Unemployment Relief, *State and Local Welfare Organization in the State of New York* (Albany: J. B. Lyons and Company, 1936), and *Work Relief Projects of the Public Works Type in the State of New York* (Albany: J. B. Lyons and Company, 1936); telephone conversation, Hopkins and Fred Daniels, March 28, 1934, FERA 196.

line from the work division director to district and local project
supervisors to job foremen and superintendents. Division engineers acted as field representatives of the state WD and in-
spected all projects. Local and district weekly reports to the
state office covered location and description, unit costs, number of employees and hours worked, and amount of work completed. The state WD served as a central clearing house for all
reports and forwarded required information to Washington.[17]

The CWA had introduced engineers into the Florida relief
administration; and although demobilization had reduced their
numbers, their influence remained substantial. The civil works
engineering staff had consisted of a chief, his assistant, 6 district engineers, and 8 office engineers. District supervisors could
have as many inspectors as they considered necessary to visit
projects daily and make periodic reports. Although the FERA
slashed the department by fifty percent, including all 80 field
men, a unique administrative arrangement saved many technical positions. The relief organization consolidated its 67 county
offices to 10 new regions, with an administrator, engineer,
auditor, and relief director. Counties followed the same system,
with the engineering representative given the title of director
of work. The WD engineering organization, which still supervised all projects, was headed by a technical advisor on the
state ERA staff, and the department consisted of a chief, 4
technical assistants, including a field man, project engineer,
architect, and estimator. They all had experience in road construction, drainage, sewage, airport building, and other public
works.[18]

Despite the patchwork remnant of engineering staffs in the
states, the end of the CWA meant the gradual resumption of
social work control over federal relief. FERA handed out grants-
in-aid to the states and responded to their demands for decentralized operations. Work projects lost their glamour as part of

[17]Pratt to O'Berry, March 29, 1934, NCERA 79; Kirk, Cutter, and Morse,
Emergency Relief in North Carolina, pp. 135–136.

[18]Arthur F. Perry, Jr., "Engineers in the Administration of Florida Relief,"
Civil Engineering, V (January, 1935), 6–9; "Reorganization," *Survey*, 225.

a "new social experiment" and became just one facet of a larger effort to sustain individual clients determined by case-work counseling. While the few CWA technicians who remained in the FERA Work Division continued to control project applications and work execution, they remained subordinate to welfare executives. Instead of social theorists or economic planners, case investigators in the FERA Social Service Division determined the overall form and amount of relief dispensed. For those "employed" on the projects, the clock had also turned back. Even if they still performed the same jobs and were supervised by the same experts, they now had to justify their need to a case worker, spend many hours of the work day idle at home with the wife and children, receive so little that beans and scrapple would be dinner fare, and once again be regarded as charity cases in their local communities. The benefits which had lifted the CWA jobholder from relief worker to public employee had gone.[19]

II

The year 1935 was one of major decision for the New Deal's social welfare policy. In January, when President Roosevelt declared to Congress that the federal government must quit "this business of relief," he found approximately 5 million on FERA rolls. Using statistics from the unemployment census, the President identified about 1.5 million as "unemployables," chronic dependents who were cared for by states, counties, churches, and private charities before the Great Depression. Pledging to supply matching grants to enable states and localities to resume this traditional burden, Roosevelt proposed legislation that ultimately was incorporated into the Social Security Act, which provided "categorical" aid for the aged, mothers with dependent children, and the blind. Roosevelt deemed the other 3.5 million people on relief as "employables," the victims

[19]Carothers, *Chronology of the FERA*, pp. 51, 52, 68.

of an industrial catastrophe that cut across state lines and thus clearly the responsibility of the federal government. For these, jobs, not the dole, would be the keystone of federal aid. Designed to provide work on locally sponsored projects for persons in need of public assistance, the Works Progress Administration would absorb the able-bodied unemployed from the FERA. Within a year after the President spoke, the WPA would hire a labor force of over 3 million.[20]

At first glance the WPA appeared to be an "emergency employment corporation" like the Civil Works Administration. The technical heritage of the CWA's general organization, finance, and engineering strongly influenced the WPA and helped to shape its administration. Like its predecessor, the WPA used outright federal grants as opposed to matching grants-in-aid under the FERA and Social Security. All executives were federal officers, U.S. Treasury checks paid the workers, and federal purchasing systems were followed. Donald Stone, co-author of the CWA *Manual*, chaired the WPA Committee on Procedures, which put out a *Handbook* in 1936, followed in 1940 by a detailed four-volume *Manual* on administration, project operations, employment, and finance. Furthermore, WPA chief engineer, Lt. Colonel Francis C. Harrington, Army Corps of Engineers, conducted a survey in the fall of 1935, which resulted in a rearrangement of the Washington staff, field offices, and district headquarters that reflected the "pronounced role" of army engineers, who had served as technical advisors and troubleshooters for the CWA. The extensive use of CWA guidelines for project control meant that the 8 million eventual WPA employees who worked from 1935 to 1943 participated

[20]Samuel Rosenman, ed., *The Public Papers and Addresses of Franklin D. Roosevelt*, Vol. IV (New York: Random House, 1938), pp. 19–21; Arthur Edward Burns and Edward A. Williams, *Federal Work, Security, and Relief Programs* (Washington: United States Government Printing Office, 1941), pp. 49–53; Joanna C. Colcord, "Divorcing Work and Relief," *Survey*, LXXI (June, 1935), 167–168; Russell H. Kurtz, "No More Federal Relief," *ibid.* (February, 1935), 35–37.

in a wide variety of projects which had been tested during the civil works experiment.[21]

Despite this strong resemblance to its predecessor, the WPA also embodied the reaction against the CWA's federal *Rules and Regulations*, the dominance by political independents or Republicans in many state and county offices, and the managerial influence on civil works policies. Although the WPA emanated out of Washington, it functioned through a network of nearly 400 state and district offices, which marked what one observer called the "relinquishment of federal control over the execution of projects." Aside from a few federally sponsored programs, like the arts projects, most WPA undertakings were planned and sponsored by state and local units, with ninety-five percent of all money going to the latter.[22] With the spirit of the CWA's national mobilization still in their minds, *Survey* editors Joanna C. Colcord and Russell H. Kurtz recalled:

> . . . a rush and power to federal authority in the fall of 1933 which is lacking now. CWA swept everything from its path with a flourish which WPA has never been able to develop. In 1933, Congress stood aside while the Administration did as it pleased with the funds at its disposal. There were no delays, no division of authority, no political interference at the top. This time Congress withheld its approval for four months, straight-jacketed the funds into eight cate-

[21]Edward A. Williams and J. Kerwin Williams, "The WPA Method vs. Grants-in-Aid," *Survey Midmonthly*, LXXVI (March, 1940), 91–93; and "New Techniques in Federal Aid," *APSR*, XXXIV (December, 1940), 947–954; Arthur MacMahon, John D. Millett, and Gladys Ogden, *The Administration of Federal Work Relief* (Chicago: Public Administration Service, 1941), pp. 206–207, 214–215; John Charnow, *Work Relief Experience in the United States* (Washington: Committee on Social Security, Social Science Research Council, 1943), pp. 84–85.

[22]Corrington Gill, *Wasted Manpower* (New York: W. W. Norton and Company, 1939), pp. 183–184; Russell H. Kurtz, "How the Wheels Are Turning," *Survey*, LXXI (August, 1935), 227–229; Donald S. Howard, "As the WPA Goes On," *ibid.*, LXXII (October, 1936), 297–298; and Ruth Durant, "Home Rule in the WPA," *Survey Midmonthly*, LXXV (September, 1939), 273–275.

gories, and relinquished key jobs to be filled from its patronage list.[23]

CWA "Hoover men," like Robert Kelso, Arch Mandel, and Rowland Haynes had left the regional offices by 1935. The following year, WPA white collar and professional projects came under the Women's Division doyenne Ellen Woodward, as Jacob Baker and Arthur Goldschmidt departed from the Walker-Johnson Building. Democrats had worded the Emergency Relief Appropriation Act to require that any state official earning over $5,000 have Senate approval, which resulted in many "political" appointments to state WPA headquarters. In regional, state, and county offices, technicians made way for organization Democrats, and Colcord and Kurtz again contrasted:

> Newly created WPA organizations have stood bemused with the complexity and magnitude of their tasks while ERA veterans, many of them with a proud record of achievement under the CWA banner, have been pushed aside, discredited. Old lines of loyalty—extending under the CWA from Mr. Hopkins to the lowliest private in the ranks—have been badly snarled in the present set-up with state WPA personnel owing their jobs to their senators rather than to the WPA chieftain.[24]

The decentralization of the WPA also replaced the technical priorities of USES officials with decisions made by county case workers, who investigated each applicant to determine if he (or she) should have any employment at all, and if so for how long. In sharp contrast to the CWA (where conceivably more than one person per family could hold a job), the WPA would employ only one member at any one time; and family size, makeup,

[23]"Now—in November," *Survey*, LXXI (October, 1935), 310.

[24]Elias Huzar, "The 'New' WPA: What it Is; How it Works," *Survey Midmonthly*, LXXV (October, 1939), 300–301; MacMahon, Millet, and Ogden, *The Administration of Federal Work Relief*, p. 270; "Now—in November," 310; interview with Arthur "Tex" Goldschmidt, September 14, 1976; Donald S. Howard, *The WPA and Federal Relief Policy* (New York: Russell Sage Foundation, 1943), p. 173.

and monthly budgets figured in eligibility. Ninety-five percent of the WPA employees underwent this means test. As a consequence of these relief policies, many unemployed proved unable to qualify for the WPA. Some large industrial states took up the slack with their own little WPAs, but ran them much like the old "work-for-relief" programs of the late nineteenth century. Several states went back to old Poor Law practices and confined the use of earnings to meet family needs through formal or informal prohibitions against spending WPA pay for liquor and other extravagances.[25]

Although the WPA, like the CWA, rejected the budget deficit to determine total wages, it did not go as far as civil works *Rules and Regulations* and set minimum hourly rates. With the objective to make earnings higher than relief stipends but not so great as to encourage workers to remain public charges, the WPA drew up an elaborate scheme of differential payments. These "security wages" were based on skill, region, and community size and ranged from $19 per month for unskilled workers in the rural South to $94 for professional and technical employees in the North and West.[26] Organized labor refused to accept this policy for fear it would threaten gains in private industry; and during the 1936 election year, unions forced the WPA to adopt the prevailing rate with varying hours per pay period. In this way, the WPA could still impose maximum

[25]Don D. Lescohier, "The Hybrid WPA," *Survey Midmonthly*, LXXV (June, 1939), 167–169; Howard, *WPA*, pp. 360, 341, 345–346; Corrington Gill, "Local Work for Relief," *Survey Midmonthly*, LXXVI (May, 1940), 157–159; and Benjamin Glassburg, "Relief's Ugly Duckling," *ibid.* (August, 1940), 238, referred to people unlucky enough to miss the categories of aid in which the federal government participated. See also James T. Patterson, *America's Struggle Against Poverty, 1900–1980* (Cambridge: Harvard University Press, 1981), p. 64.

[26]Kurtz, "How the Wheels are Turning," 227–229; Charnow, *Work Relief Experience*, pp. 51–52; Howard, *WPA*, pp. 158–165. Supplementary relief was still required, however, by families whose needs exceeded WPA earnings, and they remained dependent on relief and tied to periodic case-work supervision. Gertrude Springer, "You Can't Eat Morale," *Survey*, LXXII (March, 1936), 76–77.

monthly earnings by limiting hours. To determine the rates, however, the WPA largely bypassed CWA-type wage boards. Although the state administrator could hold hearings and accept evidence submitted by interested parties, he had the ultimate decision. Wide variations resulted, as some states set uniform rates in disregard of rural-urban differentials, some consulted unions, and others had very low rates.[27] Similarly, the WPA followed the scaled-down accident benefits used during the CWA demobilization. Protests forced officials to raise payments, but amounts were limited to two-thirds the monthly earnings and proved of little help to unskilled workers in low-wage brackets. Gertrude Springer of the *Survey* concluded that WPA earnings were based upon a general assumption that "all families have an average of 4.1 children, that everyone has average good health, [and] that accidents don't happen."[28]

The WPA's general acceptance of relief priorities in hiring and wages brought sharp criticism from the technical cadre, who pointed to the havoc caused by "inefficient" job placement and interrupted work routines. Some put their finger on the limited hours, usually thirty a week or less, with most foremen and skilled workers tending to have the shortest schedules, which meant frequent shifts in supervision and lapses in continuity and efficiency. But others pointed to the development of projects around the skills of the unemployed rather than "build a work program on the soundest possible basis and recruit workers from qualified unemployed." "It is unfortunate that the needs test has to be applied at all," wrote economists Ewan Clague and Saya S. Schwartz, complaining about job positions filled arbitrarily from relief rolls without reference to ability. The requirement that ninety percent be hired from relief rolls led to chronic shortages of skilled supervisors, while the use of barely employable, often elderly workers low-

[27]Nels Anderson, "The War for the Wage," *Survey*, LXXII (March, 1936), 76–77; Beulah Amidon, "WPA—Wages and Workers," *Survey Graphic*, XXIV (October, 1935), 493–497, 504–505.

[28]Charnow, *Work Relief Experience*, pp. 77–78; Howard, *WPA*, pp. 265–266; Springer, "You Can't Eat Morale," 76–77.

ered productivity as well as the morale of others. Even the able-bodied were frequently unsuited to the projects to which they were assigned. "We suggest that instead of trying to push these many and diverse workers into occupations for which they are untrained or ill-equipped that the Works Progress Administration make a place for them in large-scale training and rehabilitation," continued Clague and Schwartz. "To organize a training and rehabilitation section of the work relief program would improve the status of the participants as normal wage-earners and at the same time safeguard the public works projects."[29]

In vain, Corrington Gill, assistant administrator in charge of WPA Research, Statistics, and Finance, recommended that the WPA train the unemployed to improve the organization of the labor market, the efficiency of the workers, and thus reduce joblessness. He urged the "abandonment of traditional relief notions in the operation of a comprehensive work and employment program." But those CWA technicians, like Gill and his assistant Paul Webbink, who stayed in the WPA, would have little influence on work relief policies, although their proposals laid the foundation for what eventually became the federal "manpower" programs of the 1960's. In *Wasted Manpower*, published in 1939, Gill suggested that the WPA be reshaped into a training agency, but his ideas would not take hold until the United States faced production shortages in the 1940's.[30] As part of the national mobilization, the WPA eventually sponsored courses in welding, sheet-metal work, and aircraft

[29]Ewan Clague and Saya S. Schwartz, "Real Jobs—Or Relief," *Survey Graphic*, XXIV (June, 1935), 293–295; Patterson, *America's Struggle*, pp. 64–65; Gill, *Wasted Manpower*, pp. 273–274; Harry Greenstein, "Work Programs and Relief Measures," *Proceedings of the Delegate Conference, AASW 1936* (New York: American Association of Social Workers, 1936), pp. 72–73.

[30]Gill, *Wasted Manpower*, pp. 252–275; Paul Webbink, "Unemployment in the United States, 1930–1940," AER, XXXI (February, 1941), 248–272; William Haber, "The Mobilization of Manpower," NCSW, *Proceedings* (New York: Columbia University Press, 1943), pp. 15–25; John J. Tessari, "Training and the War Effort," *ibid.*, pp. 33–46; United States War Manpower Commission, *The Training Within Industry Report, 1940–1945* (Washington: United States Government Printing Office, 1945).

mechanics. Applicants had to show past employment records and aptitudes for shop instruction, and they received WPA learners' rates agreed upon by employees and management in cooperating plants. During fiscal 1941, about 118,000 were trained in defense occupations, and by April, 1942, over 232,000 had enrolled. The WPA also sponsored training for workers in private essential industries under its Training Within Industry (TWI) program, which operated under the War Manpower Commission. In June, 1943, the WPA set up a Division of Training and Reemployment, ironically, just before its appropriations were killed by congressional conservatives determined to end the New Deal's commitment to relief.[31]

The coalition of fiscal conservatives, organization Democrats, and social workers that had beaten down the CWA in 1934 would never again permit public employment policies on federal work relief. All future programs, like the WPA, would be carefully executed by social workers, not engineers, managers, or USES personnel. Wages would depend on need. The states, rather than Washington, would assume more administrative and financial responsibility, especially for compensation, safety, and tools and equipment. Because the WPA adhered to these policies and appeased these interest groups, it survived to aid the needy unemployed for eight years and became fixed in the public mind as the model federal job program in the postwar years. But to Corrington Gill and his contemporaries, the distinctions between WPA work relief and the CWA's emergency employment corporation remained clear. To them, the Civil Works Administration stood out as the most daring response to unemployment during the New Deal.[32]

[31]Howard, *WPA*, pp. 128, 164–165, 237–238, 241–243; Gertrude Springer, "This Thing Called Relief," *Survey Midmonthly*, LXXVII (June, 1941), 171–174; Seward C. Simons, "Attention, WPA," *ibid.* (August, 1941), 239; Gertrude Springer and Kathryn Close, "Relief in These Times," *ibid.* (November, 1941), 315–321; Patterson, *America's Struggle*, p. 65.

[32]Carothers, *Chronology of the FERA*, pp. 51–52, 68; Kurtz, "Work—and More of It," 275–277; William W. Bremer, "Along the 'American Way': The New Deal's Work Relief Programs for the Unemployed," *JAH*, LXII (December, 1975), 643–644.

Epilogue: From CWA to CETA

IN FIFTY years since the New Deal, no subsequent administration from the Fair Deal to the Great Society to the Jimmy Carter Administration has embarked upon such a determined commitment as the CWA to provide the unemployed with public jobs. Despite ups and downs in the business cycle, Americans have not confronted a catastrophic depression with one third the nation in dire need. As a result, despite chronic joblessness, the public has grown indifferent toward the unemployed as well as come to realize that remedies for idleness and poverty seem to involve far more complex considerations than simply providing work. The era since World War II also witnessed the passing of unorthodox social workers, like Harry Hopkins, and the flow of industrial engineers into production management—the two professional groups who had spearheaded the movement for civil works. Despite pronouncements of the federal government's responsibility as an "employer of last resort," post-war policy makers have preferred to handle the jobless with a "manpower approach" of relatively inexpensive programs (compared to job-creation) oriented toward specific "target" groups among "employables."

Although full employment has not been achieved since 1945, inflation and balanced federal budgets have become more important domestic concerns than public works for the unemployed. Even with institutional controls over the economy and federal commitments, like the Employment Act of 1946, the post-war years were blemished by periodic downturns marked by a "hard core" of jobless who lingered on. Beginning with the first Eisenhower recession in 1953, unemployment rates reached 2.5 percent in 1954, 4 percent in 1958 and 5 percent by 1961. While these figures represented millions out of work, they scarcely approached the massive numbers who stood on the breadlines in the depths of the Great Depression. The overwhelming majority of Americans held steady jobs, and they were far more concerned about the effect of federal spending on rising prices. Astute political observers, from Samuel Lubell to Richard Scammon, concluded that a rough equilibrium had become established between the public's fears of recurring hard times and nagging worries about runaway inflation. As a consequence, this anti-inflation consensus, operating after World War II, accepted a "reasonable" jobless rate of between four and six percent.[1]

While the number of unemployed remained at "acceptable" levels, their very presence in an otherwise "affluent society" lent to them faintly exotic characteristics. Since the Second World War, most Americans did not think much about the poor until the early 1960's, when social critics like Michael Harrington and Dwight MacDonald discovered "pockets of poverty" in the isolated valleys of West Virginia, the crumbling tenements of Harlem, and the aging textile towns along the Merrimack River.[2] At the same time, social scientists began to view persistent idleness less as the result of a faltering economy than as one symptom of the "culture of poverty," a distinct way of life with its own norms and patterns of behavior. Its foremost theoretician, anthropologist Oscar Lewis, identified the salient characteristics: families structured along matriarchal lines, with absent fathers and bruised male egos; a craving for immediate gratification that destroyed any possibility to plan for the future; an indifference toward public is-

---

[1]James L. Sundquist, *Politics and Policy* (Washington: Brookings Institution, 1968); Samuel Lubell, *The Future of American Politics* (Garden City: Doubleday Anchor Books, 1956); Richard M. Scammon and Ben J. Wattenberg, *The Real Majority* (New York: Coward McCann, Inc., 1970).

[2]John Kenneth Galbraith, *The Affluent Society* (Boston: Houghton, Mifflin Company, 1958); Michael Harrington, *The Other America* (New York: Macmillan Company, 1962); Dwight MacDonald, "Our Invisible Poor," *New Yorker,* XXXVIII (January 19, 1963), 82–132.

sues and a mistrust of officials, particularly social workers, health inspectors, and the police; and a pervasive apathy that frustrated attempts by outsiders to help.[3] This "underclass," chronically unemployed and badly scarred by generations of psychological abuse, seemed incapable of holding down regular employment. Although sociologists like Daniel P. Moynihan, Lee Rainwater, and Herbert J. Gans urged public job efforts, they nevertheless injected a note of skepticism about whether the usual federal work programs, equipped with bureaucratic guidelines and nine-to-five routines, could reach alienated victims of the poverty cycle.[4]

The influence of social scientists on federal policies for the unemployed contrasted with the eclipse of social work and scientific management, the two professions that had provided the vanguard for the CWA.[5] For social workers, the post-war years marked a retreat from active lobbying for federal relief and bold experiments like civil works back to orthodox case work, group work, and community organization. With the Social Security Act and the institutionalization of welfare in states and counties, emergency relief agencies ossified into public aid depart-

[3]Oscar Lewis, *Five Families* (New York: Basic Books, 1959); *Children of Sanchez* (New York: Random House, 1961); "The Culture of Poverty," *Scientific American*, CCXV (1966), 19–25; *La Vida* (New York: Random House, 1964); Robert H. Bremner, "Poverty in Perspective," in John Braeman, Robert H. Bremner, and Everett Walters, eds., *Change and Continuity in Twentieth Century America* (New York: Harper and Row, 1964), pp. 263–280.

[4]Daniel P. Moynihan, *The Negro Family* (Washington: United States Department of Labor, Office of Policy Planning and Research, March, 1965); Lee Rainwater and William L. Yancey, *The Moynihan Report and the Politics of Controversy* (Cambridge: Harvard University Press, 1967); Lee Rainwater, "The Problem of Lower-Class Culture and Poverty-War Strategy," in Daniel P. Moynihan, ed., *On Understanding Poverty* (New York: Basic Books, 1968), pp. 229–259; Herbert J. Gans, "Culture and Class in the Study of Poverty: An Approach to Anti-Poverty Research," in *ibid.*, pp. 201–228.

[5]Daniel P. Moynihan, "The Professors and the Poor," in Daniel P. Moynihan, ed., *On Understanding Poverty* (New York: Basic Books, 1968), pp. 3–35; Nathan Glazer, "A New Look in Social Welfare," *New Society*, VII (November, 1963), 6–8; Daniel P. Moynihan, *Maximum Feasible Misunderstanding* (New York: The Free Press, 1969), pp. 21–37.

ments, huge bureaucracies that processed applications for thousands of clients. As administrators of assistance for the blind, the disabled, dependent children, and unemployment compensation, social workers found themselves burdened with hundreds of cases and endless paperwork. No longer the independent force struggling for social change, the profession had grown detached from social action, as symbolized by the demise in 1952 of the *Survey*, a magazine which staunchly supported the CWA.[6]

Scientific management experts, whose talents contributed to the success of the civil works program, dispersed after the spring of 1934, with the reaction against the "emergency employment corporation" idea. Jacob Baker, who studied cooperative enterprises in Europe after he left the WPA, became a planning consultant of the Federal Works Agency in 1942 and for the Econometric Institute in New York before becoming chairman of the board of the Economic Forecasting Institute. John Carmody, assistant to Morris L. Cooke of the Rural Electrification Administration, headed the Federal Works Agency in 1939, served on the Maritime Commission during the war, and directed production assistance for the Economic Cooperative Administration in France. Carmody's top assistant on the CWA and later WPA chief engineer, Perry Fellows, led a mission to Ethiopia and remained there as one of Emperor Haile Selassie's principal advisors on industrial organization.[7]

CWA economists and statisticians, like Corrington Gill and Paul Webbink, who remained in the Works Progress Administration, urged training programs, but their ideas did not take

[6]James Lieby, "Social Work and Social History," *SSR*, XL (September, 1969), 316; Frank J. Bruno, *Trends in Social Work* (New York: Columbia University Press, 1948), pp. 367–436; Walter I. Trattner, *From Poor Law to Welfare State* (New York: Free Press, 1974), pp. 248–264; Clarke Chambers, "Social Service and Social Reform: A Historical Essay," *SSR*, XXXVII (March, 1963), 76–90; A. D. Green, "The Professional Social Worker in the Bureaucracy," *ibid.*, LX (March, 1966), 71–83.

[7]*New York Times*, September 20, 1967, p. 47 and November 12, 1963, p. 41; The Reminiscences of John Michael Carmody, Vol. II, p. 302, in the Oral History Collection of Columbia University.

hold until World War II. The immediate stimulus was the preparedness crisis of the 1940's and the War Manpower Commission, which made federal retraining programs a patriotic necessity. From the highest levels in Washington came a group of defense and managerial experts, like James V. Forrestal and Vannevar Bush, who decried the low production skills and education levels of the work force.[8] A coalition of labor economists, personnel advisors, union apprenticeship supervisors, and vocational education administrators emerged from the war production and reemployment agencies convinced that joblessness represented one vast task of labor reeducation. Their arguments assumed that the postwar economy would generate full employment, with idleness limited to temporary technological displacement, particularly among poorly educated or unskilled workers. Federal action would therefore not require massive CWA-type job creation but rather programs to measure deficiencies in the labor pool, then educate and retrain the work force for an optimal fit with both existing and anticipated occupational demands. The Harry S. Truman and Dwight D. Eisenhower Administrations, as a consequence, undertook new federal programs, such as the National Science Foundation, the National Defense Education Act, and increased federal grants for vocational training, in response to these imperatives.[9]

[8]Morris Llewellyn Cooke, "Labor and Management under the Defense Emergency," *Advanced Management*, V (October-December, 1940), 165–167, 176; Wallace Clark, "Production Planning in This Period of Industrial Preparedness," *ibid.*, VI (January-March, 1941), 25–27; A. A. Potter, "The Problem of Labor Supply and Training: Technical Education and Defense," *ibid.*, 32–34; "War Manpower Commission," *MLR*, LIV (June, 1942), 1325–1327; "Training Services, War Industries, and Agriculture," *Education for Victory*, I (January 1, 1943), 7–9; Carl Gray, "Manpower Employment after the War," *ibid.*, IX (January-March, 1944), 36–39, 45; Vannevar Bush, *Modern Arms and Free Men* (New York: Alfred A. Knopf, 1949), pp. 226, 245, 257; J. Frederick Dewhurst and Associates, *America's Needs and Resources* (New York: Twentieth Century Fund, 1947), pp. 557–559.

[9]Sumner Rosen, "Social Policy and Manpower Development," in Margaret Purvine, ed., *Manpower and Employment* (New York: Council on Social Work Education, 1972), pp. 189–202; Eli Ginzberg, *Manpower Agenda for America* (New York: McGraw Hill, 1968), pp. 2–7, 11–22; Garth L. Mangum, "The

By the 1960's, inflation, the Cold War, and the new man-power lobby had virtually ruled out any CWA-type job pro-gram. Confronted with 4.7 million jobless in 1961, President John F. Kennedy received conflicting advice. A few liberal Democrats, like Senators Paul H. Douglas and Hubert H. Humphrey, called for emergency public employment. The Council of Economic Advisors, chaired by Walter W. Heller, favored a Keynesian strategy of monetary and fiscal stimuli, particularly a tax cut, to get the economy moving. At the same time, a number of academics, notably Professor Charles C. Kil-lingsworth of Michigan State University, warned against infla-tion fueled by any massive federal spending or work program. They traced joblessness to "sick industries" (like coal mining), plant relocations, poorly educated or unskilled labor pools, ra-cial discrimination, and other structural anomalies in a growing economy. The "structuralists" called for "packaged" programs of education, retraining, and limited public works aimed at "target" groups in specific depressed regions. While the tax cut stalled in Congress, the structuralists' recommendations led to the Area Redevelopment of Act of 1961, the Accelerated Public Works Act of 1962 (a PWA for depressed areas), and the Social Security Amendments of 1962, which provided for an experimental community work training program. The first manpower legislation *per se*, the Manpower Development and Training Act of 1962, authorized stipends for individuals en-rolled in occupational retraining. Aimed at those who had lost their jobs due to automation, MDTA required applicants to show "attachment" to the work force. Like the CWA and WPA training during World War II, the manpower ideology of MDTA was aimed at those upwardly striving among the working poor.[10]

Development of Manpower Policy, 1961–1965," in Sar A. Levitan and Irving H. Siegel, eds., *Dimensions of Manpower Policy* (Baltimore: Johns Hopkins University Press, 1966), pp. 29–42.

[10]Sundquist, *Politics and Policy*, Chapter Three; Eleanor G. Gilpatrick, *Structural Unemployment and Aggregate Demand* (Baltimore: Johns Hopkins University Press, 1966); William Spring, "Manpower Programs: the Lessons of the 1960's," in Alan Gartner, Russell A. Nixon, and Frank Riessman, eds., *Public*

The Kennedy Administration's emphasis on manpower strategies rather than job creation continued into the Great Society and even prevailed amid the controversial measures of the War on Poverty. President Lyndon B. Johnson, confident that the economy and the job supply were fundamentally adequate, turned down Senator Gaylord Nelson's proposal for $1 billion for conservation work on U.S. Park Service lands and a subsequent suggestion by Secretary of Labor Willard Wirtz for another WPA. The Administration chose instead a relatively inexpensive War on Poverty designed to bring the hard-core unemployed into the economic "mainstream" with a variety of education, health, legal aid, child care, and other community services. The Economic Opportunity Act of 1964 contained no major provisions for public employment, despite all the hoopla that its programs strongly resembled the New Deal's. The Neighborhood Youth Corps provided limited work opportunities for some 278,000 youngsters in 1965 on projects sponsored by government agencies or nonprofit organizations. Work Experience offered training for youths and for adults, primarily heads of families on relief. The Job Corps operated on the assumption that youths must be removed from their adverse environment to undergo effective training and relocated selectees in special centers to provide basic education and motivation to re-enter the labor market. The most innovative legislation, the Community Action Program, with its goal of "maximum feasible participation" by the poor, furnished a variety of social services and employment projects to target neighborhoods, but created far more controversy than real jobs.[11]

Service Employment (New York: Praeger Publishers, 1973), pp. 157–159; "The Question of Federally-Subsidized Jobs for the Unemployed," Congressional Digest, L (March, 1971), 69–79; Charles E. Gilbert, "Policy-Making in Public Welfare: the 1962 Amendments," PSQ, LXXXI (June, 1966), 196–224.

[11]Sar A. Levitan, The Great Society's Poor Law (Baltimore: Johns Hopkins University Press, 1969), pp. 9–104, 273–291; Nathan Glazer, "To Produce a Creative Disorder: the Grand Design of the Poverty Program," New York Times Magazine, February 27, 1966, pp. 21–64, 69–73; Adam Yarmolinsky, "The Beginnings of OEO," in James L. Sundquist, ed., On Fighting Poverty (New York: Basic Books, 1969), pp. 34–51.

Although OEO programs, like the CAP, generated enormous publicity, the Johnson Administration avoided any large-scale CWA-type program and allowed more funds and influence to go to a host of education and training programs controlled by manpower advocates in the Department of Labor. Beginning with the Area Redevelopment Act of 1961, Labor had the responsibility to select and place applicants through the USES. MDTA appropriations went to Labor, and the Secretary took charge of research and demonstration projects, as well as preparation of the influential *Manpower Report of the President*. The USES and the Bureau of Apprenticeship and Training came under the Office of Manpower, Apprenticeship,. and Training, the pet creation of Secretary Arthur J. Goldberg. By 1963, the new Manpower Administrator presided over USES, BAT, OMAT, and also ran programs funded by the Vocational Education Act of 1963, the Youth Employment Act, the Economic Opportunity Act of 1964, and the National Youth Corps. When criticism mounted against the OEO's Community Action Program, especially its anti-establishment ideology, and HEW's poor handling of Work Experience and Training, their job programs were also transferred to Labor.[12] By the late 1960's, the Department handled the War on Poverty's Work Experience, as well as training, employment counseling, and job development activities, plus several new efforts, including Operation Mainstream, New Careers, and Special Impact.[13]

During the course of this manpower buildup, Labor admin-

[12]Garth L. Mangum, *MDTA* (Baltimore: Johns Hopkins University Press, 1968), pp. 43–50; and *The Emergence of Manpower Policy* (New York: Holt, Rinehart and Winston, 1969), pp. 78–86; Sar A. Levitan and Joyce Zickler, *The Quest for a Federal Manpower Partnership* (Cambridge: Harvard University Press, 1974), pp. 1–13.

[13]Operation Mainstream provided jobs and training for middle-aged and elderly workers in stranded rural areas. New Careers gave work experience in paraprofessional jobs in human services. Special Impact offered manpower training to enable poor people to rehabilitate their neighborhoods and provide needed community services. Sar A. Levitan, *Programs in Aid of the Poor for the 1970's* (Baltimore: Johns Hopkins University Press, 1973), pp. 112–113; Arthur Pearl and Frank Riessman, *New Careers for the Poor* (Glencoe: Free Press, 1965).

istrators understood that special interests in the poverty program had to be placated. Accused of "creaming" (skimming
off) the more "advantaged" of the unemployed, the Department was particularly sensitive to charges that MDTA and other
training efforts had failed to reach the hard-core jobless. Secretary Willard Wirtz responded with a special survey of inner
cities in sixteen metropolitan areas and developed a "sub-em-
ployment index," which revealed startling percentages of ghetto
residents who were jobless, on part-time work, or on full-time
poverty wages. Even though Wirtz had supported a large-scale
federal job program, he had to concede to the strong manpower
advocates in his department and work within the limits set by
the Administration and the Congress. His memo to President
Johnson in January, 1967, recommended training and "categorical" assistance only for target neighborhoods in the largest
cities. Eventually this Concentrated Employment Program provided demonstration grants to twenty-one poor communities to
develop intensive training programs nominally sponsored by
Community Action Agencies but really administered by Manpower. Complementary efforts, such as Job Opportunities in
the Business Sector (JOBS), which paid employers to hire
and train the disadvantaged, and Work Incentive (WIN), an
amendment to Social Security to train those on welfare, also
came under the Manpower Administration. By the fall of 1968,
the Labor Department handled 80 percent of the budget for
job-related programs.[14]

Despite the Johnson Administration's decided preference for
manpower training, sentiment for a CWA-type job-creation
program began to grow, particularly as the black ghettos burned
during the long hot summers of the late 1960's. In the first

[14]The New Orleans metropolitan area, for example, had an unemployment
rate of 3.3 percent, while the ghetto's subemployment index was 45.3 percent.
East Harlem showed comparable figures of 3.7 and 33.1 percent. Spring,
"Manpower Programs," p. 160; and "Congress and Public Service Employ-
ment" in Harold L. Sheppard, Bennett Harrison, and William J. Spring, eds.,
The Political Economy of Public Service Employment (Lexington, Mass.: D. C.
Heath and Company, 1972), pp. 133–134.

major Congressional push for public employment since the Great Depression, Senators Joseph S. Clark of Pennsylvania and Robert F. Kennedy of New York proposed an Emergency Employment Act in 1967, granting the Secretary of Labor $2.5 billion for fiscal years 1968 and 1969 to assist public and private agencies that offered work opportunities in health, education, and related fields. But the Johnson Administration remained opposed, as Presidential aide Joseph A. Califano denounced the bill as one that would only "make work." Spending for the war in Vietnam would allow little leeway for emergency employment, not to mention any dramatic increase in funds for jobs in poverty areas.[15]

But support for a federal employment program inevitably grew. In 1968, the National Advisory Commission on Civil Disorders recommended legislation to create 1 million new jobs in the public sector within three years. The National Urban Coalition sponsored a survey by Dr. Harold L. Sheppard of the Upjohn Institute for Employment Research, which pointed to ominously high unemployment among inner-city teenagers. By the end of 1970, Congressional Democrats passed the most ambitious work program since the New Deal, the Employment and Training Opportunities Act, which provided $9.5 billion to create 310,000 jobs over three years. President Richard M. Nixon, however, responded with a veto and lectured the Congress:

> WPA-type jobs are not the answer for the men and women who have them, for the government which is less efficient as a result or for the taxpayers who must foot the bill. Such a program represents a reversion to the remedies that were tried thirty-five years ago. Surely it is an inappropriate, ineffective response to the problem of the 1970's.

[15]"Public Service Jobs," *New Republic*, CLXVI (October 2, 1971), 11; Bennett Harrison, Harold L. Sheppard, and William J. Spring, "Government as the Employer of First Resort: Public Jobs, Public Needs," *ibid.*, CLXVII (November 4, 1972), 18–21.

Although Nixon conceded that "transitional and short-term public service employment can be a useful component of the nation's manpower policies," he found no solution in "public employment that is not linked with real jobs or which does not try to equip the individual for changes in the labor market." While Nixon's gibes at the WPA were predictable, his veto message had, in fact, left the door open to the manpower approach of retraining the salvageable among the jobless.[16]

President Nixon's hand was ultimately forced by his first recession, coupled with Democratic victories in the 1970 Congressional elections. A downturn in 1970–71 had increased the jobless rate from 3.6 percent in 1968 to 5.9 in 1971 and created special hardship for particular groups: 325,000 Vietnam veterans, 75,000 scientists and engineers laid off by NASA cutbacks, and an estimated 500,000 in the ghettos of the 100 largest cities. The AFL-CIO joined the National Urban Coalition in clamoring for public service employment. The National Conference of Mayors packed Congressional hearings with 14 members who testified about unemployment and declining public services. "Never before had such an impressive panel of witnesses been lined up to testify before the Senate for any manpower legislation," wrote the committee staff director. Democratic leaders latched onto the words "temporary and transitional" from Nixon's veto and drafted a new bill that also relied on the Administration's original Manpower Training Act, which proposed appropriations for jobs "triggered" by a period of high unemployment. The new bill expanded the trigger concept to provide $500 million for public service employment when the jobless rate reached 4.5 percent for three months, with another $100 million for each increment of 0.5 percent. The Emergency Employment Act of 1971, signed by President Nixon, represented a major departure from the manpower training policies of the 1960's and a return to the New Deal

[16]Harrison, Sheppard, and Spring, "Government as the Employer of First Resort," 18–21; veto message quoted in Spring, "Congress and Public Service Employment," p. 141; Cabell Phillips, "It Wasn't All Leaf Raking—Why Not Another WPA?" *New Republic*, CLXIV (February 6, 1971), 19–20.

strategy of direct job creation. EEA appropriated $1 billion the first year and $1.2 billion the second for a Public Employment Program in state and municipal governments for the unemployed and underemployed in specific target groups, including Vietnam veterans, teenagers, welfare recipients, and displaced scientists and aerospace workers.[17]

The Public Employment Program more closely resembled the CWA than the WPA, although observers drew parallels only to the latter.[18] The EEA was not conceived as anti-poverty legislation, but was designed, like the CWA, as a "short-term bridge" to create jobs for those forced into idleness during high unemployment. Just as technicians launched the civil works program in a few weeks, the Manpower Administration of the Department of Labor designated 700 state and local units as PEP agents and got the program into gear with similar dispatch. President Nixon signed the bill on August 6 and hiring began right after Labor Day. Like the CWA *Manual* of 1933, the guidelines of PEP required that project applications give a formidable accounting of the local area and population, public service needs, job descriptions, and cost breakdowns. Just as civil works employees were paid minimum hourly rates according to PWA scales, the "PEP generation" received either the federal minimum wage ($1.60 an hour), state or local minimum, if any, or the prevailing rate of pay for persons employed in similar occupations. And, as CWA jobholders were protected by the Federal Employees Compensation Act of 1916, PEP agents were also required to pay workmen's compensation, health insurance, unemployment insurance, and other

[17]"Funding of Public Service Jobs Opens $1 Billion Manpower Program," Manpower Information Service, *Current Reports*, II (August 18, 1971), 556–557; United States, Department of Labor, *Manpower Report of the President, 1973* (Washington: United States Government Printing Office, 1973), p. 42.

[18]Phillips, "It Wasn't All Leaf Raking," 19–20; "Another WPA?" *Newsweek*, LXIX (May 8, 1972), 98–99; Donald Powers, "Bridge to a Better Future," *Manpower*, III (October, 1971), 2–5; "Public Service Jobs for the Unemployed—A New WPA?" *U.S. News and World Report*, LXXI (August 23, 1971), 22.

benefits at the same levels and to the same extent as other employees.[19]

Despite its fair labor policies, the broad scope of job placements, and the speed of its initiation, the Public Employment Program of 1971 did not match the massive scale of the CWA. While $1 billion could fund jobs for 4 million in 1933, the EEA could only pay for a mere 185,000 at its peak in the summer of 1972. PEP reduced the jobless rate only about 0.2 percent and could scarcely meet the needs of all target groups. When divided among 700 state and local units and distributed to 5,300 sub-agents and 17,500 employment offices, the funds did not amount to much. Those who supported long-range public employment considered PEP a piddling effort, inappropriate for the six percent of the labor market out of work. "Powerful antibiotics were needed," wrote economist Robert Lekachman. "Congress offered a bandaid."[20]

PEP also failed to satisfy the aims of anti-poverty reformers and affirmative action groups of the 1970's. Just as the CWA had sought to reach the middle- and working-class unemployed, PEP agents enrolled a disproportionate number of fairly skilled whites and too few blacks and other unskilled minorities. A Labor Department study showed PEP jobholders were sixty-four percent white, twenty-one percent black, and only

[19]Powers, "Bridge to a Better Future," 2–5; "The Job Program Gets into Gear," *Business Week*, September 4, 1971, pp. 28–29; "Shift in Public Employment Goal Spurs Job Creation, Quick Hiring," Manpower Information Service, *Current Reports*, II (September 15, 1971), 612–613; Sar A. Levitan and Robert Taggart, III, eds., *Emergency Employment Act* (Salt Lake City: Olympus Publishing Company, 1974), pp. 11–58; Sar A. Levitan, "Creating Jobs Is One Way To Fight Unemployment," *New Generation*, LIV (Winter, 1974), 6–10; "First Aid for Recession's Casualties," *Business Week*, March 27, 1971, pp. 24–25; Sar A. Levitan and Robert Taggart, "The Emergency Employment Act: An Interim Assessment," *MLR*, XV (June, 1972), 3–11.

[20]Sar A. Levitan, "The Emergency Employment Act: An Assessment," *Manpower*, IV (December, 1972), 22–27; Robert Lekachman, *Public Service Employment* (New York: Public Affairs Committee, 1972), p. 14; "The Debate over Public Jobs for the Jobless," *Business Week*, December 9, 1972, pp. 102–104.

eleven percent on welfare. The typical employee was white, a male, a high school graduate between twenty-two and forty-four years old, and out of work for about a month. Even though federal guidelines were written to help racial minorities, PEP did not reach the hard-core unemployed (only one-fifth of the employees had not finished high school). Bennett Harrison of the University of Maryland, Robert Aaron Gordon of Yale, John Kenneth Galbraith of Harvard, and established Democrats like former CEA chairman Walter Heller pointed out that the program had done little to increase the participation of women, youth, and blacks. They sought expansion in the number of jobs and target groups, to include more of the hard-core, unskilled jobless. Caught up in controversy and conflicting goals, PEP was allowed to expire when funding ran out in January, 1973.[21]

With bipartisan backing and Labor Department support, Congress passed the Comprehensive Employment and Training Act of 1973, which consolidated MDTA and EOA programs and provided for an extension of the EEA of 1971. While CETA created 100,000 temporary jobs and gave six more weeks of benefits to the unemployed, it signaled a far more decentralized approach to manpower, attuned to the Nixon Administration's rhetoric about a "New Federalism." National guidelines under PEP gave way to a system where state and local officials chose the target groups, outlined the services provided, and designated individual recipients. Each of the 431 prime sponsors had to have a planning council, which represented clients, labor unions, business, education groups, and community organizations, to recommend services and monitor and evaluate CETA

[21]"Public Service Jobs," *New Republic*, 11; "Public Employment," *ibid.*, CLVII (June 23, 1973), 7–8; "Hiring Begins under Emergency Act: Labor Department Issues Grant Guidelines," Manpower Information Service, *Current Reports*, II (September 1, 1971), 580–581; Michael E. Sparrough, "Public Employment Program," in Charles R. Perry, Bernard E. Anderson, Richard L. Rowan and Herbert R. Northrup, eds., *The Impact of Government Manpower Programs* (Philadelphia: Industrial Research Unit, Wharton School, University of Pennsylvania, 1975), pp. 252–300.

programs. A participant had to be unemployed, underemployed, or economically "disadvantaged," reside in an area with 6.5 percent or higher unemployment for three consecutive months, and have been out of work at least thirty days. Those in on-the-job training, work experience, and public service employment received the same pay (at least the highest applicable minimum wage), fringe benefits, and promotion opportunities as regular employees doing similar work. During 1975, CETA's first full year of operation, 227,000 were in transition jobs (supposed to lead to permanent positions in the public sector) and another 157,000 in emergency work. Subsequent CETA Acts marked a return to traditional manpower policies for training rather than job creation.[22]

. . .

Can there be another CWA? Probably not on the massive scale of 4 million. The fears of deficit spending, a swollen federal bureaucracy, and a perpetual class of unemployed on the public payroll, which ended the CWA in the spring of 1934, were the fears of the 1970's that allowed PEP to be phased out after two years and confined CETA to training, target groups, and depressed areas. That climate of opinion elected Ronald Reagan in 1980 on the promise of less government and balanced budgets. It permitted his Administration first to cut CETA funds by a third, then to emasculate the public works section, and finally to terminate the program altogether. CETA's suc-

[22]Levitan and Zickler, *The Quest for a Federal Manpower Partnership*, pp. 74–102; Mary Eisner, "The Need for PEP—Public Jobs," *New Republic*, CLXX (February 16, 1974), 12–13; "Public Service Jobs—A Way to Put the Untrained to Work," *U.S. News and World Report*, LXXVII (August 5, 1974), 61–62; James A. Craft, "Public Service Jobs as Transitional Employment," *Manpower*, VI (October, 1974), 3–7; "Bumpy Road for New Jobs Program," *U.S. News and World Report*, LXXVIII (January 13, 1975), 41–42; "Unemployment: 8% . . . 9%?" *Newsweek*, LXXXV (January 20, 1975), 54–62; Lawrence A. Mayer, "First Aid for Recession's Victims," *Fortune*, XCI (February, 1975), 74–77, 158, 160; *New York Times*, January 17, 1982, Sec. 1, p. 32.

cessor, the Job Training Partnership Act of 1982 was funded at a mere $618 million and carefully placed in the hands of state governors and local private industry councils.

More remarkable than this general reaction against federal job creation has been President Reagan's capacity to ride out the most severe post-war recession without giving in to liberal Democrats on even a temporary work program. Although the national unemployment rate soared to almost eleven percent, the American public showed no commitment to public works for the jobless beyond the innocuous pronouncements of the Humphrey-Hawkins Resolution. Even when the Congress finally managed to force the passage of a $5.5 billion transportation repair effort, the White House refused to concede that it was an anti-recession measure. Calling the program a sound "infra-structure" investment, President Reagan emphasized that it was financed by a gasoline tax and would not raise the federal deficit by one penny. At the same time, the great majority of Americans seemed to trust the Administration's promises of an economic recovery based upon Reagan's assurances that deregulation and "supply-side" tax cuts would create millions of new jobs in the private sector. From the depressed timber industry in the Pacific Northwest to the quiet assembly lines in Detroit to the idle steel mills in Ohio and Pennsylvania, the jobless clamored for extended unemployment benefits and food stamps and seemed appeased by the highway repair program and occasional distribution of surplus food. They pinned their hopes on recall notices from local factories and mills, while the President cajoled businessmen to react positively to his economic incentives.

Yet some vague job program was undeniably taking shape, fitted to the ideological constraints of Ronald Reagan's America, the persistent skepticism about federal spending on "unemployables," and an anxiety over national efficiency not seen since the progressive era. Its roots lay in the country's response to the Japanese challenge and the growing conviction among business executives and industrial management experts that increased productivity would require a vast retooling of industry and a far-reaching program of labor education and re-training. Like the CWA, such an effort would probably be couched in terms of a national emergency and of the need to preserve vital productive skills; and it would be formulated by industrial managers, not social workers. But the similarities would end there. Any future program could not be a massive federal employment agency, but rather a job-development bank, more akin to the Reconstruction Finance Corporation, to handle training grants for private corporations and labor unions. Given the national consensus to return much federal power back to "the people," this program would probably include individual vouchers, a kind of negative income tax payment, for retraining at a labor institute, at a university, or for work experience with a "high-tech" corporation. The sharp reaction against large-scale federal involvement would permit little more than this indirect stimulus of private-sector job creation. But a determination to rescue the wasted manpower of Americans may well be the major preoccupation of domestic reform for the rest of the century.

A NOTE ON SOURCES

THE FOLLOWING is a selective summary of the materials consulted in preparing this study. Full documentation can be found in my dissertation, "The Civil Works Administration, 1933–1934: the Business of Emergency Employment in the New Deal," on deposit at the Columbia University Library.

PRIMARY

A study of the Civil Works Administration must begin with the records of the CWA and related federal relief and employment agencies in the National Archives. Record Group 69 includes the Civil Works Administration Papers and the Federal Emergency Relief Administration Papers. Other pertinent files that were useful include the United States Employment Service Papers (Record Group 183), the Department of Justice Papers (Record Group 60), the Office of the Adjutant General Central Files (Record Group 94), the War Department General Staff Papers (Record Group 165), and the National Emergency Council Papers (Record Group 44) housed in the Federal Records Center, Suitland, Maryland.

Unfortunately, the state emergency relief administrations, which were co-opted into the CWA, have not been as careful to preserve their records. The North Carolina Emergency Relief Administration Papers are an enormous unprocessed collection stored in large sealed boxes in a state depository building in Raleigh. The Illinois Department of Welfare (formerly the Illinois Emergency Relief Commission during the 1930's) has the files of the IERC, not as archives, but in filing cabinets according to cases. The IERC records for the CWA period were very disappointing, no doubt, because civil works discarded the means test and other case work procedures. I could not find any papers for the Pennsylvania SERB, the New York TERA, or the California SERA.

Many of those who participated in the national administration of the civil works program have left their papers. The Harry L. Hopkins Manuscripts in the Franklin D. Roosevelt Library, Hyde Park, contain CWA staff meeting minutes, field reports, and telephone calls, which are particularly useful. The John M. Carmody Papers, also at the Roosevelt Library, have reports from field engineers. The Reminiscences of John Michael Carmody, Volumes I and II, in the Oral History Collection at Columbia University, are especially informative on his years before the CWA. The Aubrey W. Williams Papers, in the Roosevelt Library, proved disappointing for the CWA, except for a manuscript entitled "The New Deal—A Dead Battery." A separate collection of Jacob Baker Papers, filed with the FERA records in the National Archives has very good materials for 1934 on demobilization and reconversion to the Work Division. The Frank Bane Papers, University of Virginia, and Louis Brownlow Diary at the University of Chicago both offer insights into the public administration and efficiency forces behind the creation and organization of the CWA. The lack of material in the Franklin D. Roosevelt Papers at Hyde Park reveals the President's marginal interest in civil works, except for political repercussions. The Official Files, however, have two informative memos from Budget Director Lewis Douglas on scrapping the program. FDR did receive numerous letters, mostly of gratitude for the CWA, which provide valuable sources on the reactions of the average worker to the program. Eleanor Roosevelt's Papers, in contrast, have good correspondence on the Women's Division, as well as the Ellen S. Woodward Papers, Mississippi Department of Archives and History, Jackson, Mississippi.

Many individuals have figured significantly in the CWA in particular states. The William G. McAdoo Papers, Library of Congress, have several folders on the tangled California politics and the CWA. Victor A. Olander's Papers in the Chicago Historical Society provide a rich source on the relationship of organized labor and the CWA in Illinois. The Henry Horner Papers in the Illinois State Library, Springfield, also provide some interesting correspondence on civil works in the Midwest, while the Gifford Pinchot Papers, Library of Congress, are equally revealing for Pennsylvania. The Social Welfare History Archives, University of Minnesota, have the Harry L. Lurie Papers, and the Archives of American Art contain the letters of a few participants in the Public Works of Art Project, including Edward Bruce and Julian Levi. The Norman Thomas Papers at the New York Public Library give some information on the Socialist Party's efforts to organize those on the CWA.

Numerous public documents and government publications offer rich

A Note on Sources ★ 279

details. Each state submitted a mimeographed *Final Report* at the close
of the program in March, 1934, and the FERA put out a *Monthly
Report* with many excellent articles on safety, compensation, and white
collar projects. Other informative publications include the CWA, *Manual
of Financial Procedure;* the USES, *Twelve and One-Half Million Registered
for Work;* and *Chronology of the FERA* by Doris Carothers. State relief
agencies also recorded their activities, like the California State Relief
Commission's *Review of Activities, 1933–1935, Emergency Relief in
Pennsylvania* (written by Arthur Dunham), the Illinois Emergency Relief Commission, *Biennial Report,* the New York State Governor's
Commission on Unemployment Relief, *State and Local Welfare Administration in the State of New York,* and the Pennsylvania State Emergency Relief Board, *Unemployment Relief in Pennsylvania, September 1,
1932–October 31, 1933.* Most of these state reports, however, were
compiled by welfare officials, who tended to emphasize the clients
aided and glide over distinctions between direct and work relief, let
alone provide evidence of the tug of war between social workers and
technicians.

Published works of those who participated in the CWA provide
valuable insights into the professional viewpoints toward relief and
work for the unemployed. Harry Hopkins' writings include his standard *Spending to Save* (New York, 1936); "The Developing National
Program of Relief," NCSW, *Proceedings* (1933); and "The War on
Distress," *Today,* I (December 16, 1933). Aubrey Williams wrote
"Putting the Four Millions to Work" and "A Year of Relief" in NCSW,
Proceedings (1934); and "Standards of Living and Government Responsibility," *Annals,* CLXXVI (November, 1934). The engineering
and management experts reveal their motives in creating public work
for the jobless and the details of operating such a program. Jacob
Baker wrote "Construction in Relief Service," *Engineering News-Record,* CXIV (February 7, 1935) and "The Range of Work Relief,"
Public Works Engineers Year Book, 1935. John Carmody's articles in
Factory and Industrial Management document this Taylorite's long interest in helping the unemployed: "Curing Unemployment—Whose
Job Is It?" (October, 1930); "Intelligent Unemployment Relief" (July,
1930); and "Unemployment Solutions" (June, 1930). Corrington Gill,
who unfortunately left no papers, did publish several forward-looking
pieces, especially *Wasted Manpower* (New York, 1939) and his land-
mark assessment of where New Deal social welfare should head, "How
Many Are Unemployable?" *Survey,* LXXI (January, 1935). Other in-

fluential statements by Gill include: "The Civil Works Administration," *Municipal Year Book, 1937*; "The Effectiveness of Public Works in Stabilizing the Construction Industry," American Statistical Association, *Proceedings*, XXVIII (March, 1933); "Local Work for Relief," *Survey Midmonthly*, LXXVI (May, 1940) and "A Study of Three Million Families on Relief in October, 1933," *Annals*, CLXXXI (November, 1934), which delineated the concept of the "new unemployed" and had an immediate impact on the setting up of the CWA. Louis Brownlow's *Passion for Anonymity* (Chicago, 1958) and "The Role of the Public Administrator," *National Municipal Review*, XXIII (May, 1934) deal with the organizational challenges of a federal work program. Donald Stone, a major force behind the CWA *Manual*, revealed his expertise in "The Need for Standard Units and Costs in Municipal Management," *Municipal Year Book, 1931*; "Public Works Management with the Aid of Records and Standards," *ibid., 1932*; and "Reorganizing for Relief," *Public Management*, XVI (September, 1934). Nels Anderson, assistant to Carmody for labor relations, wrote *The Right to Work* (New York, 1938); and "Organized Unemployed," *Social Work Year Book, 1937*. Perry Fellows, the CWA assistant engineer, authored "Municipal Engineers and the Relief Administration," *Public Works Engineers Yearbook, 1935*; "Worthwhile Work," *Society for the Advancement of Management Journal*, I (May, 1936); and "Engineers in Government," *ibid.* (May, 1937).

For contemporary social work opinion see Grace Abbott, *From Relief to Social Security* (Chicago, 1941); American Association of Social Workers, *This Business of Relief* (New York, 1936); Josephine C. Brown, *Public Relief, 1929–1939* (New York, 1940); Leah Hannah Feder, *Unemployment Relief in Periods of Depression* (New York, 1936); Marie Dresden Lane and Francis Steegmuller, *America on Relief* (New York, 1938); Mary Richmond, *What Is Social Case Work?* (New York, 1922); Edward Ainsworth Williams, *Federal Aid for Relief* (New York, 1939). Journals like *Survey, Survey Graphic*, National Conference of Social Work *Proceedings, Compass*, and *Survey Midmonthly* provided numerous articles which trace the social workers' early demands for direct federal relief, their growing dismay with the engineering priorities in the CWA, and their satisfaction with the return to relief standards on the WPA. *Social Service Review* and *The Family* provide indispensable sources for the case-work approach.

For contemporary opinion on engineering and public management see: American Public Welfare Association, *APWA, Our Autobiography*

(1941); Harvey C. Mansfield, *The Comptroller General* (New Haven, 1934); and Leonard D. White, *The City Manager* (Chicago, 1927). The most useful journals include: *Engineering News-Record, Public Works Engineers Year Book, National Municipal Review, National Safety News, Bulletin of the Taylor Society,* American Statistical Association *Proceedings,* and *Public Management.*

Union journals provide organized labor's official position on the CWA policies on hiring, wages and hours, and workers' grievances. They include: *American Federationist, Federation News, Painter and Decorator, Bricklayer, Mason and Plasterer, Garment Worker, Paving Cutters Journal, Union Teacher,* and *Equity.* Organizations of professionals and unemployed pressure groups put out journals which give a taste of "rank-and-file" opinion. *Social Work Today* was the "radical" journal as opposed to the established National Conference of Social Work, *Proceedings* and *Compass.* Other publications include: the Federation of Architects, Engineers, Chemists, and Technicians, *Bulletin; Unemployed Teacher; Art Front;* Association of Federation Workers, *Bulletin;* (Chicago) *Hunger Fighter; Unemployed News Service,* which are indispensable for tracing radical opinions of CWA policies. Needless to mention, no study of public policy, like that of relief and work programs during the 1930's, could proceed without articles from *New Republic, Nation, Fortune, Business Week, Literary Digest,* and *Current History.* The most helpful newspapers include: *New York Times, Washington Post, Chicago Tribune, Philadelphia Public Ledger, Philadelphia Record, Los Angeles Times, San Francisco Chronicle, Raleigh News and Observer,* and the *Wall Street Journal.*

SECONDARY

For the evolution of the general welfare state, urban liberalism and the social work tradition, see Sidney Fine, *Laissez-faire and the General Welfare State* (Ann Arbor, 1956); Robert H. Bremner, *From the Depths* (New York, 1956); Allen F. Davis, *Spearheads for Reform* (New York, 1967); J. Joseph Huthmacher, "Urban Liberalism and the Age of Reform," *MVHR,* XLIX (September, 1962) and *Senator Robert F. Wagner and the Rise of Urban Liberalism* (New York, 1968); and Clarke Chambers, *Seedtime of Reform* (Minneapolis, 1963).

Those who view the CWA squarely within this urban-liberal context include Robert E. Sherwood, *Roosevelt and Hopkins* (New York,

1948); Arthur M. Schlesinger, Jr., *The Coming of the New Deal* (Boston, 1965); William E. Leuchtenburg, *Franklin D. Roosevelt and the New Deal, 1932–1940* (New York, 1963); Searle F. Charles, *Minister of Relief* (Syracuse, 1963); Paul A. Kurzman, *Harry Hopkins and the New Deal* (Fair Lawn, N.J., 1964); James T. Patterson, *The New Deal and the States* (Princeton, 1969); Forrest Anderson Walker, "The Civil Works Administration: An Experiment in Federal Work Relief, 1933–34" (unpublished Ph.D. dissertation, University of Oklahoma, 1963); and John A. Salmond, "Aubrey Williams: Atypical New Dealer?" in John Braeman, Robert H. Bremner, and David Brody, eds., *The New Deal: the National Level*, Vol. I (Columbus, 1975), pp. 218–245.

Revisionist interpretations of reform and corporate liberalism include Samuel P. Hays's classic "The Politics of Reform in Municipal Government in the Progressive Era," *Pacific Northwest Quarterly*, LV (October, 1964); Robert H. Wiebe, *The Search for Order, 1877–1920* (New York, 1967). James Weinstein, *The Corporate Ideal in the Liberal State, 1900–1918* (Boston, 1968) details the corporate liberal interest in such issues as safety and workman's compensation so crucial in CWA employment policies. See also Samuel Haber, *Efficiency and Uplift* (Chicago, 1964); William Graebner, *Coal Mining Safety in the Progressive Period* (Lexington, 1976); Martin J. Schiesl, *The Politics of Efficiency* (Berkeley, 1977). For the businessmen's interest in employment stabilization and relief for the temporary jobless, see Irwin Yellowitz, "The Origins of Unemployment Reform in the United States," *Labor History*, IX (Fall, 1968) and *Labor and the Progressive Movement in New York State, 1897–1916* (Ithaca, 1965); Donald A. Ritchie, "The Gary Committee: Businessmen, Progressives and Unemployment in New York City, 1914–1915," *New-York Historical Society Quarterly*, LVII (October, 1973); Joan Hoff Wilson, *Herbert Hoover: Forgotten Progressive* (Boston, 1975); Carolyn Grin, "The Unemployment Conference of 1921: An Experiment in National Cooperative Planning," *Mid-America*, LV (April, 1973); Roy Lubove, *The Professional Altruist* (New York, 1969); Bonnie R. Fox, "Unemployment Relief in Philadelphia, 1930–1932: A Study of the Depression's Impact on Voluntarism," *Pennsylvania Magazine of History and Biography*, XCIII (January, 1969).

Revisionist interpretations that soundly dissect New Deal economic and regulatory agencies include: Ellis W. Hawley, *The New Deal and the Problem of Monopoly* (Princeton, 1966); Michael E. Parrish, *Securities Regulation and the New Deal* (New Haven, 1970); Grant McConnell, *The Decline of Agrarian Democracy* (New York, 1969); and

John Braeman, "The New Deal and the 'Broker State': A Review of Recent Scholarly Literature," *Business History Review*, XLVI (Winter, 1972). Revisionist interpretations of New Deal work relief programs include: William W. Bremer, "Along the 'American Way': The New Deal's Work Relief Programs for the Unemployed," *JAH*, LXII (December, 1975); Frances Fox Piven and Richard A. Cloward, *Regulating the Poor* (New York, 1975); and Barton J. Bernstein, "The New Deal: the Conservative Achievements of Liberal Reform," in his *Towards a New Past* (New York, 1969).

federal projects (CWA), 58–59, 69, 134–39
Federal Works Agency (FWA), 263
federated fund-raising, Great Depression, 15–16, 224; the Twenties, 10, 28, 73
Federation of Architects, Engineers, Chemists, and Technicians (FAECT), background, 132, 144; *Bulletin*, 144, 152; CWA project organizations, 149; collective bargaining, 147–48; New York Committee for United Action on CWA, 154; rally against questionnaire, 153
Federation News, 106, 108
Fellows, Perry, 56, 80, 241, 263
field representatives, 71; APWA, 22, 27; CWA auditors, 67–68; CWA engineers, 55–58, 91, 234–36; Cook County CWA, 93; Department of Labor, 115; FERA, 27–30, 34–35, 39, 221, 248; Pennsylvania CWA, 83; RFC, 22, 27–29, 75
fiscal conservatives, 214, 219–21, 247, 259
flood relief projects, 184, 187, 244
Folks, Homer, 99
Force, Juliana, 138n, 139, 142, 144–45
force account, 14, 45, 64, 215, 240
Florida Relief Administration, 251
Forrestal, James V., 264

Garfield, James R., 20
Gary, Elbert H., 12
General Accounting Office (GAO), 49
Georgia Civil Works Administration, 89
Gifford, Walter S., 20
Gill, Corrington, background, 31; CWA, 41, 49, 69; FERA, 39;

unemployment relief census, 34; WPA, 258–59, 263; *Waster Manpower*, 258
Gleason, John J., 123, 125
Goldschmidt, Arthur "Tex," 47, 52, 211, 255
Gordon, Robert Aaron, 273
Gosselin, Grace, 154, 224
grants-in-aid, FERA, 26, 41, 239–40, 251–52; RFC, 72; vocational training, 264; WPA, 253; Wagner Bills, 17
Great Society, 260, 266
Green, William, 104, 108, 110, 123
grievances of CWA workers, appeals boards, 126–27; committees, 132, 204, 206, 211; white collar and professional groups, 149–50. See *also* hiring and wage disputes
group consciousness, CWA clubs, 197–98; CWA demobilization, 210; CWA gangs, 197; CWA project identity, 198, 201, 211; CWA workers, 196; California, 200–201; periodicals, 152; rank-and-file social workers, 150–51; radical stimulation, 201–210; spontaneous unions, 199–200; white collar and professional groups, 132, 143, 148, 154–55
Grundy, Joseph, 90
Guffey, Joseph, 87, 90

Hackett, Russell, 56
Hammond, Alonzo J., 78n, 80
hard core jobless, 260, 266, 268, 273
Harriman, Henry I., 218
Harrington, Francis C., 253
Harrington, Michael, 261
Harrison, Bennett, 273
Haupt, Alma, 175
Haynes, Rowland, 28, 255
Heller, Walter W., 265, 273

LIBRARY OF CONGRESS CATALOGING IN PUBLICATION DATA

Schwartz, Bonnie Fox, 1945-
The Civil Works Administration, 1933-1934.

Originally presented as the author's thesis (Ph.D.)—Columbia University, 1978.
Bibliography: p.
Includes index.
1. United States. Federal Civil Works Administration—History. 2. Public service
employment—United States—History. I. Title.

HD5713.6.U54S38 1984   353.0084'85   84-42560
ISBN 0-691-04718-9 (alk. paper)